"*Famished* is a visceral unveiling of the secret lives of Christian girls. Evangelicalism has a long history of the 'skinny white woman,' and Rollins's bold memoir not only traces the roots but also exposes the sexualized purity culture that teaches girls to fear men, their own bodies, and especially anything beyond their control. The high cost of religious scrupulosity and institutionalized religious diet culture is evident on every page of this remarkable debut."

—**TIA LEVINGS,** author of *A Well-Trained Wife: My Escape from Christian Patriarchy*

"While others write coming-of-age memoirs about discovery and freedom, Anna Rollins articulates the grief of years spent learning to disappear in a way that was sold as holiness. *Famished* honors generations of women—but especially Millennial women—who built our entire sense of self around becoming smaller, a pattern that reappears throughout our lives. This is a beautiful and haunting meditation on what cannot be rewritten and what might still be reclaimed."

—**ANNA GAZMARIAN,** author of *Devout: A Memoir of Doubt*

"*Famished* is a visceral account of the work it takes to release the chokehold of bodily compulsion, religiously inspired and otherwise. It's also a joyful rendering of the beauty that can blossom even in the midst of that lifelong work. Anna Rollins has crafted a nuanced exploration of desire that I couldn't put down. I devoured *Famished* in two sittings."

—**KELLY FOSTER LUNDQUIST,** author of *Beard: A Memoir of a Marriage*

"Anna Rollins challenges us to consider what it means to believe that our bodies were made good and what aspects of culture—Christian and secular—we need to reconsider to live into that belief. She does it by offering her own experience as a way to trace the intricate connections between purity culture and diet culture and how they work together to constrict women's bodies and souls. Many readers will recognize their own struggles in hers and will appreciate her clear thought and wise insight in working through them. *Famished* points us toward the possibility of bodies, desires, and faith that are more supple, more capacious, and more full."

—**LYNNE GERBER,** author of *Seeking the Straight and Narrow: Weight Loss and Sexual Reorientation in Evangelical America*

"In her vital contribution to the purity culture conversation, Rollins reveals a world in which the body absorbs everything religion tells us is bad about women. She takes us on a journey through the ways that she and other women learned to dominate, deny, and bully their bodies into small, quiet, controlled submission to earn the love of God—and the healing that is available when we realize we are lovable exactly as we are, body and all."

—**LINDA KAY KLEIN,** author of *Pure: Inside the Evangelical Movement That Shamed a Generation of Young Women and How I Broke Free*

FAMISHED

ON FOOD, SEX, AND GROWING UP AS A GOOD GIRL

ANNA ROLLINS

WILLIAM B. EERDMANS PUBLISHING COMPANY
GRAND RAPIDS, MICHIGAN

Wm. B. Eerdmans Publishing Co.
2006 44th Street SE, Grand Rapids, MI 49508
www.eerdmans.com

Published 2025
Printed in the United States of America

31 30 29 28 27 26 25 1 2 3 4 5 6 7

ISBN 978-0-8028-8451-0

Library of Congress Cataloging-in-Publication Data

Names: Rollins, Anna, 1988– author.

Title: Famished / Anna Rollins.

Description: Grand Rapids, Michigan : William B. Eerdmans Publishing Company, [2025] | Summary: "Exploring connections between diet culture and purity culture, this memoir tells the story of a woman who grew up in a conservative Christian tradition and struggled for years with disordered eating"—Provided by publisher.

Identifiers: LCCN 2024042503 | ISBN 9780802884510 (paperback) | ISBN 9781467468763 (epub)

Subjects: LCSH: Rollins, Anna, 1988– | Christian biography—United States. | Eating disorders—Patients—United States—Biography. | Eating disorders—Religious aspects—Christianity. | LCGFT: Biographies.

Classification: LCC BR1725.R64 A3 2025

LC record available at https://lccn.loc.gov/2024042503

Biblical quotations are from the King James Version unless otherwise noted.

Small portions of this book have previously appeared in much different forms in *HuffPost*, *Literary Mama*, *Electric Literature*, *TinyBeans*, and *Slate*.

For Alice

CONTENTS

NOTE TO THE READER

This is a work of creative nonfiction. The events described really occurred. Dialogue has been reconstructed to the best of my memory. Many names have been changed, and some composite characters are present. As in any memoir, I am telling a true story through the lens of my own subjectivity.

PREFACE

We got home late from our church's Wednesday night service—and I was hungry. I still had at least another hour of exercise to clock in before the end of the day. So, I decided to eat half a granola bar. I retrieved the box from the pantry and opened the wrapper. I broke the granola bar approximately in half, justified eating the half that was slightly bigger, placed the remaining bar and wrapper back in the box, and hurried to my room to change into my sports bra and a large T-shirt. As I headed to the stairs leading down to the basement, I walked back through the kitchen.

The clock on the oven said 9:12 p.m. When I glanced at the clock again, it was 9:25. I was stunned. I looked to the kitchen counter. A plastic container with bakery blueberry muffins sat open, each muffin ripped to shreds, each top missing. I'd dropped crumbs all over the tile floor. Like an animal. The box of granola bars was sitting on the counter, too. Every single one of the wrappers had been opened, and half of each bar remained lodged in its wrapper. I heard my dad's footsteps, and I hurried to tidy my mess. I stashed the box of granola bars, but I wasn't quick enough to hide the muffins.

My dad walked into the room. He glanced at the counter and then at me. "Why is it like we have a mouse in the house all the time?" he said.

I laughed stiffly. He seemed to notice my discomfort and changed the subject. "Better get ready for bed. It's getting late, and don't you have a math test tomorrow?"

I headed toward the bathroom to brush my teeth and wash my face. I was overcome with anxiety. I did it again. I'd eaten so many things, so quickly, again. I hadn't finished exercising. It was the end of the day. My parents would hear me if I went downstairs to work out now. I was tired. Still, I wasn't allowed to go to sleep yet.

My bedroom was dark as I quietly moved through the memorized motions of an exercise video. *If I wasn't forced to go to these evening services, maybe this wouldn't keep happening*, I silently seethed. I should have tried harder to get out of it. I didn't have time for these sorts of things. Forty-five minutes passed. I was covered in a cold sweat. *That's good enough*, I thought as I crawled in bed.

Fifteen years later, I stood over my nine-month-old baby, Alex, as he struggled to breathe. The PICU's oxygen machine beeped as I stroked his arms, kissed his soft cheeks. My thoughts were lost in the sea of pasta alfredo that I had eaten the night before. How could I possibly work it off?

Could I get into a bathroom, lock the door, and sneak in a hundred squats? Could I stream a workout video on YouTube, mute the sound, and perform exercises by his crib without any medical personnel seeing me?

Hypercontrolling my food and using exercise compulsively had always been how I coped with life, stress, expectations, and fear. With my child's life in danger, my mind was consumed with controlling my own body.

Even before my son's illness, I was in crisis. After giving birth to Alex, my second son, I became obsessed with his sleep schedule, abandoning grocery carts filled with food to adhere to rigid nap times. But even though I forced him into the model infant nap schedule I'd studied on Instagram, *I* wasn't sleeping. Instead, I woke at 3 a.m., worried about planning lectures for my graduate composition pedagogy course, responding to the several dozen emails that had accumulated in my inbox, and completing edits on my grant-funded academic article on composition tutoring. How would I finish these tasks *and* stick to my pumping schedule; prep produce for a nutritious, low-calorie dinner; fit in mileage for my half-marathon training plan; walk the dogs; and make it to the therapy appointment my husband insisted I book?

By bedtime, I was often screaming—throwing burp cloths at the wall, threatening to kill myself if a child spiked a fever or threw a tantrum.

"When I first met you a few months ago, I thought, 'Okay, maybe she's dealing with postpartum depression or anxiety,'" the therapist I'd begun seeing after the birth of my second son said. "But now that I've gotten to know you, I don't think that anymore."

The room was quiet, only the vague whir of a white noise machine's ocean waves crashing in the hallway.

"You don't?" I asked.

"No," she replied, folding her hands in her lap. "Do you?"

I paused to consider her question. Something was wrong—that much I knew. I wouldn't have been wasting my precious child-free time with her otherwise. But there was a reason Alex's pediatrician hadn't flagged my mental health with those mandatory surveys earlier. I didn't spend my days in tears or in bed. I was quite high functioning, at least to anyone who didn't see me within the privacy of my own home. I was training for races, publishing academic articles, making my students happy to ensure positive end-of-the-semester evaluations, all with a toddler and baby in tow.

"No," I replied finally. "I don't think so either."

My therapist smirked. "No—you don't have depression or anxiety. But here's what I think: You are very, very, very angry."

She looked me straight in the eyes to see my response.

Anger was my enemy. I had always tried to cover it with a smile or shrink it down to a size zero. But a wave of gratification washed over me in that moment, the pleasure of being seen.

"Well, yeah. But I don't think most people would describe me that way."

She nodded her head: "No—they wouldn't. And that's probably part of the problem. Now—let's figure out why."

This was the last time I saw her. In a matter of days, the world would shut down due to the COVID-19 pandemic.

I grew up in an Appalachian fundamentalist church that fully embraced purity culture, a movement that emphasized the importance not only of sexual abstinence before marriage but also of rigid gender roles. We lived in the mountains, where we could remain in the world but not of the world, simply by placement of geography. If you were born into this place, you inherited close family networks and extensive hospitality. But if you moved in from the outside, as my mom and dad had just before I was born? You were often distrusted, even feared. This was a place where austerity and abstinence were the highest virtues. Where rolling mountain landscapes were dotted with chemical plants. Where distant authorities made proclamations about how to move and whom to touch. A place of rules, so many rules, fixed and accumulating, as sprawling as eternity.

So when COVID happened, as we backed away from our neighbors in fear of their breath and their touch, as we became aware of danger in the air, of the threat of death in the bodies of others, it all felt very familiar.

As we washed our groceries and covered our mouths, as we retreated to our pods in fear of contamination, I was reminded of my childhood, its hyperfocus on purity and cleanliness, the ever-present threat of toxic chemicals in the air, its obsession with those who were with us and those who were against us, the stakes always life or death.

Alone at home with my two children, I turned the therapist's question over in my mind: *why so angry?* And why was it that the angrier I felt, the more I micromanaged meals, perseverated over calories, and added extra workouts to my already full days?

I considered how I'd bought into the scripts offered to me by both diet culture and purity culture: that if I controlled my appetites, I could control my world. That if I made myself smaller, I would be better, safer.

I'd expected it to be difficult to watch my body change during pregnancy—and it was. But giving birth did not alleviate my anxieties. Since becoming a mom, I felt, quite deeply, that to be good in my new role, I had to be perfect. And I felt this anxiety acutely at church—because I always had. On pre-COVID Sundays, I recalculated Alex's nap and feeding schedule, trying desperately to arrive at church on time with happy children wearing clean clothes. I'd learned since girlhood that the highest calling of a woman was to produce well-behaved, God-fearing children.

I stood and sang hymns, Alex writhing in my arms, knowing he needed to nurse, *again*. I'd quickly retreat to a back closet so I wouldn't offend anyone as I lifted my church dress to feed him. Breastfeeding was both required for good motherhood *and* immodest. I needed to complete my duty while hiding all the evidence of my work.

After finishing Alex's feeding, I returned to the sanctuary, just in time for the sermon. The pastor was speaking about total depravity, how our desires are tainted by our wickedness, and how we needed to trust in the grace of God rather than ourselves.

I was frustrated hearing sermons that mentioned grace because I felt I never could find it for myself. And I was angry when my husband tried to help me, encouraging me to let go and trust God. Since when had religion taught me that a woman could let herself go?

Instead, it had done the opposite. Religion was tight, constrictive, and ever shrinking.

I felt comfortable in the small, controlled world of COVID because restriction was in my bones. I'd never truly left fundamentalism or the behaviors I had developed in response to it.

I had never excavated the fear or anger that shaped my own

coming of age. But now I had children to care for, including my baby, newly considered high risk with an asthma diagnosis. I had a life that was not perfect but was certainly full of love. As we sheltered in our homes to flatten the curve, I determined I would work to crawl out of rigid behaviors that limited my life rather than go back.

So, struggling during the pandemic, I did what everyone else was doing. I signed up for some online therapy. I saved social-media memes on the topic of healing. At the time "you don't have to earn your food" felt moving and profound. And I joined a few private support groups on Facebook, all focused on recovering from the impacts of purity culture or diet culture.

It was in these groups that I met others who had lived parallel lives to my own. Our tales all followed similar scripts.

Young girl grows up in a church where she learns that if she doesn't cover her body, men will take advantage of her—and it will all be her fault. She battles with disordered eating behaviors, usually around the time of puberty, often in attempts to halt her sexual development. These behaviors are significant enough to take over her life—but mild enough to evade diagnosis. She gets married. She struggles having sex with her husband. Maybe she can't have it because she's in physical pain from shame or vaginismus. Maybe she's preoccupied with the fear that her husband will leave her if she gains a few pounds.

Growing up, she was fed a steady diet of sermons that told her she needed to keep up her appearance if she didn't want her husband's eyes, or body, to wander. If she didn't hear this message directly from the pulpit, she read it in the popular Christian books marketed at the turn of the millennium, like Mark Driscoll's *Real Marriage* or Stephen Arterburn's *Every Man's Battle*. And even if her husband was wonderful, kind, loving—a dream—she never felt that she could truly trust his love for her.

I heard my own story echoed when Erin described that she believed her body was not her own—her body was for her future husband. Katie expressed the same lesson that I learned at church and school: "My body was only good for sex. All I'm good for is this one thing."

In chapel services at school, I learned that if I had sex before marriage, my body would be like a glass of dirty water or a used piece of chewing gum. So many sermon illustrations compared my body to food waiting to be consumed by men.

And like so many women in these groups, I had been taught that if I didn't want men to violate me, I needed to exert tight control over myself. As Malerie said to me, we lived in "states of contradiction." She'd been told that focusing on her body was a sin—but she had to think about her body (to guard it, to keep it) all the time.

All of us had reached our own point of crisis. Maybe it was a divorce. A death. A birth. A diagnosis. Something happened that shook up our worlds. And we needed to heal our relationships with our own bodies. We wanted to experience pleasure, openness, freedom, joy. We were sick of fearing and fighting our own appetites.

So we excavated our faith.

Some of the women I met and got to know left their childhood religions. Some wanted nothing to do with Christianity at all. I spoke to hopeful agnostics, staunch atheists, a Satanist.

But others embarked upon authentic Christian journeys toward a God whose love they longed for. Like me, they asked questions such as, How can I have faith without certainty or perfection? Is the gospel actually good news? Is there room for diversity—of opinions, of identity, of personality—in the church?

I didn't want to leave my faith. But I also didn't know how to stay, either. On Sunday mornings when we were all still sheltering in place, I went for stroller walks and streamed sermons from N. T. Wright and Tim Keller on my phone. I walked through our tree-lined neighborhood, breathing in fresh air as a pastor unpacked the word of God through the headphones in my ears.

Sometimes I wanted my makeshift church service to last longer than a single sermon. This was a feeling I had never experienced.

At first, I figured this desire was following the same sort of math that had governed much of my life. Walking burns calories. More effort now means less guilt later.

But deep down, I knew this wasn't all of it. On these walks, I experienced a sense of possibility, of growth and life.

One Sunday morning after listening to a sermon, I streamed Kate Bowler's podcast, *Everything Happens*. At the age of thirty-five, as Bowler completed research on the way American Christianity has contributed to our culture's obsession with *living our best life now*, she was diagnosed with stage IV cancer. Since this diagnosis, much of her work centers on the toxic positivity of self-help culture, the pressure to always improve, the belief that we have much more control over our bodies and fates than we truly do.

I'd read some of Bowler's books, including *Blessed* on the history of the prosperity gospel in America. The message of the prosperity gospel—that one can expect blessings of health and wealth, as long as one follows the will of God—is one that has crept into most of the American church.

Purity culture follows this logic: *if I control my sex drive and abstain from sex until my wedding day, then I will have a happy marriage.*

And diet culture sells a similar formula: *If I control my eating, my body will look better, be better, and I will have a happy life.*

Dr. Hillary McBride, registered psychologist and author of *The Wisdom of Your Body*, has written about her struggles with an eating disorder. She described experiencing rigidity and suspicion of mental-health treatment while growing up within Christianity. And yet, she still identifies as finding a home within this religious tradition in spite of significant changes to how she understands and practices Christianity.

"I think that we can challenge systems and be a part of them," she explained to me in a phone conversation in November 2023.

She gave the example of being white and living within predominantly white communities—like my Appalachian hometown, for example—while still seeing the problems within such communities. I can advocate for changes that address systemic inequality and structural racism without disavowing the people or place I come from.

And she compared this to living within diet culture or even evangelicalism. "What I feel concerned about in the conversations around diet culture and purity culture is the internalized fundamentalism that has us view the world in a black and white way," she continued. "This tends to be an underlying motivational system that doesn't necessarily change even when we leave diet culture or leave evangelicalism. I know so many people who leave diet culture, but then adhere to body positivity in a similarly black and white way. This tells me they've swapped fundamentalisms." In other words, if you used to rigidly police what you ate, but now you strictly police what you and others can say, think, or feel about bodies, you are still living out the logic of fundamentalism.

During the roughly eighteen months of significant COVID-related restrictions, I wasn't the only one who felt both imprisoned and at home living with rigid rules. Fundamentalism and its restrictive thoughts and behaviors would not let me go. The more women I spoke with, the more I felt I had found a lost sisterhood trying to redefine a way to take up space and reclaim our appetites for life, love, and food, both physical and spiritual.

So, I decided to write *Famished*. It's led me on a journey that's both reflective as I go back into my own past and journalistic as I speak with scholars, psychologists, and women like me who are loosening the constrictions placed upon us, whether physical or spiritual.

In all my interviews, the most interesting thing I noticed was this: When women worked to heal from body shame, their relationship to religion was intricately involved.

At its core, this is also my story of seeking freedom from bondage—in my relationship to food and to faith. In it, I realize that the love of God doesn't depend upon my appearance or performance. And, believing that my body was made good, I can't perfect myself by restricting goodness.

GIRLHOOD

1

At twenty years old, Nicole was 5'7" like me. She also weighed about 115 pounds. In her photos, I noticed that we wore the same underwear—striped, violet high-waisted cotton briefs from Victoria's Secret.

It was the year 2000, I was twelve years old, and the Victoria's Secret Angels were thin and perfect. I stared at them in the catalogues I stole from the back of my mom's closet, her secret hiding place.

The internet was still new and there was no social media. I surfed websites devoted to my favorite celebrities, Mary-Kate and Ashley Olsen. But one afternoon following a few too many clicks, I stumbled upon The Spark, a mashup of celebrity news and contests that would predate TV programs like *The Biggest Loser* and *My 600-lb. Life*. One of the contests was called The Fat Project.

That's where I first saw Nicole. The website editors had chosen two thin, attractive young adults—one guy, one girl—and challenged them to gain thirty pounds in thirty days for the chance to win three thousand dollars. Nicole and Eric lived in an apartment together, weighed in daily, and took front and side photos wearing only ratty cotton underwear, including Nicole's violet briefs that matched mine.

A former homecoming queen from Haleyville, Alabama, Nicole was, according to her bio page, "tired of people judging her for her good looks—so she's agreed to ruin them." Bemoaning undesired attention, Nicole said, "That's all anyone ever looks at. So I want to get disgustingly fat and see how everyone reacts."

After school, I rushed home to sit in front of my dad's HP computer and log on to America Online to follow Nicole's daily consumption. I was fascinated by this young woman who didn't want attention for being thin.

Instead, she wanted to disappear by getting fat.

I read that the contestants had been fasting to lower their starting weight. After their initial weigh-in, they began to eat: three large pizzas, two liters of Coke, crème-filled donuts, and Chinese takeout. The website editors posted photos of the feast. Following that meal, the contest moderator mixed up a shake from GNC: 2,200 calories in a single serving.

Nicole capped this day of eating by posting a photo of her bare belly. She reclined on a couch wearing pajama pants. Even in a seated position, her taut stomach revealed no excess.

"Time for dinner," my mom called, and I quickly logged off. I pulled up my shirt and pinched my own belly as I made a mental calculation of how many calories I would allow myself to consume.

The Fat Project was an extreme diet standing in front of a fun-house mirror, a mean circus of gluttony. The website moderators mocked the contestants, frequently deriding them with insults about their bodies and even their morality. "She's taken to wearing socks with her undies, which I feel is a true sign of her commitment to dumpiness," the moderator wrote beneath Nicole's progress image on day ten. "I look at her feet and gurgling thighs and think of a newborn housewife—whose only daytime company is six Heinekens and a box of bon-bons, and who'll be wearing a size 20 before the leaves are off the trees. If I were her boyfriend, I'd be getting a lawyer." Nicole sought liberation, but the spectacle made her a laughingstock. Still, it felt revolutionary to watch a woman willingly sacrifice what was, I believed, her one source of power—her thin body.

I couldn't get enough of it. My appetite and I were in a battle of wills. I always needed the upper hand—and watching another woman give in to her desires made me feel even more powerful when I resisted mine.

Fat activism had not yet arrived in my corners of the internet—and it was nowhere close to my home in small-town Appalachia, either. I grew up in a part of West Virginia known as "Chemical Valley" due to the frequency of industrial spills. In school, we often sheltered in place, not because of the threat of natural disasters like tornadoes or hurricanes—the mountains protected us from these—but because of the frequency of accidents at the various plants positioned along the banks of our main river. I was familiar with the sound of the alarm, the acrid smell of a landscape washed with something like vinegar, clouds accumulating as the sirens continued, day growing dark, and we hurried inside to seal the cracks of our doors with duct tape and dish towels.

I attended a fundamentalist Christian school cloistered at the end of a curvy mountain road. As a girl, I felt safe, sheltered, and protected—as long as I stayed in line.

At school, I sat in chapel services led by preachers from churches across the state. The love and grace of Jesus were often mentioned in passing, though certainly not something to linger upon for fear that we would all begin to feel too free.

But at home, I fantasized about freedom, daydreams brought to life on the internet.

Day two of The Fat Project featured photos of Nicole in baggy overalls shopping the aisles of the grocery store for "the worst foods America has to offer." On her list were Little Debbie Cakes. SpaghettiOs. Pop-tarts. Peanut butter. Chips. Margarine. Cinnamon Toast Crunch.

Just a day into the contest, Nicole was up 3.5 pounds, though the moderator speculated that most of Nicole's new weight was still in her intestines. She still looked as thin as when she started.

But soon, Nicole's body changed. Her underwear looked tight, her belly button enlarged, and in a photo zoomed in on her midsection, two bright red arrows were drawn to point out her newly grown love handles. She "has ridges," the caption said, and her "dedication is definitely starting to show."

I felt titillated by her thighs now touching, her belly spilling over the elastic of her underwear. It was thrilling to see the consequences of her indulgence—and it was exciting to see a woman who looked so similar to me showing off excess without apology.

"I've been struggling with the sin of masturbation, Anna," Jessica, a friend of mine from school, confessed to me late one night at a sleepover, the blue light of the television illuminating a single tear on her cheek.

"What do you mean?" I asked after an awkward pause.

"What do I mean—masturbation?" Jessica looked at me in the low-lit living room, facial expression now changed to one of superiority. "You don't know what masturbation is?"

"Of course I know what it is," I said, defensive. "I just . . . I know how boys do it. But girls . . ." I let my sentence trail off with raised inflection.

I regretted making my ignorance known as Jessica began to politely explain female masturbation to me: "You know how whenever you see a guy, and he's really hot—and you touch yourself. Down there." Then she told me about her own lust, her PG-rated fantasies about men. She concluded my education with a question: "Do you know what I mean?"

"Oh. Yes. That. Of course," I said. An express train ran through my veins. I did not know what she meant—except, I realized, when I looked at Nicole's body growing, I did.

Each afternoon I was eager to look at pictures of Nicole eating. I waited impatiently for the internet to dial up, then quickly clicked over to see The Spark's daily report on Nicole's progress. And the pictures. Nicole pressing whipped cream into her mouth. Nicole eating a whole pizza. Nicole in her underwear, arm submerged into a full bag of chips.

Some days the editors posted photos of Nicole's newly developed cellulite. I was exhilarated examining her pale, dimpled skin. Each day, she hit a higher number on the scale, and I found myself thinking, *This is what I would look like at this weight.* I was disgusted even as I tightened with pleasure.

Nicole's freedom to embrace her appetites—and the images of her expanding flesh—thrilled me.

As Nicole continued to grow, the website described her as "visibly much fatter" with "jelly rolls sagging at her waist. It's like the homecoming queen is melting away." Pictures zoomed in on the skin of her belly showcasing fat folds, cellulite, "the dark side of Nicole."

Why was it described as "dark"? I wondered. Wasn't she eating what she had never let herself have? Or was the contest seeing her now as a shadow of herself, as an entirely different person because she was heavier?

Near the end of The Fat Project, close-up photos were posted of Nicole wearing the same bra and underwear set she wore at the start of the project. Her weight gain was compared with photos zoomed in on her gut, then her legs, her kneecaps, and even her fingers.

"She used to be a homecoming queen, and now even her jewelry doesn't fit," the website copy said.

"Bloated is not really a strong enough word to describe what's going on here," read another day's entry. "I offer you 'bustooned' and 'hoggled' as possible new adjectives for her current, exalted condition." Like me, they were both disgusted and turned on—perhaps their editorializing shaped my own reaction.

A tattoo in the shape of a star was etched on Nicole's right hip bone. By the end of the month-long project, after she had gained thirty pounds, it had become stretched and distorted into something more like a snowflake.

2

"Men are physical creatures," the pastor said matter-of-factly. "God doesn't excuse men for lust. But women—you need to do your part to help a brother out. Women who love the Lord should care very much about preventing a brother from stumbling into sin."

I looked around the school chapel to see the stiffened posture of my middle school friends. Though I had heard these admonitions before, that day, I felt anger rise in my chest. Not because I was being told to button up, though I resented that too. I was angry because I felt misunderstood. Unseen. And though a part of me wanted to disappear to conform and remain safe, a greater part of me longed to be known for the person I actually was.

I suddenly realized that the pastor was not ashamed of the lust of men—he was bragging about it. From the pulpit. To control me.

But what about my *lust?* I wanted to yell at him in response. *You think I don't have it, but I do. I can be just as dangerous as you. Just as powerful.*

If men were "physical creatures," I found myself wondering, what kind of "creature" was I? I was never referred to as a creature by these men, as something animal and earthly. I was regarded more highly, as more evolved than brute instinct and appetite. I was not considered animal at all—I was something closer to spiritual, to angelic.

But this angelic depiction was not true of me or other women I knew. In trying to deny that I had appetites, I was consumed by them. I thought of little else. In attempting to transcend my body, I was obsessed with my body. I wanted to be small to stay safe—and yet thin Nicole was gorging herself to become less visible. The female body was a trap with no escape, a problem with no solution.

I threw away my lunch each day and hid in bathroom stalls with a book instead. When I arrived home from school, my brain buzzed, my fingers twitched. My breath was stale. Beyond hungry, I walked into the kitchen and took a box of cereal from the pantry. I could have a handful, I promised myself. Just to take the edge off. Just to help me through the several hours of workouts I still needed to complete. Twenty minutes later, I wouldn't remember what all I'd eaten, but I'd know it had been a lot. I was still, somehow, hungry. The cookies would be torn to bits. Cheerios would be littering the floor from where I'd missed pouring the cereal straight from the box into my mouth. My mom would walk into the kitchen and see the mess I had made. Sometimes she commented—"What in the world did you do to the muffins?"—but sometimes she'd just glance and walk away into the living room. It was time for Oprah.

I'd have to pay for this, of course. I spent hours in the basement playing, then replaying, Tae Bo workout videos: jumping, kicking, jabbing, punching.

At dinner, I pushed my mom's mashed potatoes around my plate. I cut my slab of steak into tiny pieces.

"Why are you not eating?" my dad asked.

"I am eating," I said, taking a bite of green beans. "But I had a pretty big snack after school." I continued to play games with my mashed potatoes.

"You have to eat a little bit more than that," my dad said as I stood to take my plate to the sink.

"I'm just not that hungry. I had a pretty big snack after school," I repeated. "Plus, I read an article online about how bad animal products are for you. I'm going to become a vegetarian."

My dad sighed. "Vegetarians can still eat mashed potatoes," he insisted.

At night before bed, I snuck dessert into the bathroom, chewing up powdered donuts and spitting them into the toilet. After that, I brushed my teeth, put on my pajamas, and headed to my room. I turned off the lights and completed several hundred situps in bed, just in case.

I was all hunger, all need. I was ashamed. But I was also proud—funny how it worked that way. I knew that I was physical, embodied, a person with desires, despite how frequently I was told that I was not.

Still, I did have some fear that the pastor was right. That I was not as physical as a man. All my fantasies about boys had narratives attached to them. The fantasy included a relationship. A conversation. An event. A destination. Their bodies were not the point. Even in my imagination, I was not looking at them exactly. I was looking at them looking at me. I was seeing myself through their eyes. And I was critical, closed, overly conscious, hardly turned on by them or what I imagined they saw.

What lit me up were images of women gaining weight—the reasons didn't matter. A pregnant woman's distended bare belly on a beach. Renée Zellweger's rail-thin figure remade into the curvy Bridget Jones. Any female celebrity who had loosened the reins a bit, gone up a few pant sizes between shoots. These bodies that could so easily be mine doing precisely what they were not supposed to do—eating anything, wearing anything, showing anything—and doing it without remorse.

In Joan Jacobs Brumberg's *The Body Project*, Brumberg explores how the body is the principal project for contemporary girls. The body is not just something one inhabits. Its shape is associated with morality, and as such, it is "'the ultimate expression of the self.' We not only exist in our bodies. They are the prism through which we judge ourselves and interpret judgment."

Brumberg describes a shift in the content of girls' personal journals during the twentieth century. At the beginning of the century, girls wrote about their plans for improving their characters through good works. But near the end of the century, the focus moved to improving their looks through restrictive behaviors.

Girls used to gaze outward and desire the expansion of their souls; then they turned inward and became obsessed with shrinking their bodies.

As I clicked my way into rabbit trails on the internet, I found myself repeatedly drawn to visuals of "afters" becoming "befores." The transformation in reverse. Women living without apology. I was interested in the possibility, in the repercussions, in the courage it took for someone to fill more space. I was titillated by the rebellion, the willingness to transgress and to make bare the physical aftermath to the world.

I looked at these women most often when I was hungry: hungry and cold, with no period. And men scared me. I hated them, convinced that they had brought me to this place where I feared feeding myself, to a place where I was consumed by my body's needs.

The only thing that warmed me was seeing a woman, a woman saying no. No to the demand to stay small. And I assessed the overflow of her flesh, and I felt the flicker of a flame I did not know I still possessed, and in that spark there was hope, possibility.

3

The quiet, dark night amplified the sounds coming from the floorboards. At nine years old, I held my breath, tensed my body straight as a stick. I knew my mom would comfort me if I called to her, but I was fighting a spiritual battle and knew she couldn't help. I had to pray harder. *Dear Lord, dear Lord, dear Lord, please protect me, please forgive me, I am so sorry, dear Lord, forgive me, please, and help me trust in you, dear Lord. Please keep the demons away from me, dear Lord.* I would recite a version of this prayer most nights throughout elementary school.

My first obsessions were religious. My first compulsion was prayer.

I learned the correct way to pray in my elementary school Bible classes. The teacher wrote an easy acronym to remember on the chalkboard. ACTS: adoration, confession, thanksgiving, and supplication. That was what you were supposed to do, in that order. I remembered the assigned structure for the week's Bible test—but implementing it in my personal life? That was the problem. In bed, I prayed repetitively as I watched shadows move across window blinds. My prayers were heavy on supplication (*Please protect me from demons, dear Lord. Please help me get an A on my math test, dear Lord*) and almost devoid of adoration (*Of course, you are beautiful, Lord*—I had to remind myself to say).

I felt some guilt about my prayers and tried to revise their emphasis and content. I also felt ashamed of how often I repeated myself. Too many *dear Lords*. We'd recently reflected upon a verse in the book of Matthew in chapel: "But when ye pray, use not vain repetitions, as the heathen do: for they think that they shall be heard for their much speaking" (6:7–8). After listening to this sermon, I realized my nighttime prayers were practically heathen.

The local news reported on drug overdoses, and women after church told stories of acquaintances whose homes had been invaded in broad daylight. Despite these anecdotes of violence, nothing bad had happened to me or anyone I knew. Coyotes kept eating our neighbors' chickens from the coop at night. That was the biggest threat I had personally experienced.

Still, I felt vulnerable. My parents double locked the doors at bedtime, never hid a key underneath a mat outdoors. Inside, they placed a thick piece of plywood below our front door's knob. It extended diagonally to an opposing floorboard. This precaution was meant to make it more difficult for someone to break down the door at night.

I once dreamed I walked into the restroom at school, and when I opened the door to a stall, a man was hiding there, waiting for me. I tried to scream, but only air came out of my mouth.

When I told my mom about the nightmare, she said, "Oh, honey" as she rubbed my shoulders. Then, out at a restaurant that evening, we went to the restroom together. It was empty. My mom opened each of the stall doors and looked behind them.

"Your dream made me think—you should check behind each of the doors before you use a public bathroom. Make sure there's no one hiding out," she advised.

I did this dutifully for years. Even today, I sometimes fear I am inviting my own demise if I don't check for men hiding in public restrooms. As if I would somehow deserve the attack if I was foolish enough not to check. As if it would be my fault.

I'd been taught to fear men—in church, at home, and at school. Young men were not candidates for babysitting me; older men were suspect if they volunteered to serve in church nursery without their wives. They were the reason I needed to wear shorts under my skirt on the playground, why I needed to wear tops with sleeves so that my shoulder blades were fully covered.

These men were also the face of God on earth. I learned to conflate the two—authority with danger. It was reckless to come too close.

If I wanted any more spiritual guidance outside of formal sermons, I needed to receive it from a woman in the church. Women in the church were expected to offer guidance freely, to accept responsibility graciously, knowing that they would never be hired by the church.

I understood that true women of God were supposed to be willing to serve without any sort of fanfare or money or thanks. They would receive the reward for their gentle and quiet spirit in heaven. This seemed unfair to me even as a girl turning into a young woman, but I also was not sure what could be done about the situation. It was impossible to argue with the Bible.

As a teenager, I came to understand that there was a silver lining to it all: As long as I stayed quiet, I could hide my questions and frustration and fit in—sort of. I was never going to be asked to pray before meals. I was never going to be asked to pontificate on my views of *eschatology* or *epistemology* or *ecclesiology*, fancy words men liked to use. Even though I was frustrated at church, I didn't dare stop going—I considered myself too good of a person to do that.

I could continue attending church, and as long as I wore the appropriate attire and perhaps, occasionally, volunteered for nursery, I would not get any pushback. As I began to interrogate what I had been taught to believe, I posed my questions quietly (*If God loves everyone, why do people go to Hell?*) in my own journals and looked for answers in books from the library.

Having a conversation with any of the men about my questions didn't feel like an option. It didn't even feel safe.

4

I spent my summers outdoors playing in a valley lined with apple trees, splashing barefoot in the creek winding through the mountains. A neighborhood with a cul-de-sac had just been built beside our home, and within a year, a handful of families with children moved into its cookie-cutter houses.

I was excited about the additional friends. I had been praying each night before bed that God would send me friends in the neighborhood so that I could play with someone other than my little brother. My mom joined me in this prayer, quietly praying for a break for herself as well.

All our new neighbors attended the public elementary school just down the street, and most of the kids were boys. At my school, girls were encouraged to interact with our same gender, were teased when we chose to sit with a boy at lunch. In my earliest memories from school, any friendship with boys was framed as romantic, and all of the interactions were charged.

But I was hungry for friends. So, I chose to not think of the neighbor boys as boys. We congregated each summer morning by a line of evergreens. And then we dispersed to various yards in the neighborhood, tossing footballs in one, building stick forts in another. Wading through the creek, we found and jointly claimed ownership of two hermit crabs. They died after a short time under our care, so we hiked through the woods, trespassed on private property, and held a burial ceremony for them on a hill behind a horse barn. At night, we played capture the flag in my yard—we had the smallest home, so the biggest yard—and caught fireflies in mason jars as the sun set.

Around the age of nine, I began to feel guilty for spending so much time with these boys without making any attempts to intervene in the fate of their souls. We set off fireworks in the night sky, we played games of one-on-one basketball in each other's driveways, but what would that mean in the grand scheme of eternity? It was laziness on my part—laziness and a lack of care.

"You have been given such privilege!" said a local preacher from a nondenominational church speaking in our school's chapel. "Growing up in Christian homes, attending Christian schools, living in the United States of America," he continued, "but you take these gifts for granted. All around you are dying souls who will end up in the fires of hell. And how do you spend your days? Going about your activities without a care in the world."

I knew that several of the boys in my neighborhood went to church, though I was pretty sure they didn't go to the right kind of church. Regardless, I knew that they had not received the level of spiritual instruction that I had been given. So, I decided that I would become more intentional with our play after school.

Soon after this service, when the boys congregated in our yard for flag football, I walked inside, grabbed my black simulated-leather King James Bible with gold-gilded edges, and asked that the boys join me by the porch swing in the garden instead. One of the boys, Kyle, several years younger than me and not yet in elementary school, seemed happy to walk over to the swing, to sit on my lap as I read to him. The rest of the boys continued to play, and I counted this as their eternal loss—I had tried, after all.

I opened my Bible to the book of Esther, one of two books in the Bible named after a girl. I knew all the books of the Bible, could say all sixty-six books in order in under twenty seconds. I was particularly drawn to Esther, the story of a girl who saved her people by winning a beauty pageant. This seemed like a familiar story.

I liked the book of Ruth, too, though it resonated with me less, a story of a woman who saved her mother-in-law through hard work and by lying beside a man. "So, she just lay beside Boaz?" I asked a Bible teacher at school, and with the same look she got on her face whenever she explained that the wine in Jesus's first miracle was not actually wine, like the wine we have today that can get you drunk, she said, "Yes. She just lay down beside him."

I began reading to Kyle: "Now it came to pass in the days of Ahasuerus . . ." I plowed through the name of the king without stuttering. I'd learned that it was better to seem certain of your pronunciation when reading the Bible aloud than to admit ignorance with a pause or a stumble. Kyle shifted in my lap, began to yawn. I kept reading. Only three verses into the first chapter, he slid off my lap and said he was going to join the game going on beside us.

I urged him to reconsider: "Just a few more verses! This is really important, Kyle. I need you to listen to this." But I failed to persuade him. I continued to sit on the swing reading the chapter silently to myself, as if to model a standard of behavior for the boys tackling one another in the grass.

Eventually, I walked inside the house and put the Bible in my backpack for the next day of school. "I tried to witness to Kyle," I told my mom as she chopped vegetables for our dinner.

"Oh, that's really nice, Anna," my mom said to me.

"I read part of the book of Esther," I continued, "but he seemed to get kind of bored."

My mom continued to slice the onions, told me that maybe next time, I could read something to him about Jesus. I conceded that this was a good idea, though I was less interested in doing this. There was just something about Esther that felt more familiar than Jesus.

5

One summer afternoon when I was nine years old, my mom, my younger brother, and I were in the produce section of the Save A Lot, evaluating the quality of strawberries and the ripeness of bananas. As I surveyed the table of fruit, my attention was diverted for what felt like only a moment. When I turned around, neither my mom nor my brother was there. I knew immediately what had happened: They had been raptured, and I had been left behind.

I was fearful, though I had been expecting this turn of events. While my mom was putting on her makeup that morning, I'd turned the channel to Daystar, an evangelical television network. A big-haired blonde woman sat across from a portly, balding man. Together, they discussed current events I had little understanding of—something in Jerusalem, the character of President Clinton—that certainly signified that the end times were upon us. They knew that they could not predict a particular date for the rapture—the Bible had forbidden that—so instead they predicted a range of dates. "Come, Lord Jesus, come," they said as a PO box address where viewers could send their donations appeared on the screen.

"Oh, turn that channel off. Those women are ridiculous," my mom said as she walked into the room, grabbing her purse and a stack of library books to drop off on our way home from the grocery store. On the top of the stack was her overdue copy of Tim LaHaye and Jerry B. Jenkins's best-selling book *Left Behind*. Both my mom and my dad had read it. I planned to pick up a copy from church the following Sunday—they'd recently gotten a shipment of the books and were handing them out for free.

In the grocery store, my brain turned static, and I walked in a fog down a number of aisles searching for my mom and my brother. The Save A Lot was rarely busy, but I did see a number of nice-looking women and children in the cereal aisle. Their presence made me wonder if maybe the rapture hadn't happened after all. Then I saw a haggard-looking couple wearing jeans with holes in them, and I began feeling certain, once more, that we were in the end times, and I would be facing the tribulation alone without my family.

I wasn't surprised that I had been left behind. Though I'd won clubber of the year in Awana (an evangelical Scouts alternative) for the past four years, I knew my award wasn't because I was that great of a person. I was just competitive and very motivated by points assigned to specific tasks. Plus I had a knack for memorizing verses with mnemonic tricks I'd been taught in Bible class at school. None of the public-school kids at church had my extensive experience with memorization.

As I continued to wander the aisles looking for my mom and brother, I considered the state of my own salvation. I held a private fear that my faith was not sincere enough, that I had not asked Jesus into my heart with a pure enough desire or motivation, though I knew better than to admit this out loud. I'd memorized the verses about how we could have assurance of salvation, and if anyone asked me whether I questioned Jesus's call on my life, I could quote back the appropriate passages.

I was surprised that my brother had been raptured. I was pretty sure that I was a better Christian than he was, if he was even a Christian. He was loud and, though only five, a little bit lazy. He watched too much TV, and when he wasn't plopped in front of a screen, I could find him in my room ripping the heads off my Barbies. Maybe he was raptured because he was still so young, not yet at the age of accountability, I reasoned to myself.

Eventually I spotted my mom and brother in the ice cream

aisle. I ran to them, careful not to reveal the state of terror I'd just been in. Even at nine years old, I had my pride. I whispered to my mom as we walked to the checkout that I had been afraid that they had been raptured. I giggled self-consciously at this admission. "Oh, honey," my mom said, "I remember whenever that happened to me when I was a girl. My mom and Aunt Catherine disappeared in the department store, and I was sure that I had been left behind. I was very scared. I found them, of course."

As we stood in the checkout line, I evaluated a display of key chains. For the past year, I had been saving up my allowance money for my key chain collection. One of the key chains had the image of a crab, with the word "Cancer" printed beneath it. I picked it up, handing it to my mom. "We should buy this for Aunt Catherine," I said with full sincerity. Sometimes Aunt Catherine would send me key chains in the mail that reminded her of me. She had just recently been diagnosed with stomach cancer. I heard my mom talking about her illness on the phone every afternoon.

"Oh, Anna," my mom said, putting the key chain back on the display. "That's not talking about the type of cancer that Aunt Catherine has. That's a zodiac sign. You know, like a horoscope. Christians shouldn't mess with stuff like that. You know the Bible doesn't allow us to predict the future."

6

At the age of ten, I flipped through Delia's mail-order catalogs to gaze at the models—all older than me, but still, somehow, thinner than me, too. They looked so happy and sophisticated with shimmering lip gloss and closely tweezed eyebrows. It appeared they had places to go, social lives full of trips to the mall and the beach and the movies.

I didn't just covet the models' clothes—I wanted the lives I imagined they were living. I longed for the freedom that a girl who wore a shirt that revealed a smidge of midriff must have.

I circled the items I wanted the most, knowing fully that I would never actually be allowed to wear most of their apparel. All those tiny rectangles of fabric masquerading as shirts or skirts, one of my mother's friends might say.

Our school dress code was strict: Everything needed to be feminine and long and loose. Ankle-length denim skirts. Boxy floral tops covering my shoulder blades and trying to hide the existence of my bust. It was easier to avoid form-fitting clothing when you didn't have a body that could fill a sweater out.

Delia's sold thinness as happiness. My religious system and the dress code at school placed thinness next to godliness.

After flipping through my Delia's catalogs, I would sneak to the living room and watch Total Request Live on MTV, gazing at Britney Spears in her belly-baring music videos. I tried to learn her dance moves. I coveted her abs, though I knew I would never be allowed to wear a shirt showing my midsection in public.

Later, alone in my bedroom, I tucked my T-shirt into my training bra to try to create a similar effect. I evaluated myself in the mirror, glancing from my belly—pale and soft and not quite flat—to her airbrushed image in a teen magazine I'd begged my mom for at the grocery store.

Reporters were always asking Britney about her figure, how she kept such a taut waistline. "1,000 crunches a night," I remember her saying in an interview—and this number stuck with me. I've been fixated on numbers forever.

Emulating Britney's practice, I did sit-ups on the floor of my bedroom each evening. I completed the sit-ups in sets, keeping track of the numbers in my mind. I aimed each day to make it into the thousands.

Eventually, I developed a rug burn on the skin of my spine. In school, I sat in my desk massaging the damaged skin on my back with quiet pride.

Of course, I knew I could never look like Britney Spears in real life. I was repeatedly instructed that I needed to cover my body to keep men from temptation and lust. As I was reminded by preachers in chapel services, 1 Timothy 2:9 says, "In like manner also, that women adorn themselves in modest apparel, with shamefacedness and sobriety; not with braided hair, or gold, or pearls, or costly array."

Even at the age of ten, I knew that my flesh was a liability and a stumbling block to men. The main way to control men's insatiable lusts and desires, I learned in Bible class, was to control my own body, to be fully clothed, to be chaste.

The reward for my good and careful behavior would come in the form of a savior—that is, a husband.

Any future that did not involve being a helpmeet to a husband at home was spoken of by pastors, by teachers, even by my parents (who tried to find balance in the midst of hyperconservatism) as failure. This meant I had to learn how to attract a husband. Carefully, without making him lust. I needed to be friendly but not a flirt. Outgoing but not loud. Attractive but not sexy. Submissive but not needy. It was a precarious task. I felt the weight of the situation.

I kept track of my measurements on a white sheet of printer paper. I decided I would officially measure each month. Unofficially, I would break the measuring tape out every day after school, just to see. I didn't want a surprise.

I measured the usual body parts—bust, waist, hips. I had been instructed how to do that by looking at the size charts in the back of my Delia's catalogs. That was easy enough. I wanted more numbers, though, more data points to watch. I measured my biceps, my forearms, my wrists, my ring fingers. Ankles, calves, lower thighs, upper thighs, rib cage, shoulders. I placed a messy box around the long list of numbers, labeling it with the month and year. I did this for several years starting at the age of ten and hid my log in the bottom of a drawer containing old school notebooks and insignificant photographs.

7

Grace and Dignity was a required class for junior high girls at my Christian school. One day we were given makeovers by a mom who sold Mary Kay. Our teacher emphasized the importance of subtlety. "When someone looks at you," she said, "they should see a beautiful girl, not her makeup."

It became a joke, then, when Caroline and Abby, girls still largely unaffected by puberty, left class with bright blue eye shadow, cheeks the color of cherries. They giggled ferociously down the hall, pressed their faces together, stuck out their tongues, laughed that they looked like clowns. We knew that, had any of us arrived to school that day with makeup caked on that thick, we would have been given a demerit and a washcloth.

In the next class period, we swarmed Mr. Smith's desk. Standing in front of him with our Mary Kay makeovers, we awaited his reaction. He was a skinny, balding man with round glasses and yellow teeth. My assigned seat was just in front of where he stood to lecture us about American history. As he discussed the importance of limited government, my gaze naturally fell right where he zipped his khakis.

We learned other lessons in Grace and Dignity—how to dress tastefully and appropriately. Never sweatpants—those were too sloppy. We considered the way a pair of pants hugged the curve of the butt.

Our teacher knew, realistically, that we couldn't always wear skirts, especially when engaged in manual labor like housework or gardening. But when we wore pants, we should be sure that some loose fabric hung over the backs of our thighs. My friend Jessica became obsessed with this expectation, always looking at her backside in the mirror, buying jeans that were three sizes too big, cinching the waist with a thick belt. She bemoaned her large pant size often though, really, she barely filled out a size medium.

We didn't talk about sex much. We knew we weren't supposed to do it, had to save it for marriage. It never crossed my mind that I would have sex outside marriage the same way it never crossed my mind that I would steal or kill someone.

One day, Jessica raised her hand and asked our teacher, "What do you think about saving our kisses for marriage?" Jessica had just read a chapter book released by Focus on the Family that featured a character who wanted to add value to her kisses by saving them for her future husband.

A few girls quietly scoffed at this, while our teacher considered it. "It's not a bad idea," she said after a pause.

We spoke about how to conduct ourselves with boys. With modesty, always. Our clothing should not incite lust—that was a given. We should also not call boys on the phone, should not ask boys out on dates, should not tell boys that we liked them. In future years, when we were old enough to date, we knew we weren't supposed to pay for anything.

"But also," our teacher told us, "be kind, girls—he's working hard to save up money to take you out. Order something inexpensive on the menu. Not necessarily a salad—but maybe that. Grilled chicken is a good choice. Water."

Around this time, a close friend's brother was caught with a stack of JCPenney catalogs under his bed. He'd been hoarding them, looking at the women modeling bras and underwear. We would learn in Grace and Dignity that this was natural, though inappropriate, behavior for boys. When my mom heard the story, she began to worry about her own son and started hiding her current Victoria's Secret catalogs in her closet, near a pile of old shoes. She hid them discreetly when my brother was not watching but seemed unconcerned that I knew of their location. "This is the sort of stuff you can look forward to buying for yourself whenever you get older and get married," she said.

After measuring myself and completing my sit-ups, I would sneak to my mom's closet and flip through the catalogs. I learned the models' names. Alessandra. Gisele. I studied the images, evaluating their breasts, their waistlines. Their hip bones, their collar bones. I imagined myself grown, in bed with my future husband, him looking at me, me nothing but boobs and bones in one of those tiny silk negligees.

I knew—and coveted—the figures of the Angels more than that of any boy. But this was not something we ever discussed in Grace and Dignity. Not another behavior I was taught to avoid.

8

The summer I was almost a teenager, I spent my afternoons at the community pool. Each afternoon, I'd take a brief dip in the shallow end. Then, I'd lie on a lounge chair by the moms from church who sat fully clothed on the same cluster of plastic chairs. I was interested in hearing how they sized up other women. With eyes closed, I'd listen—wet hair dripping onto the concrete between the chair's plastic slats, warm sizzle of skin in the sun. Eventually, Donna, a woman from our church, would shoo me away, just as I was beginning to feel at one with the hot plastic, just as the conversation started to get good.

Across the pool from the moms were the teenagers. I stared over the water at the older girls. They all went to public school. They wore triangle string bikini tops and similarly small bottoms. I looked at their legs, long and oiled and dark and shapely.

I dreamed of the future when I would become them. The smallest version of them.

One summer night after a day at the pool, my mom and I shopped at Value City. From a metal rack in the juniors' section, I pulled a bikini that looked like the ones those teenage girls wore. It was pink and yellow and floral. I imagined that wearing it would be all I needed for my transformation. I held the top against my flat chest. I wore an oversize gray T-shirt over my brittle, chlorine-dried one piece. My mom immediately said, "No way."

"Please—let me just try it on. We don't have to buy it."

My mom slowly nodded her head, giving me permission. I headed to the dusty line of changing rooms in the back of the store to see what I looked like.

"Keep your panties on, Anna," my mom called from outside the room. "Who knows how many people have tried that thing on."

I evaluated my image in the cracked dressing-room mirror. It was hard to envision myself poolside with my Fruit of the Looms peeking out from beneath those tiny bottoms. I struggled to tie the top. The triangles kept shifting. They hung lopsided across the beginnings of my breasts. The fluorescent light highlighted some dimples near my belly button. My legs were pale. I was dissatisfied.

I fantasized that in a new location and with some effort, I, too, could appear like those girls at the pool.

Back at the pool, Evan, whom I knew from church, grew tired of us all playing in the deep end. "This is boring," he said. "Let's play something else."

"How about Marco Polo?" I suggested. No one seemed interested.

"Let's have a chicken fight," Evan said after a moment. Dustin cheered, "Yes!"

"I'll be a base since I'm the biggest," Evan, twelve, skinny and tall, said without hesitation.

"I'm about as big as you," Dustin, eleven, short but wide, replied.

Stephanie (a girl from my church) and I were the only two left. We would both be on top. She and I were small for our age—we took pride in it. We wanted to keep it that way.

Stephanie looked me up and down. I wore a pink one-piece with three rhinestones embellishing the suit's scoop neck. I looked Stephanie up and down. She wore a black Speedo with flecks of turquoise blue, the swim team uniform.

"I weigh eighty-five pounds," Stephanie said.

"I weigh eighty-eight pounds," I told Stephanie. Really, the scale blinked ninety-three when I stepped on it in my mom's bathroom that morning.

"I'm a year older than you," Stephanie replied with a look of superiority.

"I'm pretty sure I'm taller than you," I responded.

Stephanie sighed. "I am never going to weigh more than one hundred pounds. Never," she said.

I paused to think about this. I believed her. I believed that she could foresee and determine her future.

"Oh, me neither. No way will I ever weigh more than one hundred pounds."

She looked at me. "You might, though. You're pretty close."

I knew she was right. I really did not see how I could stop it.

"C'mon," Evan yelled, interrupting us. "Get over here for the chicken fight!"

Together, we swam across the shallow end to where the boys stood. I climbed on top of Dustin's fleshy, pasty shoulders. I found my position. He was solid.

"On three," Evan yelled. He began counting down. I wobbled in the air, arms out, hands ready. I wanted to do some damage. I was going to win.

9

“We must decrease, so that he can increase,” the pastor bellowed from the podium. Twelve years old, I sat in the bleachers of our school gymnasium hunched over, legs crossed, arms pressed tightly into my stomach. I pushed my arms more forcefully into my abdomen, could feel the softness of my flesh through the thick wool of my sweater. Still, the waistband of my long denim skirt shifted with ease. There was finally room to breathe.

“Is there anything in your life that you need to give up so that you can follow the will of God?” the pastor asked. “With eyes closed and heads bowed, reflect upon the message we heard from the Lord this morning.”

My stomach grumbled loudly. I pressed my arms in more forcefully, an attempt to muffle the sound of my hunger. Our principal’s wife began to play the first verse of “Just as I Am” on the piano.

The pastor called over the instrumentation: “Is the Lord speaking to you? Our earthly loss is heavenly gain. Do not ignore his call. Come! Come!”

The song concluded. No one came. We were dismissed. It was time for lunch.

As my friends filed toward the cafeteria, I headed to the lobby of the gym. I threw the turkey sandwich my mom had packed for me into a metal trash can. I’d been discarding my lunch for several weeks. At first, I’d felt guilty about the waste. Still, I was relieved to be rid of the temptation.

I darted into the bathroom. Alone, I gazed at my appearance—thick, frizzy brown hair and plain brown eyes rounded with eyeliner applied with an unsteady hand. I lifted my sweater to evaluate my bare, empty belly—still, somehow, too much. I sucked in, counted my ribs, stroked them like my most precious possession. Then I pulled *Wuthering Heights* out of my backpack so that I could sit and read and escape to another place entirely for the rest of lunch.

Every evening after school, I stepped on the scale barefoot wearing only an oversize gray T-shirt and cotton briefs. My parents kept our old porcelain scale in the cupboard in the unfinished portion of our basement. Cans of green beans, tomatoes, and corn towered around it—our stock of nonperishables. We were always prepared should disaster strike.

One evening, the dial hovered just below a number that had taken a good deal of effort to achieve. I stared at the number. Double digits. I was finally back under one hundred pounds. I held my breath, giddy with excitement. I stepped off the scale, pushing it back to the corner of the cupboard. I ran to the finished portion of the basement to press play on another workout video, a VHS in which Paula Abdul coached viewers through fat-blasting dance routines choreographed to her own music. I finished the video. I ran back to the scale. The number was the same, despite my strenuous workout. I was disappointed. I wanted the number lower, my previous goal so quickly status quo. I no longer had a specific number in mind. I just knew I loved to feel the high of loss.

"Some of you care about sports more than you do the word of God," one pastor said during a chapel service. He went on to chide us for wanting to remain *comfortable* rather than witnessing to our friends. We were chastised for wanting to play ball and laugh and talk about television, rather than telling our friends from public school the truth: that unless they repent, they would go to hell.

Then, he proposed a harder question: Perhaps we did not care because we were not actually saved. Had we considered that if we had no drive to rescue the lost from eternal damnation, perhaps we, too, had not experienced salvation?

And the Bible says that because we know the truth—because we were sitting in chapel, listening to speaker after speaker preach the word of God—eventually, God would harden our hearts. We had been given the blessing of godly teachers and preachers, mothers and fathers. Even then, we still rejected the call of Christ. So much worse would our eternal torment be.

I acted as if I was unaffected by the grim prognosis, the harsh evaluation of my behavior. That because I wanted to go bike riding with my friends in peace, I was setting myself up for suffering in hell.

This is what I remember most distinctly: When faced with impossible standards or unreasonable expectations, I did not challenge them. I distracted myself. I looked away.

One of the pastors who preached frequently in chapel also worked part-time as our typing teacher. His church was small; only a handful of families attended. It met on a dusty back country road in a neighboring county. He supplemented his income by supervising students learning to type using Mavis Beacon software in the computer lab. For unknown reasons, typing class was segregated by gender—girls met for instruction at one time, boys at another.

Our teacher had rosy cheeks and steel-blue eyes. He looked like a young Santa Claus without the beard. He was friendly—suspiciously so. He complimented us, seventh graders, on haircuts—this was nice enough—and then on outfits.

He compared Emily's outfit to one worn by his wife: "My wife used to wear dresses like that when we first got married. She looked beautiful. She's gained some weight since then, isn't able to fit into those types of things anymore. That type of dress looks great on you, though, Emily."

Emily, a girl I pegged as stupid at the time, smiled and thanked our teacher for the compliment. Then she bemoaned her own size, complained that when she stepped on the scale at the doctor's office, she was up to 125 pounds.

"No way," our teacher replied. "You, 125 pounds? It all has to be in your big toe!" Then he told us how much his wife weighed—now and also on the day they got married. I was learning.

In class, I was a fast typist. I took pride in how quickly my fingers could move on the keyboard. Using the software's timer, I treated it like a footrace for my hands. "That's very good, Anna," our teacher would say as I typed with intensity to beat a personal best.

One day, our teacher noticed that Emily was wearing bright-red nail polish. He complimented her on the color, moved closer to her chair, inspected the curve of her nails. She thanked him, told him she and her mom had gotten manicures the previous weekend. He expressed his approval. He turned to the rest of the class: "There is nothing more disgusting than for a girl to have dirty hands." He paused. "I might start considering this whenever I grade you. Deduct points for unkempt nails."

In elementary school, I collected nail polish with my allowance money. I took pleasure in creating an ombre effect by painting each nail a different shade of blue. I'd wanted to paint my babysitter's nails this way, too, several years prior. She refused my offer, said she preferred more classic shades, red or pink, or no color at all. I quit painting my own nails shortly after that. In class, I looked at my hands. My nails were unpainted but clean, trimmed with little excess. Still, I felt exposed by our teacher's comment. I found myself glancing down at my hands with hesitancy as I typed for the duration of the class period.

Our teacher preached in chapel one day soon after this class period. His message was about idols of the heart. In the Old Testament, he reminded us, the heathens worshiped idols of stone. Our present-day idols were not so obvious. They were the secret sins that we held on to, those precious things that we were just not willing to give up.

"What is it that distracts you from Christ?" he interrogated us. "What keeps you from witnessing to others about him?" He paused for effect. "Is it television? Music? A particular boy or girl? A sport? Money? Sex? Pornography?"

I sat in my seat, heart racing. I felt exposed, even though he had not included my idol in the list. I knew the answer to his question: I idolized my body. I felt consumed by its demands. I was frustrated by its hungers, its weaknesses. I found myself hopping on and off the scale all evening long. The numbers were all I could think about, dream about. The numbers were a great distraction from his list of possible idols. I didn't care much at all about any of the other things he mentioned.

Slowly, I raised my hand. My palms began to sweat as I considered the implications of this quiet admission. Would teachers in the room be squinting to see whose hands were up? Would I have to admit to my obsessions? I imagined this scenario, imagined a teacher approaching me after the service, asking if there was something I needed to talk about. This fantasy evoked dread and relief in equal measure. I was ashamed of my sin, and I felt trapped. All of it seemed bigger than me, bigger than something I could just decide to give up.

When we opened our eyes, the principal's wife began to play another hymn on the piano. Our teacher added another requirement to the service: All who raised their hands were told to walk forward to the front of the room and kneel by the stage. He wanted us to confess our sin for accountability and receive pastoral prayer.

Only one person walked to the front of the room—a lanky high school boy with floppy hair whose idol I assumed was pornography. The rest of us remained seated. When the principal's wife had finished playing her song, the pastor commended the bravery of the boy.

He turned to the rest of us then and spoke disdainfully: "There were many more of you who raised your hands. When we ignore the conviction of the Holy Spirit, we harden our hearts to the Lord. Walking forward requires courage. Those of you who raised your hands without walking forward ignored the call of the Holy Spirit. He will not continue to pursue rebellious, unlistening souls."

Math class was scheduled immediately after chapel. I retreated briefly to the bathroom. I felt shaken and ashamed. I also felt relieved. I couldn't believe I'd been stupid enough to raise my hand. What was I thinking, anyway? I didn't have an idol, a real problem. What would I have even said if I had walked forward? *Oh, sometimes I worry about eating lunch.* I mocked this admission in my head, imagined the pastor mocking me, too. I glanced in the mirror as I left the restroom. I noticed the hard bone of my hips jutting through my denim skirt, and I rubbed it, as if for comfort, or courage, or distraction.

10

In math class, my teacher told us that just before her wedding, she prepared to fit into her dress by eating only a couple hundred calories a day. *Did you know that's not enough for even a toddler to live on?* She said it with feigned disgrace, but even as a twelve-year-old, I knew she was bragging. I sat in class hunched over, arms pressed tightly into my abdomen, squinting at the chalky haze of numbers on the board. I had a prescription for glasses, but I'd quit wearing them that year for appearances. I had a headache by the time the final bell rang each day.

For extra credit, we were to write down everything we ate for a week and the corresponding number of calories. *We would be shocked!* she said. *Done*, I thought to myself, gratified by this challenge. I'd been logging this information in a burgundy Mead notebook for months, and I'd developed a sort of shorthand, a cover for my notes should they be discovered by my mom or dad. "One apple, eighty calories" was expressed as "1 a, 80 c." I was tall and thin, but I'd packed on twenty puberty pounds over the summer, and this felt like a situation that needed to be managed.

When I turned my records in, I received my extra credit, but there was no response to the strict content of my submission. I wanted acknowledgment. I wanted a look of concern. I knew my dietary log revealed something more pernicious than basic discipline. I wanted to be seen. I wondered if she read the numbers, if she thought I had miscalculated, if she just really didn't care. I continued to keep these records in notebooks buried at the bottom of my underwear drawer. They were a kind of release valve, a log of the pressure inside that gave me the stamina to remain calm outside, still in line, still the quiet girl in school.

My best friend in elementary was known at school as the *other* quiet girl. She lived in a log mansion at the top of a giant hill deep in the woods. We would jump on her trampoline at night, exterior lights shining on the springs, and it felt as if we were flying through the trees.

Her mom, Judy, was a successful realtor, her fresh, blue-eyed face plastered on billboards. One day after a home showing, a man began calling Judy repeatedly. Later, he appeared at her house, driving up and down their long driveway. Soon after, they came home to find their front door open, lingerie pulled from her chest of drawers, bras dangling from the deer mounts decorating the walls of their family room.

They packed up immediately and left town. I didn't learn of the circumstances surrounding their move until the hurt of my only friend suddenly moving had healed to a scar.

"Poor Judy," my mom said quietly, reflecting upon the consequences of a woman becoming too big, revealing too much. "You should never put your picture up on a billboard."

11

"You all know me, and you know that I've been yo-yo dieting since high school," Tammy said, wiping a tear away from one eye as she stood behind the pulpit in the sanctuary. Women weren't typically allowed to stand in the preacher's place on Sundays, but for this, the elders made an exception.

"I'd just about given up, accepting the fifteen extra pounds I packed on after each baby. Thanks for that, Kelly and Michael," she said, winking at her children seated in the pews. "But you might have noticed that, over the last year, I've lost twenty pounds—and I've kept it off, too! And here's the secret: This time, I didn't go on a diet.

"One day, I was at Lifeway looking through Sunday-school curriculum. I noticed materials for something called First Place. It's a weight-loss ministry. I flipped through a booklet, and right away, I was impressed. And I've done all the programs: low-fat, Weight Watchers, the Zone, SlimFast.

"But something felt different about this program. You're given meal plans that can be modified. You learn about what Scripture has to say about food. They even have you study the way Jesus probably ate in the first century!

"And here's the clincher: The program is Christ-focused. It is centered on *prayer*. Our bodies are the temples of the Holy Spirit, after all. It is our duty to make sure that they are healthy.

"I'm so impressed with this program—and I feel closer to the Lord now, too. After speaking with Pastor Steve, I've decided to organize a churchwide group that will meet on Sunday nights, for anyone interested in trying out First Place."

After church in the parking lot, I heard my mom talking to her circle of friends about the group. Her best friend, Linda, a short woman with large glasses, said, "I guess I'm going to join the Fat Club. Tammy kept making eye contact with me after she stopped crying up there." The women took turns reassuring the others that they didn't need to join the group, but they all planned to join the group. That is, everyone would except for my mom.

When my mom was a young girl, her friends teased her for having bird legs and a bony chest. When she grew into herself, even after having children, she easily maintained a figure that drew little criticism. She didn't talk about her body much to me, never spoke about dieting. One time during the summer, my brother and I were drinking milkshakes before bed, watching Nick at Nite on the small television in our kitchen. My mom refused a milkshake for herself, told us, "It's too late for me to have ice cream." That's the closest I ever heard my mom come to talking about a diet.

I knew my mom would not join the group, but more significantly, I knew that she pitied the women who felt they needed to. After attending a Southern Baptist women's conference one weekend, she complained that all the speakers spoke about were the women's poor body images. "*Jesus thinks you're beautiful! Your husband thinks you're beautiful!* That's not true," Mom vented to my dad in our living room about the sessions. "Some of their husbands do not think they are beautiful—because some of them are *not* beautiful!"

"They're not going out to eat with us after church because they are so *legalistic*," my friends whispered about my family in the pews.

We all believed in adhering to a particular moral code. But if those morals were lived out in a way that made another person feel guilty or uncomfortable or judged, the victimized party might call the other person legalistic. This criticism was meant to be harsh. The Pharisees, we learned in sermons, were *legalists*. They were very religious, had high standards, and Jesus absolutely hated them.

We all found it thrilling to have permission to judge others for being too good, and not just for being too bad.

When I was a child, our family did not eat at restaurants on Sundays after church. This was a law born out of loss. Mom gave up the Sunday after-services restaurant ritual most people at church had after she graduated from college. On the bus home from music class in downtown Atlanta, my mom spotted her childhood next-door neighbor, Lisa. As they caught up with one another, Lisa told my mom that she was doing okay, though she'd dropped out of college because she couldn't afford her tuition payments. She was working as a bartender at a local restaurant to save up some money for the next semester.

Mom, who did not even take a sip of champagne at weddings, stiffened at the word "bartender." Her own mom had always said, "Never marry a man who drinks." Most marital strife, according to the women in my family, was connected to the consumption of alcohol.

Lisa's mom had died when she was a baby. After elementary school each day, she and my mom ate fistfuls of chips from the family-sized bag in Lisa's kitchen, while Lisa retrieved the gin from the cupboard to mix her father a welcome-home-from-work drink. She left the glass waiting for him on the television stand beside his La-Z-Boy.

Sometimes my mom heard yelling coming from Lisa's house at night. Sometimes my mom heard the sound of objects being thrown against walls. Once, Lisa had a black eye when she arrived at the bus stop. She said one of her friends had accidentally hit her with a baseball. Often, she wore scratchy turtlenecks on hot summer days.

Now Lisa was a bartender. My mom tried to help in the best way a Baptist girl knew how—she invited Lisa to church.

"Oh, no," Lisa said without missing a beat. "I can't get off work on a Sunday. We're too busy. And I need the tips."

Years later, my mom read the *Atlanta Journal Constitution* and learned that Lisa had been in a car accident late one night. She died upon impact. "The accident was related to *alcohol*," my grandmother said quietly.

As my mom processed this loss, she kept thinking of Lisa's refusal to come to church. Maybe if tips had not been so good, if church people had not flocked to restaurants immediately after services, Lisa would still be alive. Or, if not alive, then maybe she'd be in heaven. Mom was pretty sure Lisa was not in heaven. So she vowed never to eat at a restaurant on Sunday again.

The rule was explained to me this way: The Sabbath is a day of rest. We should do everything possible to contribute to the rest of others. "How is it really a day of rest when you have other people working for you?" my mom said.

No one else at our church shared this view, despite my mom's lengthy explanations to her friends in the vestibule after services. I could hear the smugness in my mom's voice as she turned down invitations to the Chinese buffet across the street. I felt both embarrassment and pride.

When I was a teenager, one of my private food rules was *no restaurants*. I kept this rule quiet to avoid scrutiny, but *thou shalt not eat at a restaurant* might as well have been inscribed in my own personal Bible. I devised many arbitrary rules about food and my body, the list much longer than the Ten Commandments. Breakfast was fine. Lunch was not. Pilates counted as exercise. Walking did not.

There were so many rules, I didn't even know all of them explicitly. I often did not become aware of their existence until I was asked to break one, until I felt a familiar rise in my chest, heart beating faster, palms sweating—the anxiety of adhering to a restriction without allowing anyone to know about its presence in the first place.

Sometimes, of course, I needed to break a rule. To break a rule, I had to plan ahead of time; barring that, there were consequences. I administered my own consequences, just as I made my own rules. I could make a rule permitting my breaking a rule, but I could not make that decision spontaneously. Adherence to these rules required a very orderly, predictable life. Routine. Few parties. Self-imposed isolation. Vacations were more stress than they were worth. My survival felt incredibly fragile.

Thou shalt not eat at restaurants became a rule for me as a young teenager because I could not find the specific calorie counts for dishes on the menu. Michelle Obama had not yet begun her First Lady work of requiring the labeling of every menu item with corresponding units of energy. Because restaurant food was so mysterious, I simply made a rule that I would not consume it. Magazines frequently talked about how cooking at home could prevent the scale from creeping up, all those sneaky oils and fats added in the kitchen without your knowledge. Even salads were not safe, these articles continued, the romaine tossed in calorie-dense dressing. The seemingly purest options were still pernicious.

In Sunday school, we learned about Jewish dietary laws, the laws of kashrut. *No birds of prey. Land animals must eat grass and have cloven hooves. Seafood must have fins and scales. Dairy and meat cannot be mixed.* We bemoaned their extensiveness. We considered the rationale behind their existence in the first place. Sunday school teachers spoke about how these laws were to protect the health of God's people, to diminish the growth of tumors, to reduce the likelihood of food poisoning, but really, I learned later, this was just speculation.

Some of the rules did not seem to have a rationale at all.

The consequences of breaking the rules, too, were open to interpretation. The Torah stipulated no penalty, though the Talmud advised the administration of thirty-nine lashes, corporal punishment.

We knew that gentile New Testament Christians were no longer bound to these strict codes. Whatever reason there was for such rigidity in ancient times, observance of those codes was not necessary at our dinner tables. Jesus had declared all foods clean. He offered himself up as a meal. He was the bread of life.

Praise the Lord, we were free! Though of course we were not. At church potlucks, I watched women at the buffet line judiciously choose the smaller dessert plate to limit their portions, piling it high with raw vegetables. I saw their secret laws because they were mine too. If they had spoken these rules aloud, if they had connected them with their religion, we might have all cried, "Legalist!" It was such fun to identify the presence of a good legalist in the crowd, even for those of us who received the label frequently ourselves. Whether we felt the need to keep our rules private or felt at liberty to discuss them, we women had our own codes for bodily protection. There was great power in believing that what we put in our mouths could have eternal consequence.

12

Shortly before my aunt Catherine died, she was given tickets to visit Benny Hinn at one of his healing conventions.

"It's worth a shot," the ladies at church told my aunt. They spoke of people who had been healed from chronic diabetes, from the debilitating pain of car accidents.

"I'm not getting my hopes up," Aunt Catherine said, after she wrote in to Hinn's organization, giving notice of her future attendance: thirty-something mom of a young toddler, stomach cancer, several rounds of chemo and radiation, ovaries just removed. She never received a reply. Those healed in the service were heavily made up, dripping emotion, performative plants.

"I should have known better," she said angrily to my mom over the phone. All she had left were her doctor's appointments, her diminishing medical options. Hope began to seem just as ridiculous as Benny Hinn.

After Aunt Catherine died, we received stacks of lasagnas left on our front doorstep, piles of Hallmark cards in the mail.

Soon, though, people at church moved on with their lives and forgot about my mom grieving her only sibling. They began asking her to volunteer again, to lead children's activities.

Mom, exhausted and depressed, turned these requests down. She started to receive critical glances. She realized that the people who used to rely on her volunteerism were annoyed that she was no longer pitching in.

On Sunday mornings, she still woke early, got us all dressed, and loaded us up in the car. But then she'd sit at the wheel for a moment: "I can't do it today," she'd finally say. "Let's just stay home."

Thrilled, my brother and I would bound upstairs in our nice shoes and fancy outfits to turn on the television.

After we repeatedly missed services for several months, I heard women—*bossy women*, Mom would call them behind their backs—approach her after church when we were present, chiding her for our poor attendance.

"It's important to model Christlikeness for our children," I heard one blonde woman say. "That includes making church attendance a priority in our lives."

Mom began doubling down. In a surprise to us all, she quit choir. Singing in the church choir had been the biggest part of her identity, outside of being our mom. I was confused.

"It just isn't something I value anymore," she said when I looked to her for an explanation.

13

My mom put a kettle of hot water on the stove and set out the Royal Albert fine bone china with gilded edges and country roses. These teacups were one of the many items my mom inherited after Aunt Catherine passed away.

A pair of freshly baked scones cooled on the kitchen counter. Chocolate chip with whipping cream, slabs of butter, crystallized sugar. Mom made them while I was at school for us to enjoy together.

The occasion was simple: I was home. And we were going to sit and talk about our day.

I loved her scones, and I hated her scones. Sometimes, in study hall at the end of the day as my stomach grumbled, I worried that my mom had these scones at home, waiting for me. They were nearly impossible to resist.

At the kitchen table, I allowed myself a quarter—no, half—*fine*, a whole one. I crunched some numbers and willfully underestimated my calculations.

My mom didn't seem to know about my math, and I wanted it to stay that way. If she knew about the math, she might make me stop. Or it might make her sad.

I didn't want to make my mom any sadder than she already was.

Snow fell. A red robin appeared at the bird feeder by the window. My mom had hung several of these on the porch, and they were always stocked with seed.

Here, at home, it was warm and safe.

I changed out of my school clothes into workout gear. I was going to sit with my mom, just for a minute, but I had trouble getting back up once I'd plopped down. It was as if I'd come out of the cold to recover in a warm bath.

I dissected the pastry on my plate into pieces, but Mom didn't say a word about that.

"How was your day?" she asked.

And I told her. I told her about the geometry test that I was so stressed about, and I told her that this year's fall social theme was going to be "Hawaiian." I told her that Josh asked Sarah to go to the social with him, and I told her that I hoped Billy would ask me, though I knew he never would.

I told her all sorts of things, most everything, really, but I would never, ever tell her about *this*—my secret math.

Because *this* was all mine.

An hour passed. And then another. We poured many cups of tea, and I nibbled too many pieces of scones. I began to worry about how I was going to get rid of it all that evening. I was running out of time.

"I'm so overwhelmed with schoolwork," I heard myself say. "I have so much to do. It's just so much. I don't know how I'm going to get it all done."

Of course I wasn't really thinking about schoolwork.

My mom looked at me and nodded. "Well, how about you take a mental health day tomorrow?"

I was thrilled at this. I was so relieved to think that I'd have a whole day to get all my exercise in. "But what will I say at school about why I'm absent? I don't want to lie."

"Well, do you feel sick?"

"I do feel sick."

"Then let's just say you're sick, then."

14

When fall of my freshman year in high school came, a girl at my church named Sierra returned looking like she had been stretched. She was both grown and shrunk. Each Sunday, her head—the biggest part of her entire body—blocked my view of the pulpit. As our pastor preached about the state of Israel, of America's certain destruction if we did not support the chosen people of God, I examined the top half of Sierra's back in her shift dress. Her shoulder blades were sharp. There was no flesh poking around the elastic lines of her bra. She'd dismissed the frivolity of girlhood, trading it in for the sophistication of adult minimalism. There was no longer anything extra about her.

"Did you see Sierra this morning during the service?" I overheard Linda say to another woman as they walked across the parking lot to a First Place meeting. I didn't have to hear the rest of the conversation: I knew they were discussing Sierra's body. I imagined each of the moms stepping on the scale at the front of their meeting room, sharing their goals for healthy-living accountability, continuing to discuss their concern over the protruding ribs of a fourteen-year-old as they ate their platefuls of melon wedges.

After some months, I'd practically forgotten the Sierra I'd idealized as a child. Instead, when I heard her name, I did not envision her face or hear her quiet, breathy voice. I heard the words "sick." "Too thin." "Problem." And I heard them in the voices of my mom's friends.

But even acquaintances in casual, unrelated conversation brought Sierra's name up as a topic of concern.

My friend Noah also expressed concern about Sierra. Everyone was worried, he told me; she appeared to have lost even more weight, and I agreed with him that she did look sick. Though, really, I thought she looked great—I always had. She had always been just the sort of girl I aspired to become.

In youth group, Sierra didn't say much. When I heard a noise that came out of her, it was rarely in the form of words. She laughed often, high pitched with a pinched face, and she was usually responding to some boy, a joke he had presumably made. I never heard her banter back. It was as if she had nothing humorous to contribute but still was determined to not appear unpleasant.

Sometimes when I would arrive late to youth group, the other kids would still be eating. I'd see a cold slice in front of Sierra on an oily Styrofoam plate. "Here, have a piece," I imagined one of her concerned friends insisting as Sierra sat cross-legged in a metal folding chair. I figured she didn't want to seem difficult, so she went along with the game. I wondered why she didn't just skip the beginning of the meeting altogether as I did, wandering the stairs behind the baptismal, flipping through old church directories in the choir room. I realized, though, that she did not skip because she would, in fact, be missed. And this was what made me most envious of her. Not her sharp hip bones still visible in jeans. Not her sunken, bony cheekbones brushed with rose blush. I envied that she, so quickly, had become a part of the group, that people noticed when she was gone, that others were concerned as she slowly disappeared.

One evening after youth group, my mom stopped by the Save A Lot across the street to pick up some bananas and milk. While standing in the checkout line, I noticed an advertisement for the upcoming *Growing Pains* reunion on the cover of a tabloid magazine. I watched the show in syndication. So many of my classmates had crushes on the show's main character played by Kirk Cameron. "You know he's a Christian?" Jessica would say as she taped a magazine cutout of him from an advertisement for his latest inspirational film to the inside of her locker. We'd nod our heads, indulging ourselves in this celebrity fantasy.

I was a dedicated viewer of *Growing Pains*—not because of Kirk Cameron, but because of Tracey Gold. I noticed how her body changed over the course of the show: from a little girl, to a curvy teenager, to a frail young woman. That final iteration of her appearance looked much like Sierra: thinning, teased hair, a skeleton with skin. I watched reruns of the show primarily to observe Gold's character, Carol, waste away on screen. I was convinced her body was saying something, and I was sure I could translate the message. I felt we were speaking the same language.

When I saw that the show's finale was scheduled to air, I taped it on VHS. For months, I watched that episode privately, the Seaver family eating one last meal on the set of their iconic home, pizza on a picnic blanket spread across their empty living room floor. I rewound the tape repeatedly to watch Carol. I wanted to see her take that piece of pizza and act out a performance of eating. I analyzed the way her mouth moved with the introduction of the slice. And then, again, in that same scene, I'd observe her nervous eyes. She never actually placed the pizza to her lips. She just held it like a prop, an unfortunate encumbrance, and I, too, felt this way eating meals in the company of others. As if everyone else had a natural talent for consumption, while I was playing a barely learned game with rules I didn't understand, always on the verge of losing.

After some months, as Sierra continued to shrink, I learned from Noah on AOL Instant Messenger that several of the older kids in youth group were making plans for an intervention. "We're just so worried about her," he typed in the chat screen. "Have you seen how thin she's become?" And of course I had—it was all I could do not to stare at her during the entire church service. I found her body's message much more fascinating than anything our pastor had to say. "She looks very thin," I typed in response, and Noah proceeded to tell me of the plan: They were all going to talk to her. To express their concern. To tell her she looked fine as she was. To make her eat.

I knew this wouldn't work. I imagined that if I had been on the receiving end of an intervention, I would have felt embarrassment at first, but mostly, I would have been thrilled at the concern. To be sick enough to be seen. It would have been just the encouragement I'd needed to keep going. I wanted to press Noah about their plans: *So, how, exactly, are you going to make her eat?* I believed that their schemes were laughable and ridiculous. *You can make her do a lot of things*, I wanted to say to Noah, *but you can't make her do that*. Instead, I typed back, "Good luck."

At the end of youth group one evening as I walked toward my parents' car, I saw a circle of older teenagers surrounding Sierra in the grass. She looked uncomfortable, arms crossed, and I saw her nod her head several times. I wanted to linger and watch the show, but my mom had already started the engine and was ready to head home. About an hour later, I saw Noah log onto AOL Instant Messenger. I immediately said, "Hey!" I hoped he would offer up details about the evening without my having to ask. Sure enough, he told me early in the conversation, "Well, we all talked to Sierra after youth group today." Like the moms meeting in First Place, all of us in youth group also craved forms of accountability.

"How did it go?" I asked in response. I was pecking at the keyboard, typing with one hand. My other hand was filled with a fistful of cereal, my dinner. I told myself that was all I was allowed for the evening.

"She seemed to appreciate us showing concern," Noah responded. "She told us she's been having a hard time, that she's been stressed. But she agreed with us—that she was starting to look too thin. She promised us she'd try to start eating more."

"That's great," I said simply. *Stress*, I laughed to myself. *Did they really buy that?* I felt certain that their intervention did nothing, or perhaps even provided the support she needed to continue in her game. I was interested in what would happen next.

I had decided that at the next youth meeting, I would arrive on time. Pizza had just been dropped off at the door, and the cardboard boxes were placed on a table at the front of the room. I sat in the back, fiddling with the pen I kept in my Bible, watching Sierra from the corner of my eye as she laughed with her friends. Her friends stood up, walking toward the line of food, and Sierra joined them. They each took a Styrofoam plate. Everyone grabbed two slices, while Sierra took one. They all returned to their chairs. I watched them eating, chewing and laughing and talking, and I observed Sierra tear a piece of crust from her slice of pizza and softly place it to her lips. She ate it slowly. And then she tore another piece, again, with such careful chews. The rest of her group had already finished their meal. Several of them were walking to the trash cans to discard their plates. Sierra popped up, too, darting into the hallway with her plate and pizza, returning to the room empty-handed and smiling.

As I watched the scene, Noah sat down beside me in the back of the room. He never hung out with me at youth group, even though there were only about thirty of us. We just chatted online. I assumed I was too young, that he preferred spending his time with kids his own age, and so I was not too offended by his disinterest. Still, I was excited to have him join me as I sat quiet and alone.

"Hey!" I said to him with some enthusiasm.

"Hey!" he responded. "Aren't you going to get some pizza?" he asked me. I glanced away from his gaze. "Oh, I already ate dinner," I told him without pause. He looked at me slowly. I watched him assess my arms, my waist, my thighs. I was pretty sure it was the first time he'd ever looked at me.

I felt a shiver of pleasure in being seen.

"C'mon," he said to me. "You should at least get a slice. I don't want you turning into Sierra."

"Oh, no," I said with a laugh, and I stood up as if to approach the table. But then I walked to the door, out into the hall. I decided I would wander outside for a bit, completing a lap or two around the perimeter of the sanctuary. I would return once the meeting officially began. And if Noah asked where I had gone, I'd tell him I'd forgotten something in my car.

But when I returned, Noah had moved from our chairs in the back to a circle with Sierra and the rest of the older kids. He did not notice my reentrance. He did not glance in my direction. The main show, it seemed, was up front, with the loud boys and the giggling girls. And though there was nothing stopping me from joining the group, I sat alone in the back waiting for the sermon to begin.

15

I studied diligently for the SAT, checking out stacks of prep books from the library, taking practice test after test. I didn't know what I wanted to do for a career, precisely—I wasn't even sure I was allowed to have a career. But I knew I wanted to succeed. I believed college would take me where I wanted to go.

"No one can have it all," Mom told me quietly one afternoon as I studied in the kitchen. She was reflecting upon her own life and my future one. "It's a lie to believe you can." She paused. "But don't let anyone tell you that your education is wasted whenever you become a stay-at-home mom. A woman's education is never wasted. When you educate a woman, you educate a whole family."

All the girls in my class at the end of high school had the same plans: We were going to college. College was a given. There, we'd have this brief taste of the outside world and then immediately retreat into the home under the authority of male headship to start a family. I wanted to be a mom. I had trouble imagining anything else. I wanted other things, too—an updated wardrobe, a Tudor home in the English countryside, a floor-to-ceiling library of my favorite books. But I had been told more times than I could count how dangerous it was to "want it all."

So this was our map for life: to test-drive the foreign, professional world but then to ultimately buy into the domestic. Though this road seemed familiar, that did not mean I was not intimidated by it. I hadn't had much success with boys. I was uncomfortable and awkward in my body. I didn't know how to flirt. I believed I was invisible to boys, and even if I wasn't, I tried to make myself disappear from them anyway.

Unfortunately, my body appeared to be the primary currency for my future life transactions.

I loved children. They were the only creatures that made me feel at ease, not under constant scrutiny. But to have a baby meant that you had to have sex. I supposed I could figure that out. But then I would have to grow a baby in my body. I'd have to gain weight. I didn't see any way around that. And then I would be talked about, examined. I listened intently to how people spoke about the bodies of pregnant women at church. They praised them to their faces. They mocked them behind their backs. This duplicity was almost enough to make me reconsider my plan of having children at all. Almost. I told myself it would be a familiar challenge—to try to control an impossible situation.

Before our class's Christian leadership retreat, I studied the daily schedule. The order gave me comfort. I looked immediately for the slots labeled "free time." There were several chunks each day. This would be when my classmates would throw Frisbees, gossip, flirt. This is when I would exercise, preferably alone. I wasn't sure where or how.

I would hide in a bathroom stall to run in place, roll into a ditch to complete sit-ups, if I must.

When we were not attending sermons, we were allowed some leniency in dress. Upon arrival, Jessica and I changed into loose-fitting athletic pants. She suggested we run the grounds together to become acquainted with the layout of the conference center. She didn't run as fast as I would have liked, and she was satisfied with her work far earlier than I was, but I didn't say much. I didn't want to appear too desperate.

Jessica had read all the books I'd read—Elisabeth Elliot's

Passion and Purity, Joshua Harris's *I Kissed Dating Goodbye*, two purity-culture staples. She was prepared to save herself for marriage and to submit after. But I really couldn't imagine Jessica submitting to anyone. For all her faults, she knew what she wanted and wasn't afraid to go after it. She was forthright. She didn't tiptoe around people. I admired this about her, which was why I kept hanging around her.

Jessica didn't seem to lack confidence, but she was very concerned with the modesty of her own clothing, never wanted to "make a brother stumble." She was also on a perpetual diet. She sprinkled Splenda in her water and drank SlimFast at lunch. She and I were both obsessed with what we put in our mouths. But while I hid my preoccupations, she was unashamed to turn down a sandwich to drink her meal in a can. When she ate pizza slices, she blotted the grease with a napkin. "Oh, Anna," she'd say to me, "just have one slice. It's not going to hurt you. You know you'll work it off later. Here—" she handed me a napkin—"blot it like this. Tear the cheese off, if you must."

I blushed furiously when she gave me these instructions. My shame was layered. I was uncomfortable with my body, frustrated by its hungers. But I didn't want anyone to see these fears or frustrations. That felt just as needy. All I really wanted was to get to a place where I could exist, airy, light, without any real demands of the world or others. In achieving that, I hoped to be above reproach.

Any need exposed my inherent sinfulness. I had been taught that I was totally depraved, which meant that everything I desired was bad, too. If I wanted a boy, this revealed my lust. If I wanted a higher score on my math test, this was pride. If I wanted, eventually, a good job, a career that fulfilled and fed me, this was greed. If I wanted to be thin—to be pretty, or accepted, or safe—this was vanity. Between church and school I heard sermons six days a week. Over and over again I listened while everything I wanted was traced back to everything that was so very wrong with me.

My exhaustive efforts toward goodness—and my ongoing inability to quash my own desires—only proved my deviance.

It wasn't all hopelessness. We were offered a solution, of course: Jesus. Jesus was good when we were not, and all his righteousness could be ours with a sincere, precisely worded prayer. I prayed this prayer over and over; I tried, truly, but maybe that was the problem—that I wasn't supposed to try; I just needed to learn to stop wanting so much and receive. But I didn't know how. And I didn't know what to do with my body. It felt like an impossible problem.

And so it seemed logical to numb my needs. To do the opposite of what my body told me to do. I couldn't trust it, after all. If I saw a cute boy, I immediately looked the other way. If I wanted a deeper friendship with a girl, I tried to spend more time alone, cultivating contentment in my inner life. And if I was hungry, I tried very hard to no longer be. Or, at least, I tried to hide my hunger from others, from them seeing me so needful and chomping and open.

16

As we headed to dinner the first evening at the conference center, I was excited to see a hiking trail just behind the cafeteria. The trail, according to the wooden sign posted beside it, led to a lake in the middle of the woods, just over a mile away. I decided I would run this trail up and down for the duration of each of my free times for the rest of the trip. There was a place I was able to go when I was moving. It was anywhere other than here.

On the menu for the day, there were grilled chicken, green beans, mashed potatoes, a salad mix, rolls, and brownies. I did my usual math. *Okay, grilled chicken is probably, what, 250 calories, but I don't know what it was cooked in. I could dab the oil off with a napkin. If I only eat half, that's 125. Green beans are 30, but I think I see bacon, so maybe bump it up to 80 to account for the grease. I can eat the salad plain. That's probably 20. The mashed potatoes are tricky. I don't know if there's butter or sour cream. I'm sure there is. Maybe 300? I'll only eat a few bites of it, just to be safe. Skip the brownie. The roll is small, so with no butter it would maybe be 100? So, 125 + 80 + . . .*

"Anna. Anna!" I startled to Jessica's voice. "Why are you so spaced out? Where do you want to sit?"

"I don't know—wherever. You pick."

While I tried to finish my calculations in my head, Jessica chose an open spot beside a sickeningly clean-cut boy. He wore a button-up shirt tucked into khaki slacks. He was skinny, a redhead with what appeared to be curly hair, should he ever be permitted to grow his hair out. He looked like a preacher boy, and sitting all alone, preacher boys were always in search of their preacher's wife. I certainly wasn't interested in this job, but Jessica had remarked on multiple occasions that this was the future ministry she felt called to.

Jessica introduced both of us to the preacher boy, whose name was Brian. He pretended to shake our hands but pulled away with a tired joke—"Oops! Can't break the six-inch rule."

Jessica responded with a big laugh: "I better scoot my chair over, then, to not violate our codes of conduct."

Brian had a huge grin. He liked this, the flirting. This was how you did it here—you spoke of all the stupid little things you were not allowed to do or touch. I smiled weakly, pushing the mashed potatoes around on my plate.

They began talking about their future plans for college. "What do you want to major in?" Jessica asked Brian.

"I want to go to Bob Jones and major in music ministries."

"What's your instrument?" I asked him. I didn't want to appear totally checked out, and even though I found him repulsive, if he seemed interested in me, I was ready to revise my initial assessment of him.

"Piano," he said quickly, continuing to gaze at Jessica. I decided that was enough—no more questions. He seemed like an even bigger loser than I originally thought.

"Who are your favorite musicians?" Jessica asked with wide eyes. He named a string of classical composers, but then he leaned in to Jessica, cupping his hand to his mouth to whisper another name. Jessica began to laugh ferociously.

"What did you say?" I asked, confused. Jessica responded with an exaggerated whisper: "He said, 'the Beatles.'" Brian's facial expression changed to feigned embarrassment.

"Oh," I said.

"Don't tell anyone, please," he begged us. "I'm about to graduate. I wouldn't want to get kicked out." He winked at Jessica. She flashed a smile and winked back. She grabbed my hand: "Secret's safe with us!" I nodded slowly in response.

I tried to make my way out of the conversation after that. I turned to Emily, a classmate beside me. "I feel kind of sick," she told me. "I just started my period."

"I feel kind of sick, too," I said.

The first sermon was scheduled after dinner. As we sat in the main meeting area to listen to our first speaker, Emily was jittery, toes tapping. After we sang the first hymn, headlights approached the log-cabin meeting room. We heard several honks. Emily jumped up, grabbed a bag of her belongings from beneath her chair, and ran out of the building. Her mom's boyfriend had come to rescue her, we found out later. A few of the teachers had perturbed looks on their faces, but still, they didn't stop her exit.

I hadn't known that illness was a way out of the retreat. Many of us wanted out. The retreat had a reputation: It was often said that if you wanted to break up a dating couple, send one or both to the leadership retreat. Something in one of the sermons nearly always led to romantic collapse. I wasn't dating anyone, but I knew even for single people, there was something about the conference that was meant to break you.

In the first sermon, the preacher gave a list of five principles necessary for leading others toward the will of God. After the sermon concluded, our class—about thirty students—moved to a smaller room. We circled up. Our principal, Mr. Watson, a potbellied transplant from Louisiana, asked each of us to share which point we struggled with most.

There was one principle in the sermon that struck me: *Silence is approval.* The pastor elaborated—staying silent as others sin is the same as participating in sin yourself.

I was often silent. I frequently felt my existence was out of alignment with truth. I couldn't articulate what was wrong, exactly, but I felt I was living in a way that didn't mirror who I truly was inside. I was a very good girl—but I knew I wasn't that good. In fact, I was beginning to believe that the things that made people consider me good—my smallness, my silence, my sweetness—were actually a pathological facade.

The pastor mentioned the sin of staying quiet when you knew others were drinking at parties, sleeping with their boyfriends, but this was not what resonated with me. I couldn't care less about these things, thought very little about the after-school activities of my peers. Still, I knew deep in my soul that my sin was connected to silence and complicity, though I wouldn't have used these words at the time.

My palms were clammy as each of my classmates shared. I didn't listen to what anyone else had to say; I was so focused on crafting a succinct contribution of my own. There was little I hated more than coercive large-group intimacy. I was still under the delusion that because my peers could reply with confidence, with voices that did not crack or shake, that they truly believed what they were saying. I was envious of this assurance. I wasn't sure when I would ever cultivate it for myself.

My turn came. I swallowed, then quickly said, "I think I struggle most with *silence is approval*." Mr. Watson began laughing loudly, as if I'd told a funny joke. "You? Silent?" he continued to cackle. "I can't imagine," he said with a wink. "Sometimes I forget you're even in the room, you're so quiet."

I stared at him, felt the eyes of my classmates on me. I blinked back a single tear as he moved on to the next person. I spent the rest of the time in the circle attempting to control the expression on my face.

Aside from that one initial tear, I felt I succeeded. When we were dismissed, I bolted from the room quickly and tried to find a bathroom where I could be alone. Jessica followed me. She ran to me, gave me a hug. "Anna, I'm so sorry. Mr. Watson is such a jerk. What he said was cruel." I looked at her and asked, "Could you tell I was upset? I kept trying not to cry."

She looked at me expressively. "Of course I could tell you were upset. I didn't see you cry, but you were doing that thing you do when you're nervous. You kept crossing your arms, pushing them into your stomach."

I hadn't realized my body betrayed my discomfort. I tried to smile at Jessica while I thought of what to say next. "Thanks for checking on me," I managed. I still wanted to be alone.

The next day, our class participated in team-building exercises by the lake. "We're going to yell, 'We're number three! We're number three!'" Mr. Watson said. "You see, as Christians, we should always put God first, others second, and ourselves third." He began to repeat the chant. He jumped up and down to build excitement. It was as if we were at a football game, except no one was playing a sport, and we were all chanting maniacally across the still water. "Louder!" Mr. Watson screamed. We projected our voices. He slapped the backs of the boys who cheered the loudest. "Attaboy!" he said with approval. That was one of his catchphrases—*attaboy*.

We had a block of free time after team building. I dropped my Bible by a nearby tree and sprinted straight to the trail behind the cafeteria. At home, I usually ran with music on an MP3 player. Here that was prohibited—both the music and the technology. The woods were quiet, and I noticed that my other senses were enhanced without the addition of outside music. The light cast shadows through the fur of the cedar trees. I heard fallen leaves crunch beneath my sneakers. I smelled deer droppings and a hint of smoke. There was a bird chirping in the distance.

When I reached the lake, I saw a boy from my class on the other side of it. I didn't know him well, though I'd made assumptions about his confidence and character. He was an athlete, quiet, but well-liked. Here he was alone, running away in the woods, just like me. We nodded at each other. We continued to move on separate paths for the next few hours. Occasionally we crossed one another, nodding, still remaining silent.

17

During the summer at the end of high school, I stayed up late watching television in our living room after the rest of the house fell asleep. Before Netflix made binging a show possible, multi-episode marathons of *America's Next Top Model* ran every night. There was something gritty about this show that was not present in other reality television. The film was low quality, the lighting shadowy. All the girls competing on the show were hungry looking, except for the one contestant who was not. This contestant was a token—even I knew this at fifteen. The judges praised her curvy, womanly figure as they parroted body-positive clichés. She would make it a few rounds into the season and then would be voted off. Not for her weight—of course not for that. For literally anything else.

Then many seasons featured a contestant with anorexia or bulimia. This girl maybe weighed a handful of pounds less than all the others, was perhaps a bit more pale, somewhat more sad. I felt sorry for this contestant. I assumed all the girls on the show had eating disorders, even the curvy one who was maybe a size 6. The contestant with an eating disorder was a token, too, a scapegoat to virtue signal that what the judges ultimately cared about was health. After catching a contestant throwing up in the bathroom, Tyra Banks counseled the girls in the common room. I recalled her reminding the contestants that *health is the most important thing*. I assumed this contestant was just worse at hiding her eating disorder than the others, and the television producers made her pay for her indiscretions by making the incident part of the show.

This glamorization of thinness (while decrying the behaviors so many use to get there) was typical of pop culture at the turn of the millennium. Like so many women I would later meet, we were catechized by Kate Moss and "nothing tastes as good as skinny feels." We were sold the dream of protruding ribs and overflowing bras in Victoria's Secret catalogs. On the news, we heard panic about "the obesity epidemic."

"[The Millennial] generation was caught in the crossfire of a specifically heinous, fatphobic time in cultural history that has left us seriously screwed up," noted Michelle Konstantinovsky in an article for *Glamour*.

The messages from both purity culture and diet culture were clear: Our hungers did not give us valuable information about our needs. Appetites were forces to fight. The reason these philosophies are so powerful and resonant is that, at least on some occasions, this can be true. But not always.

In our living room there was a mirror that extended the length of one wall. Its presence made the room appear more spacious and inviting. As the *America's Next Top Model* contestants posed in themed photo shoots for charitable organizations, I evaluated my front and side profile in the mirror. I rubbed my hip bones, took pleasure in seeing their hard knobs. I lifted my tank top, sucked in, counting ribs, then flexed, then released. I tried to take a natural breath. Filling my diaphragm with air looked like excess.

I could hardly stand the thought that others saw me breathing throughout the day.

Despite the explicit language of the judges, there were unspoken, contradictory rules. I knew that for any of these girls to succeed, they had to be thin. The more insidious message was that they also must pretend not to care about being thin at all. You had to maintain an air of nonchalance. The secrecy, the unwillingness to talk about what was happening, was what entrenched you completely. First you're caught with the desire to be thin. Then the trap clamps down harder as you pretend not to want it at all.

I got hungry staying up late, had not yet learned that one way to control your appetite was just to sleep more. During commercial breaks, I would grab a package of donuts from the kitchen. My mom kept many baked goods on hand. She bought them for me. She knew how *picky* I was, but the bakery items always seemed to disappear when I was around. I rushed to the bathroom to chew the pastry with careful, controlled bites. I spit the saliva-coated cake into our vintage mint-green toilet. I poured myself a glass of water. I swished the water around in my mouth, spitting into the sink to wash away lingering residue. I would do this until the commercials concluded, until the show came back on. This wasn't a ritual I practiced at school or anywhere else. Only here, alone, at night.

18

I became obsessed with reading about other people's eating disorders as a teenager. I secretly searched for titles of books on our desktop computer in the den, deleting my search history once I found lists of recommendations. I memorized titles and authors for my trips to the downtown library. I didn't write anything down. I didn't want my list to be found—*I* didn't want to be found.

I felt embarrassment checking the books out, as though the librarian would learn what I was as she scanned each title. I had a method for hiding. I would find the one book I was actually interested in. Then, I would gather other books that I had no interest in at all. Inspirational romance novels. A popular YA book. A "how-to" about gardening. I would tuck the book about eating disorders in the middle of the pile, front cover down. I held my breath as the librarian scanned each title, hoping she wouldn't linger or, worse, make a comment about my choices aloud.

I read the classics: *The Best Little Girl in the World*, *Second Star to the Right*, *Stick Figure*. Marya Hornbacher's *Wasted* was *the* classic. I couldn't get enough of it. After checking her memoir out dozens of times, I found a way to secretly order a copy of my own. The book arrived in a box with two other books—for school, I told my mom with put-on nonchalance as I rushed with the package to my bedroom. I kept the book hidden under my bed, beneath a stack of devotional books and my Bible.

Hornbacher's memoir, published when she was only twenty-three, has received substantial criticism for glamorizing eating disorders. Her account became, for many, a how-to manual in its specific descriptions of behaviors, its inclusion of startlingly low numbers related to weight and calorie counts.

As a teenager, I read this memoir before bed nearly every night for years. I would read a few pages of Hornbacher's text after finishing a chapter from the Bible. This was my devotion. Often, I would open the book at random, indulging in whichever pages I landed upon. While I was conscious of the book's ability to instruct, what I found was that her words triggered my interest in feminism more than self-harm.

Her story, however graphic, sparked a revelation in me: Perhaps I was drawn to disappearance because it was precisely what I had been told I, as a woman, needed to do.

19

The summer I was fourteen, my parents announced that we were going on a beach vacation.

"Is there a TV?" I asked my parents, though I didn't care that much about television. I was trying to determine whether I could play my workout videos.

"Yes," my dad said.

"And VHS? Do they have a VHS player?" My dad checked the condo's brochure. Again, he nodded his head yes.

My dad handed me the brochure, and I scanned through the condo's amenities. Two beds, two baths, full kitchen. "We'll probably make most of our meals at home. Stock up on groceries at the beginning of the trip. Just go out to eat someplace nice once or twice." I nodded. It was as if he'd read my mind. I looked at photos of the place. I assessed the size of the living room where the TV was located. There would be enough room to do Tae Bo if I pushed the glass coffee table to the corner of the space.

I can do this. A beach vacation, I thought quietly to myself. At the grocery store, I could buy my usual, safe foods. I could complete my many daily workouts—just as if I were at home. Maybe I'd even go for runs along the beach. I'd seen this done in movies. It fulfilled a sort of fantasy for me: an experience of heightened living—and I wouldn't have to modify the way I lived at all. A pleasure without consequence. There seemed to be so few of those.

"The entire island has a bike path along its perimeter," my dad continued. "We're going to rent bikes so that we can explore. The path looks pretty shaded, too. I don't want to spend too much time by the sand. I don't need that much sun." He reflexively rubbed the scar along the tip of his nose.

I flipped through the brochure. *Twelve miles of tree-shaded bike paths!* the advertisement boasted. I looked at a photo of a family peddling leisurely beneath a line of weeping willows. There were small children, and they were smiling, making a memory, going, it seemed, quite slow. *This could probably count as half*, I thought to myself. *Or a third. Probably a third, just to be safe.* So, I quickly did the math: An hour of biking would count as twenty minutes of my daily required exercise. Not very efficient. But still, nice to have some variety. A change of scenery.

The island was manicured and quiet. Weeping willows and palm trees lined the main streets. Gas stations and fast-food restaurants eschewed their signature colors to conform with a unifying brick brown mandated by local code. We purchased groceries. I watched my parents pile the shopping cart high with bread and peanut butter, muffins and milk. Frozen pizza. I added apples, a negative-calorie food. Carrots. Special K—the way it was marketed, the cereal diet, had made the carbs less suspect. Less damning. It was 2003, and the demonization of carbs was only beginning.

It was calories that I feared. I was puzzled as to why I was so tired all the time.

We unloaded our luggage and groceries at the condo. The space was just as inviting as the pictures I'd studied from the brochure. The muffins taunted me from the counter, and I coached myself to stay away. After all, I'd been sitting in the car all day. I hadn't done anything to earn them.

We headed to the beach early the next morning. The jellyfish were still washed up from the tide. I waded carefully into the water, shivering in the surf. I walked back on dry sand to my beach towel, and I lay down to soak up the early morning rays. A breeze blew. My arms had goose bumps; my nipples were erect. I used a portion of my towel as a blanket for my feet. My hand reflexively stroked the hard bone of my ribs. This was when I felt most at ease—horizontal and skin stretched, close to the earth, as visible as a sheet of paper, a slice of bread.

Other families began to arrive with coolers and tents. My dad looked to the sky, then to his watch: "Time to head back," he said as he gathered our water bottles and chairs.

"What do you mean? We've been here for, like, an hour? I'm just now not cold," I said.

"This is when the UV rays are the strongest," my dad said as a middle-aged woman with loose, leathery skin walked past. "Better watch out, or you'll end up like that," he said nodding to the woman, now out of earshot.

I shook my head. Still, I gathered my supplies. Our condo was just over a mile away. *I guess I do need to head back to get one of my workout videos in*, I thought to myself.

I looked at my mom. "Later, when it's cooler," I asked, "can I go for a run along the beach?" She looked at me as though I'd asked to join a cult.

"No way!" she replied.

"Why not? I run at home all the time. How is this any different?"

My mom glanced at my dad: "Did you hear that, Steve?"

"What's that?" he said.

"Anna wants to go for a run along the beach. By herself."

"One of you could run with me, I guess," I said.

My dad laughed. "My teenage daughter wants to run by herself along the beach. Sounds like a newspaper headline. Good way to get kidnapped. Trafficked."

I rolled my eyes. "People do it all the time," I said under my breath.

"Anna, we are in *South Carolina*. Not *West Virginia*," my mom said.

I knew I wasn't going to win the fight. I decided I would run in place in my room for the amount of time it would take to run outside instead. It would be boring, but I could play music. I could use the time to calculate the number of calories I'd allow myself each day of the trip—prepare ahead of time for any dinners out.

"Why'd we even come here if we're not going to spend any time on the beach?" I said, disgruntled on our walk back to the condo.

"Oh, you'll have fun," my dad said with a smirk. "You'll see. We're going to bike around the island tomorrow."

20

The next morning, we woke early and began biking with the sunrise. We stopped for breakfast at a Starbucks in a clean brick building. I ordered coffee, black, and a cup of ice water. My mom ordered a scone, and she offered to share. “I’ll just have one bite,” I said as I tore off a hunk. She walked away to use the restroom. I tore off another piece of the cakey pastry. Then another. Then another. When she returned, I’d eaten half of the scone—not something I’d planned to do. My mom glanced at the remaining pastry in the paper bag. I cast my eyes down to the table. “I’m sorry,” I said under my breath. A reflexive apology—to whom, my mom? She looked relieved. “I was planning on splitting it with you,” she said without additional comment. I was apologizing to myself, I realized. To the part of me who had made a rule, for the other part of me who had broken it.

We walked back outside to bike the twelve miles around the island. There was an ocean breeze, and we were peddling leisurely on a wide path, my mom riding slowest of all, my dad instructing us to pause at crosswalks to wait for her to catch up. We peddled for half an hour, and all I could think about was that scone I had not planned on, how I would account for it later. *Biking feels too easy*, I thought to myself as we crossed over a wooden bridge. It felt like walking. Less than walking. Could I even count this as exercise? I felt certain that this would not count.

An hour passed. "How many miles do you think we've gone, Dad?" I asked as we rode past a shopping center.

"Ah—I'd say about four miles. Maybe five," he said.

I panicked. We were not even halfway through this sprawling activity that was supposed to count as a third of a workout that I'd decided no longer would count at all. I began trying to factor in where I would fit in the additional hours later that day. A Tae Bo workout once we got back to the condo? And then another one in the evening? I was exhausted just thinking about it.

The morning had gotten hot. I was dizzy, drenched in a cold sweat—dehydrated from that coffee. I looked down and saw my pasty, peddling thighs, a stark contrast to the black concrete below. I felt that I had expanded since we set out that morning. The button on my denim shorts was digging into my abdomen. I could feel a roll of skin creeping over my waistband. I took one hand off the bike's handle to push my flesh back, to contain it. Once I'd done this, I couldn't stop touching my stomach, pressing its soft skin, readjusting my shorts to keep my girth from exploding out of the bounds of my clothes.

"It's getting hot," my dad said. "Let's make a water stop." I was relieved but also frustrated—how long was this bike ride going to last? I had *things* I had to do.

We stopped at a McDonald's in another clean, brick building. "I'll order us waters and a snack," my dad said as he walked into the building. *A snack?* I grumbled to myself.

"Didn't we *just* eat breakfast?" I said out loud to my mom and brother. I was angry at their weakness, their need.

"Well, I'm hungry," my brother said.

"Me, too," my mom added.

I was silent, seething. I was hungry, as well, but I knew I shouldn't be. It wasn't time. This wasn't when I allowed myself to eat. This wasn't part of my schedule. Shaking, I sat on a plot of grass and leaned back, hoping to catch a breeze, hoping for a second wind to overtake me so that I could tackle all that was required for the day.

My dad hovered above me, head glowing with the light of the sun. "Here," he said as he handed me a large cup of water, a paper bag of fries.

"I don't want the fries," I said, and he laid them on the ground beside me. I sipped my water as the rest of my family sat quiet, eating. The water helped, but the world felt hazy. The McDonald's appeared to be moving. There was a stop sign in the distance—I knew that's what it was—but still, I stared at it. It almost looked like a man. I finished my water. My mom heard me sipping the empty cup with my straw. "Want some of mine?" she offered. I nodded my head yes.

My hand inched toward the bag of fries in the grass. *I can eat two*, I decided. The salt tasted so good in the heat. *Two*, I told myself again. And I ate two—and then two more. And soon, I'd consumed nearly half the bag. I stood up and quickly walked to a metal trash can to toss what remained. "Oh, good," my dad said lightly. "I bet we'll all feel better for the rest of the ride."

And I did feel better. Less dizzy. Less weak. We hopped back on our bikes, back to the path, and we were near the ocean. I saw that wide expanse of water and sun. It was glittering, beautiful. But I couldn't stop touching my stomach, removing my hand from one bike handle, pushing my belly in, trying to compress the excess air, to flatten it like an out-of-use inflatable pool toy. It still felt distended. I lifted my shirt, adjusted my jeans. I saw the imprint of a zipper, a red mark on my pale flesh. I was so distracted. I wobbled on my bike, but I caught myself. Still, I kept grabbing my belly.

I tried to adjust the numbers for the day. To make a plan to pay for my sins. And as I calculated—an extra hour this evening, a hundred less at dinner—I felt defeated. Somehow, I was still so tired. Somehow, I was still so hungry.

We were near the main road, away from the beach. I was startled by the honk of a semi barreling through a green light.

I could feel the impressive rush of it pass me. For a moment, my mind was quiet. Blank. Then: the voice.

You could swerve.

What?

Just turn your handles. Veer toward the road. No. *You think this is ever going to get better? You think you're ever going to be able to stop?* I don't know. *You won't. You'll always fail. You'll always feel awful. You'll always have to pay.*

I'm going to get it right soon. I'll eat better. And I'll get things under control. I'll feel better. *You know that's not true. You would've done it already. You're never going to do it right.*

Another semi rushed down the main road.

Just swerve. No. *Do it. Now.* No. *Just do it.* Dear Jesus, Dear Jesus, please make it stop, please make it stop.

I was still peddling. I was no longer touching my stomach. I was quietly crying. I lifted a hand to wipe the tears away before my family noticed.

There was a block of quiet. And then, the voice returned: *So what's your plan? You think you can keep this up your whole life?* I don't know. *You won't have much of a life.* I'll try harder to manage it. *You think you'll ever get a boyfriend?* I might. *Ha! Why would anyone want to be around you like this?* I can figure it out. *And a job? Think you'll ever hold a real job?* I get good grades—sure, why wouldn't I? *You can barely go on a trip to the beach. No way could you hold a real job.* A pause. *And kids? You think you'll ever have a family of your own?* I don't know. It could happen. *Let's pretend it does. Can you even imagine it? Pregnancy? You would really be fat, then—ballooning bigger and bigger by the day.* Well, that's a long way away. There's no point in thinking about it now. *But really, can you imagine—if you stay around for the future, you may end up even fatter than you are now.* Stop. *But you can make it end now.* Stop. *It would be so easy. Just veer toward the road. This can end.* Stop. *Swerve.* No. *Do it now.* No. *Do it.*

NO! I probably wouldn't even die. I'd probably just get hit and injured—and then I wouldn't be able to exercise. Then I'd really have to kill myself.

Fair enough.

We were back at the condo. I propped my bike up against the porch. My dad turned to me as he secured the bikes by threading a bungee through all their interiors: "Now, that was pretty fun, wasn't it, Anna?"

I mumbled, "I guess so." I paused. "I'm really, really tired," I added.

21

Grace and I bonded over our mutual desire to escape Appalachia. We hoped to attend pricey Christian universities that we imagined were "liberal" because they had professors who taught evolution as fact and engaged critical theory, even though they still booked Republican politicians for convocations. Together Grace and I collected extracurriculars and studied for the SAT and ACT in the hopes that we could get substantial scholarships and make it out of our fundamentalist West Virginia home.

Grace didn't need a scholarship to escape. Even though she wore name brands only whenever they were on sale at Value City, we all knew her family was rich. Her dad was a plastic surgeon, and her family lived in a wealthy neighborhood bordering a holler just outside our capital city.

Grace and I decided to join the track team that spring. Grace said she was glad we could be on the team together, but she resented having to participate. She hated running.

"My dad's making me join," she said with a shrug. "I guess it will be something else I can list on my college applications."

I was genuinely confused. "Why's your dad making you?"

"Oh, he keeps talking about how thick my thighs are and doesn't want me to get any fatter," she explained. He wanted to give her a nose job, too, but Grace's mom told him to leave her nose alone. She agreed with him that Grace should join track, though.

I was excited about joining track. It was an excuse to exercise as much as I already did, and I could get some credit for it on my college applications at the same time. I'd dropped out of most after-school activities at that point so that I could devote additional time to exercise. I'd even quit basketball, despite enjoying the sport. There just wasn't enough movement. All the dribbling exercises without running, the standing around plotting defense strategies, and especially the lengthy travel to games at Christian schools in mountain towns hours away—and not to mention the ritual meal at Wendy's beforehand—were things I simply could not accommodate in my life anymore. I didn't provide much explanation about dropping out. I just said I didn't enjoy basketball anymore, and no one questioned my story.

But track was nothing but running. Our school didn't actually have a track, so we ran in the woods. The trails were not marked with signs, but I knew them well—all of us did. In elementary school, our teachers would take us on nature hikes to collect bugs and leaves for identification. The trails began at the back half of campus and extended for miles, winding through residential neighborhoods, eventually ending on an open mountaintop near a set of steel generators extending toward the heavens.

Our coach was a volunteer teacher who seemed to receive no compensation for his additional service. Perhaps because of this, he provided us with very little oversight: "Go run the trails in the woods. Be back in an hour. Stay with someone. Don't get hurt." Then he retreated to an office to grade papers, showing little interest in whether we even made it to the trails at all.

I was exhilarated by this freedom. Each afternoon, Grace and I changed into knee-length, baggy gym shorts. I ran through the woods light and buzzing, high on fresh air and hunger. I loved when my hunger shifted in presentation, when it moved from a grumbling stomach to a humming energy, despite my having never consumed anything at all. It felt like flight. It felt like power.

Though I ran with Grace by my side, I never told her about the power I felt. About the hunger. There was nothing that thrilled me more than quiet control, a private project no one else knew about. I loved hearing our coach congratulate us on our run at the end of practice, on the miles we clocked in the woods. And I loved hearing that voice in my head silently congratulate me further: "And *you* did it on nothing at all."

Grace's mom looked like an older version of Grace, a bit more pale, an even mix of blonde and gray hair. While Grace pulled her thick, long blonde hair into a ponytail, Grace's mom's hair hung limp. There was so little of it that she hardly needed an elastic to keep it out of her eyes. A lifelong runner, her face was all angles. It was as if she had been forced to choose between vitality and thinness, and she'd chosen the latter.

Once, while Grace's sister played in a soccer game at the same time as track practice, I saw Grace's mom park her car in the lot across from the soccer field. Rather than watch her daughter's soccer game or talk to the other moms and dads in the bleachers, she hiked up a grassy hill to a plot of land just behind the school gymnasium. The area was out of sight from the soccer field, but from our vantage point on the trail, I could see Grace's mom run along the small strip of grass—it couldn't have been more than five hundred feet long—up and down, head to the ground, facial expression solemn and serious.

"That's my mom," Grace said when she noticed my noticing. "She always gets so frustrated when our activities make it difficult for her to run." I nodded as if I understood, because I did. This was why I'd joined the track team, after all—it was an activity that still allowed me to "get my run in." One of my runs, at least.

From afar, I watched Grace's mom quietly tracing and retracing a small section of land, all alone, covering no real distance, with no real purpose I could see other than staying pointy and sharp. She seemed so very sad to me. It seemed like immature behavior. Delusional. Embarrassing. Grace's mom seemed embarrassed, too—otherwise she wouldn't have hidden from the other parents behind the gymnasium.

I understood her mom's compulsions but believed that they were something one should outgrow. At least, I hoped I'd outgrow mine. I hoped I'd figure out a way to remain thin and in control without staying a slave to my stupid rituals. I found it curious that Grace's mom was still occupied by these childish, pointless pursuits. How had she sustained it? She'd birthed and nearly finished raising four children, after all.

As we ran in the woods, Grace and I talked about our college applications, various scholarships, what we would do once we were out of here, once we were experiencing independence in a place that was anywhere other than our hometowns. We made plans to quiz one another over the phone on the various portions of the ACT where we'd struggled on our practice tests.

As we approached campus again, I saw through the trees that Grace's mom was still trotting up and down that same back plot of land.

"She's been at it this whole time," Grace said under her breath.

"I guess just as long as you and I have," I replied.

Grace sighed. "It just seems more ridiculous when you're not actually going anywhere."

22

Around the time I graduated from high school, I took a job at the local diner where a friend from school worked. Leah was petite with long, shiny brown hair. The only thing big about her was her smile—but she didn't smile often. She was quiet and often looked as if she believed herself guilty of some serious offense. She seemed like someone with experience, regrets, as if she'd tasted some of what the world had to offer, and she had some indigestion. Maybe she paid too much for the meal, too.

As the restaurant sat empty and other servers leaned on counters, Leah and I consolidated ketchup bottles and lined newly washed bread baskets with crisp white napkins.

We quizzed each other on the shorthand during these tasks. We were still turning in handwritten orders to the cook. *K* was for carrots, and *c* was for corn (which happened to no longer be on the menu). *B* was for baked potato, and *i* was for broccoli—"don't ask me why," the cook said.

I asked Leah what her favorite meal at the restaurant was, trying to stockpile ideas for items to suggest.

"I don't really like to eat the food here," she said.

"I don't think I would either," I responded, and she looked at me, and I looked at her, and I think that was the day we became friends.

"The biscuits and gravy meal is pretty popular," she said.

"That sounds gross," I replied.

"I agree," she said, "but people really love it. You should see the way the gravy sticks in the bowl even after it goes through a wash on dish tank. It's basically glue."

Sometimes customers would ask me what my favorite meal was, and I would say, "The biscuits and gravy meal is really popular." This would usually suffice. But sometimes a customer, often a middle-aged, moneyed man, would say, "But what do *you* like?" And I would want to respond, *I don't like anything. I don't like anything at all.* Though really, I loved the cinnamon hotcakes. I ordered them sometimes when I was much younger and my family would visit this diner. I loved them with big slabs of butter, exorbitant amounts of syrup. I loved the way the batter smelled as the cook flipped the hotcakes on the line, and I could almost taste those square flecks of crystallized cinnamon as they melted beneath the warming lights.

But I didn't admit this to customers for years. Eventually I would. Eventually, I would eat them again, too, though never without some hesitation and calculation of calories. Instead, I would respond to the man's question with an order from a recent table, maybe an open-faced roast beef sandwich. And I would describe the umami aroma that hit me as I delivered the dish from kitchen to table, and I hoped that this would sound vivid enough that he would believe I'd actually eaten one of these sandwiches.

Every few months Leah's boyfriend would come to town, and she would ask that I and several other servers help cover her shifts so that she could devote time to being with him.

I slowly got to know the other servers. They scared me at first. They seemed so worldly. The ones who were teenagers went to public school, and I imagined they had some secret knowledge of the way the world worked, and they drank and danced and were so free in their bodies. I imagined they could tell that I was not free, that I was brittle and hard, that I would always be rigid and fearful of my own flesh, much less open to the flesh of others.

I felt a strange mix of shame and pride before them. I felt superior and good. I also felt broken and hopeless.

Soon, I was going to have to go to public school, too. I'd been studying hard, taking and retaking standardized tests to receive higher scores, to qualify for scholarships to make it into private Christian universities. But it hadn't been enough.

"No loans," my dad said. "We don't want you taking out any loans to go to school. Besides, it'll be good for you to go to public school. Maybe it will chill you out a little bit."

I was enraged. I wanted out. I wanted out of West Virginia, and I wanted out of fundamentalism. But I didn't have the confidence to defy them, to take the loans out anyway. This meant that I would go to a local public state school, which I felt was both beneath me and terrifying.

Leah also planned to enroll in the same public state school. She didn't seem that upset about it. She wasn't scared. She was disappointed that she wouldn't be able to go to the same school as her boyfriend—he would be transferring to Liberty University in the fall. But she seemed resigned to this as well. Perhaps she was used to disappointment. She hadn't felt entitled to whatever her heart desired.

"What'd you think of today's chapel service?" I asked her one afternoon as we carried dishes from the back of the restaurant to the line. A recruiter from Appalachian Bible College had been the speaker during the service. No one from our graduating class was enrolling at ABC, and he challenged us, with some degree of fury, to give our desires over to God. He urged us to pray every day for thirty days—*surely you can give God thirty days*—about whether he desired for us to attend Bible college. If after thirty days God said no, then we could know we were following the will of the Lord if we went to school elsewhere.

"But what if he says yes?" the speaker continued. "What if he says that you need to change your hopes of making money, of becoming a doctor or lawyer or banker, to enter the ministry instead? What if he calls you to Bible college to become a pastor? A pastor's wife? A missionary? Those whom the Lord loves, he also disciplines. He will not quit pursuing you, even if you ignore his call."

"Oh, I barely even listened to him," Leah said as we began lining bread baskets at a back table. She looked completely unruffled. "Anyway, ABC's unaccredited. I have to get a job after college. I don't understand these people who take out money to go to school without having anything to show for it in the end."

I nodded my head, agreeing with her. "They're manipulating us," I said after some consideration.

"Of course they are," she said. She stood up, grabbed a tray of silverware and a stack of napkins, and brought them back to our table.

"So, you're going to the public school down the road?" she asked me as she sat down.

"I guess so," I said, rolling my eyes slightly as I grabbed half of the stack of napkins.

"I am, too." She paused. "We'll be best friends," she said, as though she'd come to a considered conclusion.

"I'd like that," I said, beginning to smile. I'd never had anyone refer to me as their best friend before.

"We'll eat dinners together. And we'll go to the gym together. We'll visit Bible studies and churches together." She listed off each of our activities with some emphasis.

"That would be great," I said.

"And you know? I was kind of sad that I wouldn't be able to go to Liberty with Levi. But I think it's good. God's teaching us patience. Levi and I will get married after college. And we're saving ourselves for marriage. It's good that I won't have that temptation in front of me every day," Leah continued.

"Yeah, that is good," I said, trying to sound supportive. To my new best friend.

"Do you know what you're going to major in?" I asked her.

"I'm pretty sure I'm going to study dietetics," she said. "How about you?"

I'd considered dietetics, too—I was almost going to say this to her. *I'm obsessed with food, too.* But I was reaching a point where I knew I no longer wanted to be obsessed with food. I wanted out.

I was pretty sure that majoring in the thing that had enslaved me was not the way to do that.

"I'm going to major in English," I said after a moment.

"What do you do with an English degree?" Leah said with some degree of disapproval. Maybe she was reconsidering her previous proclamation about the status of our friendship.

"Oh, there are lots of things," I said. I listed off a variety of jobs I'd read one was qualified for with an English degree after a quick Google search. I noted some celebrities who were English majors, and I quickly regretted this. She didn't seem impressed by the celebrities.

"Okay," she finally said after I gave my defense. "That's nice."

23

Doug was my trainer during my first weeks at the diner. At first, he was annoyed that I slowed him down. Still, he quizzed me on the menu, helping me memorize the side dishes that accompanied each entrée, green beans with the meat loaf, baked potato with the fried chicken. At thirty-four years old, he was a diner veteran. He taught me the little things: Place the check in front of the oldest man at the table. Always suggestively sell. And if a pretty young woman orders a soft drink, fill her glass with diet instead.

"I think she ordered regular," I said, watching Doug press the lever for diet at the soda fountain.

"This is what she needs," Doug said, glancing in our table's direction before balancing the beverages in the four corners of his round tray. "She's right on the edge. She'd thank me, eventually, if she knew."

I followed Doug around the back of the kitchen, assembling side salads, lining bread baskets with paper napkins. I wouldn't have noticed Doug had he not spent so much time evaluating women. This made him interesting to me—his consistently critical eye.

He wasn't unattractive—floppy brown hair, deep brown eyes. But his face was lined and pockmarked, as if he hadn't had a glass of water in a decade. He had a bit of facial hair. He looked grizzled, aged, but this dishevelment had its own appeal in a man.

I envied him this—that his sins, his missteps could still be counted in his favor.

"Do you want me to take the order this time, or you?" I asked him as the hostess seated a couple in our section.

"I think it's time for you to try," he said. "Just remember to suggestively sell. Tell them our special is the turkey dinner."

"It is?"

"No—but it can be nuked in three minutes flat. Never suggest the slow food. Never suggest grilled chicken. The faster the food, the bigger the tips."

"That's smart," I said.

"Well? What do I look like? Some dumb, middle-aged waiter?" he asked with a big grin as he tucked the bottle of ketchup into his apron pocket.

During lunch breaks, I would often find Doug eating a salad in the back of the restaurant with his head in a book.

"I love that one," I said to him one day as I saw him reading *Angela's Ashes*.

"You've read *Angela's Ashes*?" he asked me with some surprise.

I nodded and mentioned my favorite moment in the book, just to prove I wasn't pretending my literacy. "I read a lot," I said. "I'm planning to major in English."

"I was an English major," he said, looking up from his book and directly at me for, perhaps, the first time.

The next day, I found a book in my locker in the break room: *Breathing Lessons* by Anne Tyler. There was a two-page note, folded and tucked inside the front cover. At home that evening, I read the letter—messy print, red ink. In it, Doug described what brought him to this part of the state, his failed marriage, his halted career. It was mostly autobiography. But then, he concluded with compliments.

Thank God I have someone like you at work with me, the note ended.

I reread the note multiple times as I completed leg lifts on the floor of my bedroom. Then, I pulled out a sheet of paper to form a reply.

This became our practice: exchanging notes tucked in books hidden in lockers. After about a month of this, he shared his cell phone number. *Would you ever be up for talking on the phone?*

"I'm going for a walk," I told my mom that warm summer evening, flip phone shoved into the pocket of my jeans. I made my way toward a dusty, tree-lined road with few houses. Then I dialed his number.

Our conversations were, primarily, one-sided. "You're such a wonderful listener," Doug told me one night as he described to me, again, the way his wife had cheated on him, stolen from him, and how fat she'd gotten since the divorce.

But he seemed to know just how to pull me back in whenever the conversation was starting to become tiresome. He complimented my intellect, my manners, my meek and quiet spirit. "You're not like other women," he often said at the conclusion of a call.

And after a few months of this, one night I confided in him. "I think I have an eating disorder," I said, voice trembling. "I mean, I know I don't look sick. But, I have a really hard time with food."

I was sick of my secrets and shame. I wanted to be seen.

And for a few minutes, he listened. I continued talking. And finally, he said, "It makes me sad to think about that. You don't need to worry about those things. You're beautiful," he said. "Way more beautiful than Sherri."

Then we spoke for another hour about his ex-wife.

Eventually, we made plans to get together outside of work. At his apartment, where no one could bother us—no one could talk. My birthday—my eighteenth birthday—we decided, would be as good a day as any. We could celebrate together.

I got off work early. My manager cut me from the floor: "Hon, it's your birthday. And we're dead. And I can't believe you didn't call off work on your birthday, of all days!"

I was not the type to call off work. Too responsible. But after I finished rolling a tray of silverware, I went to the restaurant's bathroom to change out of my black and white uniform. I pulled on some blue jeans and a low-cut gray tank top that I'd only ever worn underneath blouses.

I inspected myself in the mirror, underwear lines visible along the backside of my jeans, peek of cleavage hanging out of my top. I pulled a tube of concealer from my purse to dot the fiery red pimples along my neck and chest with cover-up not quite the same shade as my skin.

I walked out of the restaurant quickly. In my car, I called him.

"I'm coming over," I said quietly into the phone's receiver. "Tell me, again, which road do I turn down to get to your apartment?"

He directed me, and I drove and drove, until finally, I rolled up the gravel road to his apartment. He lived alone—no roommate, no neighbors—in a small building nestled deep in the woods. My headlights illuminated his figure at the doorway. I parked, turned off the ignition. The screen door made a creaking sound, and he invited me in.

"Hey there, birthday girl," he called.

He looked different. Different from how he did at work. His hair was dark—*but did it have* this *much gray when I saw him the day before?* I thought to myself.

His voice sounded strange—not how he sounded each night on the phone.

I walked inside to his living room. It was mostly empty, beige carpet with a wine stain in the corner of the room. There was no furniture except a lawn chair, a box television set.

Along the windowsill, there was a line of lit tea candles.

He poured me a glass of wine—my first ever *real* drink. He knew this. I watched him. Glass down. (*Is the glass empty?*) Pour wine. (*This is just alcohol, right?*)

"Cheers! To your eighteenth birthday. To celebrating your eighteenth birthday with me," Doug said.

"Cheers!"

I smiled back, raising the cup in his direction. I pretended to take a sip. His eyes were already glassy.

"So, how does it feel to be an adult?" he asked after we toasted.

"I guess I've only been an adult for a day. Not even a day."

"You're so mature, though. More grown up than so many adults. You're not like those silly, giggling high school girls at work. Their parties. Their stupid boyfriends. They're nothing like you—you're light years beyond them.

"Does anyone know you're here?" he asked after a moment.

"Yes," I replied.

"Who?"

"Leah."

"You told Leah?"

"Yes."

"And what did she say?"

"She said, 'Be careful, Anna.'"

"Do you think you need to be careful?"

"Well," I paused, adjusting the fabric of my jeans. "I'm here, aren't I?"

"You know me. I mean, you *really* know me," he said, moving in closer, a puff of cigarette smoke to my hair. "And I know you. We understand each other. Not many people do—but we do. What did I do at work before you? Surrounded by those idiots. Cokehead Justin, doing lines on the clock out back by the dumpster. And Sally—poor, fat Sally and her stupid blue eye shadow, always smelling like shit with that colostomy bag. If you ever leave, I might kill myself. I'd have to get another job, at least."

"Don't say that. You know I'm going off to college this month."

"Let me show you some of my stuff," Doug said, changing the subject, gesturing toward a hunter-green storage container. He took off the lid, revealing a pile of magazines and notebooks.

"Some of this is what I've been working on. But I'll show you the published stuff. They pay in contributor's copies, and I haven't had a chance to get my furniture out of storage, so I keep them all in here."

Doug pulled out a decade-old issue of his college's literary magazine. He pointed to his name on the back cover.

"So cool," I said, as I flipped through its pages. I found his piece, and I felt that I should read it. I felt the need to show him I cared.

"You don't have to read it now," Doug said, quickly. "Maybe another time—the next time you come over."

I smiled and nodded my head yes.

"So, want a tour of the place?"

"Sure."

"There's not much. Kitchen, just beside us. Bathroom, right by the kitchen. Living room," he gestured broadly. "And bedroom."

A pause. "Want to see the bedroom?"

"Um, sure," I said.

He stood. I stood. He gestured for me to walk ahead of him. I moved toward the dark room. He lingered behind me, in the doorway. I saw a mattress on the floor, a pile of sheets.

"What do you think?" he said, moving in closer, breath hot on my neck.

"It's . . . nice," I stammered.

"And today's your eighteenth birthday, right?"

"Yeah."

"Not tomorrow. Not this weekend?"

"Um, nope. Today."

"You are eighteen today."

"Yes."

Then, my phone rang. I retrieved it from my purse, hands trembling.

"Who is it?"

"My mom," I said, looking at the caller ID.

"Does she know you're here?"

"No. I mean, I don't know."

"You don't know?"

"Maybe Leah told her."

I let the call go to voicemail. Then it rang again. My mom, again.

"I . . . I . . . I think I need to go."

"Really? Couldn't you just answer it, tell her you're somewhere else?"

I paused. "No, I can't," I said, suddenly resolved. "I've gotta go."

And then I fled to my car. I opened the door and ran down the front steps, hands searching through my purse for my car keys.

I heard the screen door swing shut. I heard his footsteps behind me. I heard his breathing.

It was dark. So dark. I couldn't even see my hands in front of me, searching for my keys. Where were my keys? My keys, my keys, so dark, it was so dark, and I couldn't find my keys.

When I think of a dark and stormy night, that's the night that springs to the front of my mind. And there was not a cloud in the sky.

I started the ignition to my car, pressing the gas hard as I reversed on the gravel road. As I made it to the main road, I sniffed the air, and I reeked of smoke. *I can't go home like this.* I stopped by Walmart and changed back into my sticky serving uniform in the bathroom. I ran to the makeup aisle and found myself some lavender body spray. I squirted it all over my body, all through my hair.

At home, Mom stood at the front door. And when she asked me where I'd been, I told her the truth.

I was grounded. Until college. Could I even be trusted to go to college?

I was mad about this—but also, I was relieved.

"*What* were you thinking?" my mom asked the next morning. "He could've done anything. Have you lost your mind?"

24

When I first began going hungry, I thought I was trying to control how my body looked. But as I neared high school graduation, I saw that maintaining strict control over what I ate was also my way of staying in control of my emotions. It was a psychological coping mechanism—and it was growing increasingly unsustainable. I realized how much it had shrunk my life and would continue to shrink my life.

I'd said no to a ski trip I wanted to attend. I'd skipped a class trip to Washington, DC. A guy I liked was about to ask me out, and I discouraged him—all because I was too nervous to eat in front of people. All because I was not sure how to fit in my required amount of exercise. As I approached college with all its possibilities, I wanted more out of life.

At my public university there was no dress code. No signed lifestyle agreement in which you promised to avoid drinking or dancing and to tell on those who broke the rules. No hellfire-and-brimstone sermons. No ever-watchful eye. It was as if I had slipped through the bars of the strict moralism that had encircled me my whole life and could finally see the shape of the cage clearly. And I could also see how the rigid food rules I'd developed for myself hung like a complex padlock on its door.

"They'll make you so open-minded, your brain falls out" was a familiar refrain criticizing secular liberal-arts education that I heard from countless pulpits growing up. But in college, I began to consider the notion that maybe my body would not actually fall apart without my micromanagement. Maybe I didn't have to constantly be on the defense, ready to go on the offense any time an assigned reading forwarded the "wrong" views. Maybe being healthy didn't mean planning each meal meticulously, having a rigid schedule that would always accommodate long blocks of exercise.

I would never have the energy to study, to meet new people, to find a boyfriend, if I continued going hungry and organizing my life around burning calories. I wasn't able to give up all my rules—this was still beyond me—but in a more relaxed environment, I was able to drop many of them. Slowly, cautiously, I started to get to know my own desires—meeting friends from class to eat late-night sugary cereal in the campus cafeteria, skipping studying for an art history exam to play soccer with a boy I had a crush on instead.

The first week of college, I stood in line with my suitemate Christy in the cafeteria. Rather than thinking about what I should eat or what I was allowed to eat, I considered what I wanted instead.

"A buffalo chicken flatbread," I told the grill cook. There were no calories posted on the menu at the time—there would be several years later, and the number would be high—but that day, I took a blind chance.

"Want bleu cheese for dipping?" the grill cook asked.

I hesitated. I'd said no to dressings for nearly a decade. "You do," Christy said, and I slowly nodded a yes to the cook.

We sat down at a booth. I watched her dip her own sandwich into a ramekin of dressing. I imitated. "Whoa," I said, overcome with how delicious cheese and chicken and hot sauce tasted with a dash of creamy dressing.

"Good?" she asked. She had no reason to consider that this was a sort of revelation for me.

"So good!"

"You've never had bleu cheese dressing before?"

"I thought I didn't like it."

"Who wouldn't like it?"

We talked and ate, and at the end of the meal, she'd eaten three-quarters of her sandwich, while I devoured mine whole. But I didn't care. Something had shifted. It had started months earlier—and it felt like a true change once I was living on the campus of a public college. The rules here were simple, basic human decency stuff. No killing, no slandering. My mind didn't spin wondering whether I would be kicked out and damned to hell if my T-shirt was a bit too tight.

I believed I was growing out of the fear of my own body. And I began to consider new ideas about the world. Perhaps women were not eternally subordinate to men. Maybe a limited government was not God's ideal form of government. I relinquished the fear that broadening my perspective was the first step toward destruction.

My life expanded. I forged friendships over late-night snacks in the dorms. I went to parties where I danced and drank and didn't worry about *liquid calories*. I planned weekend road trips, skipping early morning runs, eating fried foods along the side of the highway. There were moments I would look around at my dieting friends and roommates and think, *I don't know how this is possible, but I think* I *have a healthier relationship with food than they do*. This is how quiet the voice would become.

25

During my sophomore year in college, I enrolled in a course about Gnosticism in film and literature. Gnosticism, our professor told us, was an early church heresy. Those who followed its tenets believed that the body was bad, but the spirit was good. According to Harold Bloom, Gnosticism—not Christianity—is America's real religion.

I was hooked on the first day. This, I thought to myself, this was the key to understanding the landscape of my childhood. I was sure that I was raised in a religion that hated bodies. Black bodies. Female bodies. Fat bodies. Poor bodies. Disabled bodies. This is why we were obsessed with perfecting the self: We were fearful of our own flesh and blood.

I saw a direct connection to myself in what I learned about Gnosticism. I was so fearful of desire. I believed my body was bad. I desired for it to be reduced to nothing: to have only spirit remain. This was the first time I saw my disorder as symbolic of what I believed about religion.

At night, I'd return to my apartment after class and reflect on the course's content. I felt I'd been handed a key to a door I'd been desperate to unlock. On my laptop, I searched "Gnosticism and eating disorders." And I found dozens of sermons.

Lying in bed one night, I streamed audio for hours and listened to men and women speak of the body as good, of a God who came to earth in a body, of a God who was interested not in destroying the world but in making it new. I opened my window to the cool March air. I breathed in asphalt and crabapple. I felt I'd heard the gospel for the first time, though I was not overcome by the guilt of endless repentance. I felt light—but not reduced. Bodies as good was good news.

I learned about binary dualism—or black-and-white thinking—and how, even though it allows us to make tidy reactions to phenomena, it can be an oppressive cultural constraint. Binary dualism includes things like good and bad, up and down, mind and body, light and dark, and man and woman.

I read about how, historically, men were associated with minds and women with bodies. Women had long been seen primarily as bodies: the sites of life, nourishment, and death. As Emmeline Clein writes in *Dead Weight: Essays on Hunger and Harm*, "For figures like Plato, Augustine, and Descartes, transcending the dichotomy between mind and body—what Descartes called dualism—was humanity's ultimate challenge. . . . In their quest to unshackle mind from body, the philosopher-kings needed somewhere to trace their disgusting, desirous urges back to, a vessel for shame and blame. They found one in a figure they saw as the epitome of the bodily, a sexual receptacle that also offered food: woman."

I began to understand that my own fixation on my body—my fears of its hungers and needs and capabilities—was not simply personal or even cultural. This narrative dated back as far as Genesis: when Eve ate and offered forbidden food and was subsequently cursed with pain in childbirth.

I began reading the work of N. T. Wright, and I was specifically drawn to his discussion of the way binary dualism has affected Christians' thoughts on heaven, hell, and life on earth. He writes in *Surprised by Scripture* that because Western Christianity has embraced binary dualism, we often view heaven as a place distinctly separate from earth. With this perspective, the goal of Christianity becomes escaping earth to inhabit heaven. When we think about matter as a very bad thing that we want to abandon, it affects the way we live in space and time. Or, as Wright says, "Why wallpaper the house if it's going to be knocked down tomorrow?" If this world is temporary and passing away, in other words, it is fruitless to focus on making this place wonderful.

All these beliefs are rooted in Gnostic philosophy. Among other teachings, Gnostics believed that the body was bad and that the spirit was good. The belief that the flesh is sinful and a source of shame is still present in the church today. This demonization of the body is central to the evangelical purity culture of the 1990s. And evangelical purity culture was not just a religious phenomenon—it was a political force. As a reaction to both the sexual revolution and the AIDS crisis, large amounts of money were poured into abstinence-only sex education and True Love Waits campaigns.

And there is significant overlap between modern-day purity culture and diet culture. Both are concerned with keeping women small. Both frame appetite as suspect. Both glory in self-denial.

Part of the power in these systems is that they hit on some partial truths: There is something to be said for self-denial. Our capitalistic system runs on the gratification of desires, many of which are stoked within us by corporations. Sometimes our cravings can hurt others and us. But not always. It's important to look at our desires with a critical eye and eschew fundamentalist interpretations of them.

"Disordered eating is common in purity culture. It requires adherence to a strict hierarchy: the body must submit to the mind, and the mind must submit to the spirit," Linda Kay Klein told me when I spoke to her over a decade after I took this course. "Women in purity culture are taught that there is a correlation between how they approach food and sex."

The author of *Pure: Inside the Evangelical Movement That Shamed a Generation of Young Women and How I Broke Free*, Klein recounted a conversation she had with a woman named

Alma. Alma confessed to a religious leader that she struggled with masturbation. The advice she was given to control the urge to masturbate was to regulate her intake of sugar. The self-control she supposedly lacked with food was assumed to be the same self-control she lacked with masturbation.

The solution to the difficulties of desire was simple: refrain. Say no to all of it. And the promise for this self-denial was a desirable body and a happy marriage. The more you withheld, the more blessings you would receive. It expanded the health-and-wealth gospel to include romance, reducing Christianity to a simple equation of sacrifice and reward.

As a teenager, I learned that there was no sin that seemed more egregious and unforgiveable than sex before marriage. Women's bodies—what we could not do with them—was the focus of many sermons and Bible studies in my youth group. Years later, when I would speak to women in purity culture and diet culture recovery groups, they would all talk about how the messages in their religious upbringing led to disassociation and disconnection from either sex or food or both.

26

In a 2021 episode of *This American Life* titled "Secrets," Susan Burton details her decades-long struggle with binge-eating disorder and anorexia. She interviews others with similar experiences: women whose eating disorder was the biggest thing in their lives that they never spoke about. Women whose psychological struggles with food grew below the surface, like a tumor, out of adolescence and into adulthood.

"That eating disorder memoir I was writing? I told people my book was the cultural history of the teenage girl," Burton says, explaining that she tried to conceal the true nature of the subject of her book due to stigma and her own embarrassment. "For years I was ashamed of my own story," she added.

One woman named Martine noted, "You can say I'm an alcoholic, I feel, or I'm a drug addict. That's okay. It's like, you know, kind of interesting, but just saying, I have an eating disorder, I just want to eat, it's so unattractive, it's so disturbing. I just was never able to tell that to anyone."

Nearly all describe the shame in the continued existence of their struggle. Most had not spoken to anyone about it—some not even to their lifelong partners. The women describe the profound loneliness in this secrecy. Nearly all confess to a fear that if they were to share, others would think of them as shallow.

Despite my own fears, I decided it was scarier to keep the secret. I told it because the secret had power and because I wanted a life. One without counting. I wanted a life with pizza in public minus the side of secret shame. I told it because I wanted a boyfriend, and most boyfriends take you on dates to restaurants. I wanted a job, and it's hard to balance full-time disordered eating with a career.

But perhaps most importantly, I told it because in my new environment, I had the sense that the things I wanted were within reach.

I decided to talk about it. This time, not to a lecherous man. To someone who I believed could have actually helped me. I decided to share some of my story with a Bible study leader from a campus Christian ministry.

She was kind. She assured me that it was normal for all women to struggle with food and their bodies.

"That's true—I know it's so common," I nodded.

"It's very normal," she said. "It's not a big deal at all." Which was precisely my fear. That my pain was not a big deal. That something that had stolen so much was actually hardly anything at all.

Shortly after this conversation, I quit going to the Bible study. I decided, never again. I would never tell another person about this part of me ever again. I became convinced that no one would believe my problem was that bad.

I knew how bad my problem was, but I was managing. I was smart. I'd read a dozen books about eating disorders and their causes and their treatments. I convinced myself that I could put as much effort into recovering as I had put into staying sick. I believed I could organize my world carefully so that I could prevent my future relapse. I thought that all of it could remain a private affair.

After quitting this Bible study, I put real effort into finding a church that was both different and familiar. I didn't want to stray too far from the straight and narrow path. Still, I wanted less legalism. A bit more alcohol. I hoped to avoid sanctuaries that displayed the American flag beside an image of the cross and sermons that centered on the United States being the chosen people of God. I was increasingly drawn to the concept of grace, to the emphasis of God's love over good works.

American evangelicalism is divided on its view of salvation. In one camp, there are those who believe that salvation is something you receive after praying the sinner's prayer, a prayer of repentance with the desire to receive salvation. And just as you can choose salvation, you can also choose damnation again by living a life contrary to God's commands. These are broad strokes, but this is the Arminian camp, and it's where I grew up.

The other camp, the Reformed or Calvinist camp, does not believe that you choose Christ. They believe that Christ chooses you. Over in that camp, the sinner's prayer is a "work," and no work, no matter how good, is enough to merit the grace of Jesus Christ. Praying to accept Jesus's gift of salvation is a sort of "pull yourself up by your bootstraps" theology. Reformed theology does not believe that we have any bootstraps. Reformed theologians teach that we are shoeless, dead in our sin. They frequently reference an image from the book of Ezekiel, of human souls as a valley of dry bones that come to life only with the breath of the Holy Spirit. So, you can't choose to be saved, but also you can't lose your salvation. Because it's God's work either way.

Being told *there is nothing you can do* was revolutionary for me. In childhood, I memorized hundreds of verses, all to prove myself as a Christian. I chided myself nightly for praying incorrectly, for having sinful or impure thoughts. Though I didn't know it at the time, I struggled with scrupulosity, a form of religious obsessive-compulsive disorder (OCD) that causes you to have intrusive thoughts about the faith you hold dear.

Around the time the scrupulosity diminished, my intrusive thoughts were replaced with obsessions about food and my body, disordered eating, another struggle that often co-occurs with OCD.

I was desperate for someone to give me permission to stop doing so many things. I was fully convinced that I was unable to save myself. I'd tried. I was miserable. I started attending a Reformed Bible study. The lead pastor preached countless sermons about grace, and I nodded my head with relief. *Yes, hallelujah, grace.*

How can you know that Christ has chosen you? If you want to be chosen, then you are chosen. That is enough, the pastor explained. And in this Bible study, I met E—the man I would eventually marry.

27

"Tell me about you," my suitemate Liz said as we sat in the living room of our dorm the first week of our freshman year of college. "Tell me about the men you've been with."

"I haven't really dated much," I said and tried to change the subject.

In college, I still had never kissed a boy. I eventually revealed this to my suitemates, Liz and Christy, former competitive high school dancers from a holler in Kentucky. They were both tall and loud, broad shouldered, and—according to their own anecdotes—sexually experienced.

During our first weekend in the dorms, the three of us drove into Ohio to a Walmart just past the state border of West Virginia. Liz, a blonde who often referred to herself as *the blonde*, a way to contrast herself with the more plain, similarly built brunette Christy, suggested we shop out of state because there was no sales tax.

We purchased our cereal, bath mats, and other dorm accessories. On the drive home, Liz told stories of all the men she'd convinced to buy her flowers that past summer. "I had a date every night!" she told us. "Sometimes more than one in a night!"

Christy rolled her eyes.

"That sounds like a full-time job," I said.

"And I told anyone who asked me out that I expected flowers," Liz continued.

I turned my gaze to the patch of grass along the median of the highway. I imagined a pile of withered roses browning in the trash pit of her hometown.

A few weeks into the semester, Liz and Christy forced me to admit my lack of experience—that I'd never been on a real date (I certainly didn't count my birthday mistake with Doug). I'd never so much as kissed someone.

"It's embarrassing," I said. "I wish I could just have it happen so I could get it out of the way, move on with my life."

At first, Liz didn't understand my predicament. "Just go to a frat party, pick a boy, and start making out," Liz said.

"But how do I do that?" I asked.

"Get drunk—someone will start making out with you," Liz said. "It's not like you're ugly. You just look kind of frigid."

"No—don't tell her to do that," Christy replied. "We're going to find you a nice boy. A nice, safe boy. Someone who's as much of a loser as you are," she said with a wink.

Liz and Christy plastered our common room with posters of shirtless men in cowboy boots, tight jeans, defined pecs, artificial tans. They drooled over the images, catcalling to the walls in what I thought could have only been performances of desire.

"Doesn't he turn you on?" Liz said, gesturing to the image on the wall.

"I don't know. Not really." He looked like the sort of guy I imagined would be mean to me. He did nothing for me—and even if he had, I had a deep resistance to objectifying anyone, particularly someone I thought I could care for.

Liz rolled her eyes and turned her attention back to Tila Tequila. They'd been watching marathon episodes of the MTV reality show all evening long. They drank sweet tea from McDonald's, had ordered one final pizza before their joint diets began the next day.

I walked to my room, shutting the door to the common room. I heard Liz say my name in a low tone, quiet speculation about what was wrong with me. I opened my door again to show that I overheard.

Christy began to address me: "It's not like you act like you're attracted to girls. It's more like you're not attracted to anyone at all."

"Oh! Maybe she's asexual!" Liz cheered.

I gazed at them on the couch in their sweatpants, gawking over some stupid, arrogant-looking man, shoveling greasy food in their faces, pretending that their diets would last more than a day.

"Ha! Maybe you're onto something," I said as I tried to cover the quiver in the back of my throat.

About a month into college, I noticed I caught a particular guy's eye. Ryan lived one floor down from us in the dorm, and he attended the same campus ministry as me. My suitemates noticed, too—and they approved.

"Even though Ryan's kind of a dork, he's not ugly," Christy said.

"He'd be a good first kiss for you—he won't try to take advantage of you. It'll be good for you to get that out of the way with someone nice and safe," Liz added.

When Ryan eventually asked me out, Liz and Christy were more excited about the date than I was.

"Do you think he'll try to kiss me?" I asked Liz the night before my first real date.

"I definitely think he might!"

"Gosh. I hope so. I'd love to get my first kiss over with."

"That's the spirit!" she said.

I paused. "But I don't know how to kiss. What if I do it wrong?"

"Want to practice?" Liz asked.

"I do."

She grabbed a stuffed bear the size of a toddler from the end of her bed. She flipped the switch of our overhead fluorescent light off, turning on her dim rhinestone-embellished lamp. She placed the bear in the middle of her pink shag rug. Crouching on her knees, red Juicy Couture velour sweatpants stretched snugly across the curve of her butt, she leaned in to kiss the tan plush bear.

"Watch my mouth," she instructed me, and I did. She kissed the toy passionately. Performatively. A minute passed slowly.

"Wanna try?" she finally asked.

"Sure."

She held out the bear. I took him in my hands. I opened my mouth, leaned in—"I feel stupid," I said.

"That's the first thing you gotta learn—to ignore that feeling."

I closed my eyes. I leaned in again, polyester to mouth. I tasted the thread of the bear's embroidered lips and pulled him closer, opening my mouth wider, fabric to teeth. I bit him and pulled away.

"Perfect," Liz said.

"Perfect?"

"More than perfect."

The next day, Liz insisted on helping me get ready. "Let me curl your hair," she said, though I felt perfectly practiced and capable of grooming myself. "Please. It will make me so happy." She spent half an hour fussing with my hair.

I changed into my outfit. I wore boot-cut jeans and a white button-up shirt embellished with faux pearls and lace. Liz and Christy looked me up and down with hesitant expressions.

"You look like you're interviewing for a secretarial position," Liz said.

"I wouldn't wear jeans to an interview."

They continued to stare at me.

"Okay," I said finally, "but I don't know what else to wear."

Liz sighed, walked over to me, and unfastened three buttons. Christy nodded.

"Yes, that's better, at least."

I glanced in the mirror. "You can see my boobs!"

"Exactly! That's what we want."

My hand moved to my chest, and Liz slapped it away. "Don't you dare. You've got to give yourself a chance."

I begrudgingly nodded, checked my lipstick in the mirror, grabbed my purse and coat, and headed to meet Ryan in the dorm lobby.

"Have fun!" Liz called to me as I walked out the door. "Stay away from those buttons!"

I rebuttoned my blouse in the stairwell.

Ryan and I drove to a chain restaurant in a plaza near campus. He opened the door to the building—"ladies first," he said with a wide wave of the hand and the slightest bow. I smiled and walked up to the host's table.

"Two, please," Ryan said, and our host guided us to a booth by a window.

"So, you're in Dr. Tate's class this semester?" I asked Ryan.

"Yes! Have you taken him for anything?"

"I have him now, too. For an honors seminar on Gnosticism."

"Oh, that sounds incredible. He's my favorite professor in the department. You know, he's done a lot of scholarship on Tolkien. Are you a fan of Tolkien?"

"I've read *The Hobbit* before," I said, which was almost true. My father briefly instituted *family* time, about an hour block when we would sit around the living room as he read out loud. One book he'd chosen for read-alouds was *The Hobbit*. I complained about having to listen for months.

"Tolkien's a genius. A master of languages and world building," Ryan said, continuing to pontificate on Aragorn and Bilbo, Adaldrida and Smeagol. I nodded my head, trying to keep eye contact—he had such piercing blue eyes—as he made a case for the underratedness of *The Silmarillion*.

The waiter appeared to take our order.

"Ready to order?" Ryan asked me. I hadn't had a chance to review the menu, but I nodded my head yes.

"Ladies first," Ryan said nodding at me.

"I'll have grilled chicken. With broccoli—and, uh, a baked potato." A meal that wouldn't cost too much, wasn't excessive, but still—with the potato—wouldn't look like I was dieting. The safest meal I could think of. Also, the most boring.

Ryan ordered a dish that actually sounded good.

We continued to make awkward conversation. I'd never been on a date before, but this felt like a bad one. My head started to feel fuzzy, the chatter in my brain turned up to loud static. This was all my fault. Why was I so awful at this, being with boys, going on a date? I berated myself silently as Ryan downed french fries and pontificated on his favorite band, the Black Keys. I'd never heard of them, but I knew I needed to continue to look interested.

I racked my brain for something to add to the increasingly one-sided conversation. After a lengthy lull, I heard myself blurt out, "So, tell me your testimony."

I couldn't believe I'd said it. Though, I thought to myself, I wouldn't want to get in a relationship with a *nominal* Christian. Maybe this was right—the exact sort of thing you should ask on a first date.

"My testimony." He repeated my own words back to me slowly.

"Yeah," I said after a pause. "Like, how you became a Christian."

He stared at me. Then he told me a vague story from youth camp that ended in the sinner's prayer.

I nodded my head. "That's really great," I said. He didn't ask me to reciprocate, and I was relieved about this. I hated being asked to share my testimony.

Dinner ended shortly after the sinner's prayer. We drove back to the dorm and each retreated to our separate rooms. Liz and Christy sat on our common-room couch in sweatpants, eating pizza—they were off their diets again—watching a Tila Tequila marathon.

"Well—how did it go?" Christy asked.

"You're home early!" Liz said.

"It was fine," I said. "I think it went fine." I absolutely did not think it went fine.

"So did he . . ." Christy trailed off.

Liz interjected: "Did he get any action?"

"No. He didn't even try to hold my hand."

"Well, he's a good little boy," Liz said. "Next time!"

I smiled at her. I walked to the mini fridge to store my Styrofoam container of leftover chicken. I changed out of my outfit and into some workout clothes. I laced up my sneakers and grabbed my MP3 player.

"I'm going out," I called to Christy and Liz as I walked to the door. It was already dark, but I needed to go for a run.

MARRIAGE

28

"There's this guy who reminds me so much of you," friends told me.

"There's this girl who reminds me so much of you," friends told him.

E was a nice boy, a safe boy, just as much of a loser as I was. He and I met at a Bible study my junior year of college. I knew who he was—he'd attended my high school briefly, had transferred after having been homeschooled most of his life. He was older than me, and I'd noticed him from a distance—a tall, handsome basketball player with curly blonde hair.

One night at a mutual friend's wedding, he asked me to dance. We danced for hours. The next day, he called and asked me out on a date. He was in medical school at the time, on a rotation at the VA.

"They always let you go early there," he said. "Wanna ride my bike and go swimming after they let me off Friday afternoon?"

"Sounds great," I said.

He picked me up on his motorcycle, a small Kawasaki he'd bought from an older man at church. They'd worked together for several weeks, tinkering in a garage, trying to restore it.

E handed me an extra helmet—the sturdier one with a full-face shield.

"Ever been on a bike before?" he asked.

"Not this kind of bike," I replied.

"I'll go slow. Take it easy on the turns," he said.

I smiled and nodded—I typically couldn't imagine agreeing to such risk, but something about his manner made me feel emboldened to step outside myself.

We drove toward Hawk's Nest, a peak on Gauley Mountain overlooking New River Gorge. The face shield muffled his voice as he yelled, "Do you feel comfortable with this speed?"

"Yes!" I yelled back as I gripped his narrow waist tighter, squeezed my legs more firmly by his hips. I'd never felt so comfortable in my life.

We avoided the interstate, driving for an extra hour along curvy mountain roads, past stray dogs and muddy creeks, barefoot children, a Piggly Wiggly, piles of old disassembled cars scavenged for parts. Eventually, we made it to Kanawha Falls.

"There's a swimming hole near here," E said. "Want to stop?"

"That sounds great," I said.

When we parked, I pulled my swimsuit, a plain black bikini, from my backpack. E took his shirt off, unbuttoning his jeans. I saw he wore trunks as underwear.

"Just a minute," I said, ducking behind a tree to undress. I wrapped a towel around my chest and walked back toward E. He was standing on top of a large slab of rock. He waved me over to join him on the edge.

"Let's jump on three."

"Okay." I dropped my towel.

He grinned, took my hand, and began to count—"one—two—three—"

After swimming, we held hands as we lay in the sun to dry off. Everything felt natural with E—even when there were stretches of silence. Something about him felt easy. He looked at me without judgment. With him, I didn't feel the need to perform.

Eventually, we redressed in our jeans and sneakers. I pulled my damp hair into a low bun and shoved my helmet on. We continued toward Hawk's Nest, evening sun casting shadows through the thick canopy of trees. E was confident with the handlebars, taking sharp, sure turns up the twisting mountain road.

We reached a flat stretch at the top of the ridge. Suddenly, he pushed the throttle with force. We took off with a jolt, air whipping loudly, the rest of the world a blur.

It felt like flight. It felt like power. He had the power. I trusted that was okay.

"Sorry," he said, slowing down to the posted speed limit as we approached Hawk's Nest. "Something just came over me."

"It's okay," I said. "That was so much fun."

We parked and saw a line of tourists filing out to leave. The sun was beginning to set. A sign was posted at the entrance: "closed at dark."

"We still have some time," E reasoned.

We hiked a short trail to the gorge overlook. A train chugged along rusty tracks deep in the valley. E pulled a cigar and lighter from his pocket and sat on the rock ledge.

"Want to try?" he asked.

I nodded my head, leaned over, and took a puff.

I sat beside him on the ledge—close, thighs touching, then closer, legs interlocking. He pulled a bottle of water out of his backpack, extinguished the cigar, and then we were kissing, overlook now empty, sky a perfect, cloudy pink.

We moved to the grass, reclining, I on top of him, he on top of me, fireflies twinkling, mosquitoes biting, and we just kept kissing and kissing.

Time passed. Night fell. A single beam of light shone in our direction. "Park's closed," a security guard yelled, and we sat straight up, brushing dirt and stray leaves off our backs. We ran back to the bike.

"That was fun," I said as E started the ignition.

"Best time I've ever had at the gorge," he replied.

On the way home, we stopped at a restaurant for dinner. He ordered steak. I ordered grilled chicken.

"That doesn't look like enough," he said kindly, as he cut some of his meat to place on my plate.

After dinner, I held tight onto his waist as we drove in the crisp night air. When we arrived back at my apartment, I didn't change my breath or posture as he held onto my waist.

We were inseparable after that. We went for long hikes in the woods where we drank and smoked and kissed and talked about God. Even though we were both frustrated by the rigid legalism of our fundamentalist youth, we were still committed to Christianity. We still believed in sin, but we also believed in grace. We thought that Jesus was not nearly as rigid as the religious leaders who were the main speakers at our school's chapel services made him out to be.

We fell in love. I'd never been with a person who made me feel both so safe and so free.

Though E attended my fundamentalist high school, his father was a Reformed minister. E was so much more open than I was, so much more sure. I joined a Reformed church. This was a rebellion from the religion of my youth, but it was a soft rebellion. Arminians often warned others about the freedoms of Reformed parishioners. They are more likely to be drunkards and smokers and gluttons. A bunch of fatalists. *There is nothing you can do*, after all. If God's chosen you, then you are chosen. And if he hasn't, well—who can fathom the mind of God?

When we first started dating, we were disgusting—I could see the looks of repulsion from others in our Bible study as E softly massaged my back during the evening lesson. We held hands constantly, unlocking fingers only to rub the other's thigh or arm.

I was starving for physical touch. I'd been so hungry for so long. Our public displays of affection annoyed all the other, less smitten people in the room, but for all we did in public, we did little more in private. There, we followed specific rules. *All clothes remain on.* We were devoted to abstinence.

29

"Isn't it nice that we can catch up while doing something we already have to do?" Leah, my friend from waitressing and college, would say. She and I stayed friends while E and I were dating, too. Sometimes Leah and I would make plans two weeks in advance to go grocery shopping together.

When we shopped together, I bought lots of produce, organic and shining. I'd begun to feel so free with food, but when I was with Leah, I was reminded that there were certain standards I was not living up to. I wasn't all that committed to eating my five daily fruits and vegetables. Occasionally, I'd eat a meal without a single one. But Leah inspired me to be a better version of myself when we were together.

I'd unpack the produce from our grocery trips, put it in the refrigerator, and delay washing it. I'd promptly forget about my purchases and plans. Weeks later, I'd find spinach and bell peppers reduced to puddles in the crisper.

When I received a text from Leah with a photo of a ring, I responded with my congratulations and put a date on my calendar to try on bridesmaid dresses in the shade of begonia—we'd been discussing colors for some time.

I planned the lingerie shower with another bridesmaid, and we ordered a cake pan in the shape of a penis off the internet. We baked devil's food cake in the mold the night before the shower. And it was the closest I'd ever come to seeing an adult penis.

Penis-themed bachelorette parties were common for women in my part of the purity-culture world. Penis confetti. Pin the penis on the male poster model. Penis-shaped balloons. There were no strippers, just disembodied penises everywhere. We were desperate to prove waiting until marriage to have sex didn't mean we were sexually repressed.

We placed gift bags piled high with tissue paper around Leah's feet. The bags were filled with sheer lace nightgowns and panties that were barely more than strings. This was the last hurrah. The only thing next was a baby. But she hoped to hold off on that for a while. She needed some time to enjoy having sex.

Leah and Levi wanted to buy a house after their wedding, but Levi's jobs kept falling through. He was freelancing, hoping that one position or another would turn permanent. They were renting an apartment by the interstate. She found herself awake at night listening to heavy trucks barreling past their bed. They'd adopted a cat. Sometimes the cat slipped out of the house as she carried groceries in after trips to the store. There had been a few close calls.

Eventually, one of Levi's jobs turned permanent. He was working full-time for a popular conservative radio host, and he loved his new job. The salary was great, and the benefits package was a dream. "He flew all of us—employees and their spouses—out to New York last month for the company Christmas party," Leah told me one evening over a drink.

"Was it fun?"

"Of course," she said. "We were in New York."

Still, they continued to live in their apartment by the interstate. They'd been hoping to buy a house for some time, but they just kept having to put that off. She looked uncomfortable telling me this, clearly wanting to disclose personal information without complaining about her husband. Levi had started budgeting several hundred dollars a month, "for supplies," she said, her expression now shifty.

"For supplies," I repeated the phrase back to her.

"You know," she said, "for ammo. Freeze-dried food." She paused again. "Levi thinks we'll probably need it soon."

"He does?"

Leah shifted in her seat. "I don't know. You know he reads a lot. He knows things. And even more now that he works where he does."

Our server appeared once more. We both ordered additional drinks. "I just thought," Leah said after a moment, "that it wouldn't be this way. I thought that God would reward me for doing the right thing. For waiting. I mean, we could have had sex, but we didn't—for year and years, we didn't have sex. And I thought God would bless our marriage because we did the right thing." Leah's eyes were filled with tears.

"You know that's not how it works," I said. Though I wondered if I, too, believed that was precisely how it worked.

"I'm mad at God, Anna," Leah said after a moment. "I haven't been to church in months. I just can't go. I'm mad at God."

I looked at her. I was mad at God too. I wasn't sure why. My life was going pretty well. I was about to graduate. I was dating E. It appeared we would get married. This was the most I'd allowed myself to hope for.

I thought Leah's life looked pretty good, too, to be honest. I wasn't sure she had all that much to complain about. Still, I felt something had been withheld from me, and I sensed she felt the same thing too. That we had been deceived.

I sat still for a moment. "I'm sorry," I said finally. "You should probably still go to church though." She looked at me with a blank expression.

I continued. "The longer you stay away from church, the harder it will be to get back into it." This is what I'd been told. "You may feel better once you start praying about it more and going again. God will pursue you. You don't have to do it on your own." And as I said these things, I hoped they were true. I desperately wanted them to be. But I had a flicker of doubt. And I knew she did too. Shortly after I made these remarks, she changed the subject.

"So, what kind of flowers are you planning to use in your wedding after E proposes?"

30

I decided on hydrangeas and peonies, a May wedding. E proposed when I was twenty-two, enrolled in graduate school, studying applied linguistics and teaching composition classes. He had just begun his first year of medical residency. His father officiated our wedding ceremony. In the rehearsal, he pronounced us "Mr. and Mrs. E Rollins."

"No," I said. "Mr. and Mrs. E and Anna Rollins. I'm giving up my last name—but I'm not losing my first name, too."

His father raised an eyebrow. "She's right, Dad," E said, and his father made a note in pen. My sex education consisted of one textbook: Dr. Dobson's *Preparing for Adolescence* distributed by Focus on the Family. As I approached puberty, my mom and I would snuggle under a downy comforter before bed to read chapters aloud. I knew Mom loved me. All she ever wanted was to protect me. To keep me pure and safe and untouched.

In evangelical purity culture, sex wasn't always dirty—it was only dangerous and sinful before marriage. If I were to have premarital sex, I learned, I would "lose the innocence of youth, and [become] hard and cold as a person"—and I believed it. To avoid that fate, women must remain on high alert and work very hard to control both themselves and the men who could so easily fall into temptation. But that vigilance was supposed to magically disappear after I walked down the aisle to say "I do."

Before our wedding, I tried to prepare for having sex in remarkably unsexy ways. I read books with clinical diagrams.

I tried to insert a tampon. I'd never used a tampon before—Mom had not allowed it. *The chemicals in the fibers. Toxic shock syndrome.* I bought a box from the drugstore—the slim kind for days with light flow. I went to the bathroom, undressed, sat on the floor, and tried to push the tampon inside of me. I could not. I read the instructions on the box and tried again. I could not get it in. I grabbed a mirror, really evaluated my anatomy. But, again, I could not insert the tampon.

I called a close friend and asked for some tips. She seemed baffled. "You know where it's supposed to go, right?"

"Of course, I know where it's supposed to go."

"Okay—well, maybe use some lube. Just try to breathe. Stretch yourself out a bit. You'll get there eventually."

I tried all these things. I did not get there eventually, but I was too embarrassed to pursue the matter further. I would not be able to wear a tampon for another five years, until after I'd given birth to my first child.

I booked an appointment with a gynecologist for a prescription for birth control. I'd googled "side effects of birth control" for hours to read pages upon pages of message boards where women described the weight gain they'd experienced after taking the pill. I felt nauseated reading the narratives, but I resigned myself to the situation. I knew that the alternative—a baby—had the side effect of weight gain, too. I'd allowed myself more freedom with food, and my body had naturally found a set-point weight. Fortunately for me, that set point was still considered thin by our culture's standards. I was terrified of medication taking that privilege away.

In the appointment, when the doctor tried to give me a Pap smear, my body tensed with pain as she began to insert the speculum. "Just breathe," she said, as I clenched my fists and blinked back tears. I tried to be strong. I tried to push past the pain. Eventually she gave up: "I guess we don't really need to do this today."

"I'm really scared of having sex," I confided to my doctor. "I'm really scared it's going to hurt. What can I do to make it not hurt?" She barely disguised an eye roll. "Buy some lube," she told me, and then she wrote a prescription for the pill. Many women who have grown up in purity culture respond to sexual situations in a way similar to assault victims. We respond as though we've been abused. We've been taught that our bodies are a liability to our souls, that our eternal salvation is contingent upon our ability to maintain corporeal control.

I told my mom about the doctor's appointment. "Oh, honey," she reassured me. "I bet you were a breath of fresh air! A nice young woman saving herself for marriage. I'm sure it was a relief for her to see that people like you still exist." I was pretty sure this was not the case—I had the sense that no one valued my virginity quite as much as my mom and the church.

I relayed this conversation to a friend. She, too, had planned to save herself for marriage, but she and her boyfriend were in love, and they'd started sleeping together. I judged her, but also, I envied her—she seemed so free. Her boyfriend had not left her. She did not seem "hard and cold as a person." I assumed there would be consequences for her behavior down the road, but for now, she seemed really happy. She seemed as if she wanted me to be happy, too.

"You know, Anna," she said, "I wish your mom would stop telling you about how much sex hurts. It doesn't have to. It really doesn't."

"No?" I said.

"It didn't for me."

"That's great."

"I think that anticipating it will hurt is going to make it more likely to hurt."

"That's probably true," I admitted.

31

On our wedding night, we did not have sex. E booked a suite at the top floor of a hotel with a hot tub on an outdoor balcony. He made a mix tape of our favorite songs, drove over to the room earlier in the day to decorate it with dozens of roses, stocking expensive champagne and shrimp cocktail in the mini fridge.

Everything was perfect. As he kissed me and removed my shirt, my pants, my underwear, I whispered, "I can't, I'm so sorry, I can't. I'm scared." I began to cry.

"It's okay," he said. "We don't have to do everything at once. We have our whole lives," and I kissed him, and we held each other, and then we fell asleep.

We eventually had sex. And just as I anticipated, it hurt. He was so kind, and his kindness made me feel guilty. "How is this?" he asked as he slowly tried a new position. I clenched my jaw, tightened my fists. "It's fine," I said, blinking back tears.

"No—it's not. Let me try something else."

I leaned back and closed my eyes and tried not to think of what was coming next. I looked into his blue eyes and ran my hand through his curly hair, and my God—I loved him. I couldn't believe he was mine. He was so perfect. So patient. This was both a burden and a gift.

"Try to breathe," he said. "If we can just do it once, I bet that would make it more comfortable in the future."

I nodded. A jolt of pain. My eyes welled with tears.

"How are you doing?" he asked.

"I'm . . . it hurts," I whispered. Eventually, I would scream it. And we kept trying, some attempts less excruciating than others.

"Let's just get it over with," I said.

"I want it to be good for you."

"It's not going to be."

After, he held me and stroked my hair. I wondered when he would eventually lose patience with me.

He brought home roses. Wine. All sorts of things. And when we did the things we did while we were dating, I could be in my body, and I could lose myself in his. But then, he would try to go further, and I could not. Everything closed. I would coach my body to act the opposite way, but she would not respond.

I was not ashamed of having my body seen and touched. The fear I was most conscious of was the fear of pregnancy. I was not afraid of babies. Still, I was terrified of pregnancy. I was afraid of my belly expanding, its soft flat shape distending into a globe. The idea of such fullness filled me with dread.

"You're not going to get pregnant," E said. "You're on the pill. We're using double protection. It's not going to happen."

Logically, I knew. But then, he would move toward me, and I'd clench, and it would hurt, and I would imagine a tiny seed implanting, my belly expanding into a round, monstrous shape. I quivered with fear.

Sometimes I had dreams at night that I was pregnant. These dreams were not nightmares—they were fantasies. I dreamed of myself naked and full and round, and I lounged on satin sheets, and there was only me—no one else. And I was abundant. I woke breathless. I was free, open, expansive—like Nicole in The Fat Project, from my adolescence. I moved toward my sleeping husband in the dark and kissed his neck. What if it could be this way? What if I could actually experience the pleasures of my dreams?

One evening, I went out for happy hour with friends. A drink or three into the night, and they began discussing their sex lives. I sat at my bar stool quiet, smiling, uncrossing and recrossing my legs, sipping my glass of wine slowly.

One friend had recently given birth. "Sex just hasn't been the same since," she told us. The other women at the table comforted her, encouraging her to reach out for support, talk to her doctor, *something*. This wasn't something she had to keep enduring.

I was envious of her. I was envious that she had, at one point, known what good sex felt like. I was envious that she had not always been broken. Her pain was caused by something natural—something that was not her fault.

I was convinced my experience of painful sex was absolutely my own fault—and certainly not something I could admit to during happy hour.

For a year, then another, then another, I could not have sex without pain or discomfort. Vaginismus. I didn't know there was a name for it. I didn't know that it affected many women, that it was twice as common for those who had grown up in religiously conservative households. I just felt like a failure with a body that would never do what it was supposed to do.

One night, E arrived home from work with a bottle of expensive wine. "I think you need to get really drunk," he told me, uncharacteristically. "I think you need to drink the whole bottle. Something just has to get you out of your head."

That didn't fix it. In fact, I would later learn that this proposed remedy is a terrible solution for vaginismus. But eventually, something happened. Was it time, practice, a shift in mood or weather? I was lucky, I learned later after speaking to dozens of women who'd struggled in the same way. I wouldn't require professional intervention to recover. Just an excruciating amount of time. Eventually, I was able to receive. I began initiating, not avoiding sex. Sometimes I would suggest we go out for ice cream afterward. I gained five pounds. Maybe ten pounds. I wasn't sure—I'd gotten rid of my scale. I could feel it on my hips, everything just a bit softer. Was it the birth control?

I was pretty sure I was just really happy.

"Can you tell?" I asked E one night as I struggled to button a pair of jeans. I threw them aside, searched my closet for something with more room. "Do you think I'm disgusting?"

"I think you're beautiful," he said—and I believed him.

32

Years later, I went for a walk at the park with a former writing teacher who had become a dear friend. I told her that I was working on a book about disordered eating and purity culture. I described the sorts of stories I was sharing, the connections I was trying to make between desire and morality, restriction and obedience.

"Are you going to write about what it was like when you first got married?" she asked me. I'd confided to her about these problems in the past after several glasses of wine.

"You mean, am I going to write about how bad I was at sex?" I asked with a laugh.

She stopped and turned to me. "You know that's not what it was," she said.

When I got home, I decided to research what exactly it was. At this point, I had two children, and I no longer dealt with these issues. But I still didn't know the name for what had plagued me for years. All I knew was that before I had my first son, I was always in pain. And then, somehow, that pain went away after I gave birth.

I learned that my struggle with vaginismus was relatively common for women who had grown up in purity culture. It affects an estimated 1 to 6 percent of the general population. According to Sheila Wray Gregoire, "conservative religious women (like evangelicals) suffer from vaginismus at roughly twice the rate of the general population." In one large survey, 22.6 percent of Christian women reported experiencing painful penetrative sex.

I read more about the condition. My inability to use tampons? My difficulty with invasive gynecological exams? Those were connected to vaginismus, too. I thought back to my first OB-GYN appointment before marriage and the doctor's inability to perform a Pap smear. I could still see the exasperated look on her face. The way she rolled her eyes. *This should have been a sign to her*, I thought to myself. *I had a real condition. And my medical provider made me feel that I was just being ridiculous.*

As I continued to research vaginismus, I found language to describe the shame I felt for so many years. And I connected with other women who had similar stories.

I spoke to Jess Seitz, an occupational therapist who now devotes her life's work to helping women heal from vaginismus. But before she could help others recover, she had to heal herself.

Several years into marriage, she sat in the waiting room of her doctor's office, clipboard in hand. She lingered over one question: "Do you have pain during intercourse?" She circled yes, just as she'd always circled yes.

And just as had happened for years, her OB would never mention her disclosure.

"If my doctor didn't consider it a problem, maybe I shouldn't either," Jess told me.

She eventually gained the courage to reveal her struggle to some close friends in a Bible study. One friend invited her to a religious healing ceremony. At the healing ceremony, she confessed to a church leader that she couldn't have sex without pain. The leader laid hands on her and commanded a demon to leave her.

That did not fix her problem.

Eventually, she sought help from a pelvic floor physical therapist and a sex therapist. When she met with the pelvic floor physical therapist, the practitioner encouraged the use of dilators to help stretch the vagina or trigger-point-release massage to relax internal muscles.

But even these interventions were not sufficient.

So, she made it her mission to heal herself. She applied her expertise as an occupational therapist to treat her own condition. Using a biomechanical and psychosocial framework, she developed a new model for treating those who suffer from painful vaginal intercourse.

I was amazed with Jess's ingenuity, her ability to apply her own professional expertise to heal herself when no one else seemed able to.

"What ended up helping you?" Jess asked me later in our conversation.

I told Jess about our DIY strategies to heal the condition I did not know had a name. Then I shared with her that, eventually, I only dealt with partial vaginismus. And because of this, I was able to get pregnant. Then, miraculously, after childbirth, the pain went away entirely.

"You're really lucky," Jess said. She then spoke to me about how often she's worked with women for whom childbirth has resulted in the opposite.

I also knew that I was lucky to have ever gotten pregnant in the first place. I spoke to a woman named Marie who was trying to conceive but couldn't achieve penetration with her husband at all. She, too, grew up in purity culture and had spent much of her life trying to save sex for marriage.

"It was the most important thing a person could do," she told me.

Marie also self-diagnosed her condition after researching her symptoms online.

She sought out pelvic floor physical therapy, where she was taught to use dilators. And though this therapy has helped, it hasn't completely fixed it.

It's especially lonely trying to become pregnant while dealing with vaginismus, Marie shared with me. She doesn't really fit into communities dealing with infertility. She's had to search for groups on social media to find support from others who relate to her situation.

As I continued to read more, I stumbled upon the work of Sheila Wray Gregoire, author of *The Great Sex Rescue*. She argues that the teachings of evangelical purity culture have led to lower rates of female orgasm and more sexual pain in marriage.

To address this problem, she surveyed twenty thousand women about messages they grew up believing about sex and marriage to see what advice was helpful and what was harmful. In her research, she learned that the most insidious messages—things like *men are visual creatures and women are not* or *all men have lust problems*—are present in best-selling purity-culture books.

And I spoke to so many women who made this same observation. The most damaging messages they believed came from best-selling Christian books.

"I was the purity culture poster child," Morgan, an avid reader, said as she listed books she devoured during her adolescence at the turn of the century. Joshua Harris's *I Kissed Dating Goodbye*. Elisabeth Elliot's *Passion and Purity*. Jackie Kendall and Debby Jones's *Lady in Waiting*. I nodded my head. I, too, had read each of those titles. I consumed these evangelical books about sex and gender in the same way I studied the teen magazines in the back of my local library.

The lure of both was the same: to learn how to become a more perfect woman.

One of the most interesting observations Sheila Wray Gregoire made in her research was that even if the messages about abstinence or perfectionism were minimal in one's church or home, the girls who read these popular evangelical books were given a more extreme education.

In other words, bookish girls, the ones who were really invested in doing Christianity "right"? They were the ones who got hurt.

"When I first started dating my husband in college, I handed him *Boys Meets Girl* by Joshua Harris," Morgan said. "And he had to read it." The rules in this book defined both her coming of age and her romantic relationships.

"And I performed really well. I went by the rules, and I properly suppressed my sexuality," Morgan said. "I wasn't even tempted to do anything. I was surprised by how easy it was for me."

She described herself as being completely out of touch with her body and its desires—and that didn't change when she got married. She didn't know herself, what she wanted, what she enjoyed, and since she didn't know herself, she couldn't teach her husband about what she wanted, either.

Four years into marriage, she still couldn't have penetrative sex. When she got pregnant, her husband referred to it as an "immaculate conception."

"Well, I'm not doing this with anyone else but you," she replied.

Eventually, after having their son, their marriage couldn't handle the load of no sex—and they separated.

But ultimately, it was also reading that saved her here, too.

That—and breaking some rules.

A friend gave her the book *Come as You Are* by Emily Nagoski. Nagoski argues that mindset is central to a woman's experience of pleasure and desire—and that the key to being sexually whole is just to be yourself. The book was more science-based than religious, and it made Morgan feel less alone. She began to understand the mind-body connection. Eventually, she went to pelvic floor therapy and then three weeks of intensive mental health therapy for religious OCD. She probably always had OCD, she shared with me, but it was made worse in purity culture.

During their separation, their therapist prohibited Morgan and her husband from seeing each other and from touching each other. Morgan finally felt desire—longing, passion, libido. During that separation, they broke their therapist's rule and saw each other anyway—and they finally began to have really good sex.

Many of the women I spoke to about their struggles with vaginismus also confessed to dealing with disordered eating. Brooke

Lamb, a licensed marriage and family therapist who grew up in purity culture, told me she explores with clients deep connections between relationships with food and sexuality.

"I have a lot of clients who will say, 'Oh, you know, sex is fine, it's okay, whatever,' but then we'll start talking about disordered eating—and they're often not aware that those things are *intimately* connected." Both are about pleasure and body intuition. They're about desire—for food or for sex. And when we're taught that our inherent, intuitive cravings are bad, it really affects our ability to enjoy sex or food.

It's not until we can believe that our bodies are inherently good and worthy of pleasure and joy that we can begin to heal.

33

Shortly into our marriage, E returned home from a thirty-hour hospital shift bleary-eyed. He pulled a piece of folded paper from a pocket of his scrubs and handed it to me.

I looked at the paper—a graph with a bell-shaped curve. On the x-axis, it listed "miles run per week." On the y-axis, "life expectancy."

"What is this?"

"It shows the life expectancy of a runner. I printed it off a database at work. People who don't run have short life expectancies. People who run moderately are more likely to live longer—but look." He pointed to a steep drop-off. "People who run excessively die sooner than those who don't run at all."

While E worked long shifts in residency, I used my time alone to train for races. I was running ten, fifteen, sometimes twenty miles a day. I felt guilty giving myself more than one day off each week.

"So, what you're saying is that you're jealous that I can run more than you?" I said with a wink.

He rolled his eyes. "No way am I jealous of you. You're a slave. I like to run, too—but I don't want it to look anything like what you do."

I thanked him for his concern. I told him I had to continue training for a marathon in November that I'd already signed up for. He shrugged his shoulders, undressed, and crawled into bed to recover before his next shift.

He tried again in December. "There's a New Year's resolution I think you need to make," he said.

"Okay?"

"Only run four days a week. Only four days of working out each week."

"No way," I said.

"Just try it. You can work as hard as you want on those four days." He paused. "You might even lose weight."

"You think I need to lose weight?"

"Nope. But I know it's one of the only things that motivates you. I just think you need to take more days off. This is exhausting to live with."

"It is?"

"Aren't you exhausted?"

"Yes," I admitted.

"Just try it. For a month. You can always go back if something bad happens."

On New Year's Eve, I happened to run a high fever. As I lay in bed, chilled and sweating, my mind raced with my usual preoccupations: *How am I going to fit my workout in?* Then, suddenly, I thought, *Maybe this time, I won't.*

So I made the resolution: four days a week. I would exercise only four days each week. It was the best New Year's resolution I'd ever made. I binged less. I no longer nursed chronic injuries, shin splints, weak hips, back pain. For the first time in my life, I felt physically strong.

In adulthood, I developed rules to manage my disordered eating. This was a different kind of law. *I won't skip meals. I won't count calories. I won't cut out whole food groups. I will take one day off exercise each week.* I developed these rules without outside intervention. I did not go to therapy, and I did not see a doctor, and I did not consult with a dietitian. I'd thought about seeking help, but then I convinced myself that this was something best handled on my own.

I still leaned heavily on the rules. I exercised only four days a week—but it was never less. Still, enjoying a social and professional life became less of a puzzle. I was a better partner. It was easier to manage fevers and stomach viruses, long days at work and family emergencies. I was still a prisoner—but one with some recreational time. *Aren't we all, after all, prisoners in our own bodies?* I rationalized to myself.

34

Shortly after I married E, we visited a loft bookstore in Washington, DC. I stumbled upon a text about the size of a miniature Golden Book called *Anorexia and Mimetic Desire*. I pulled the book from the shelf. I glanced to my left, and then to my right, to make sure no one was watching as I began to flip through its pages.

The cover of the book was pink. It was written by a man, René Girard, a literary theorist of some renown but known as fringe—I'd learn later—for religious, conservative ideals. The book was a translation from the French. I considered standing right at that shelf to read each page, but that felt like stealing.

Still, I knew I would not buy this book. I could afford only one, maybe two books that day, and to purchase this one, I would need to buy at least five. If I were to buy this book, I would place it in the middle of a stack, title face down, avoiding eye contact with the clerk as he rang me up. This was my practice—to disguise my true interests with diversions. To avoid being seen.

I knew I couldn't buy this book on its own. It felt similar to buying a book about murder after having already engaged in the crime. I purchased another book from the shop, one I was less interested in. I don't remember its title; I doubt I ever read it. Then I hurried back to our hotel, the title of Girard's text memorized, eager to find an electronic version that I could download privately on my laptop.

I spent that evening beneath the scratchy Holiday Inn duvet staring at my laptop, reading an old man's interpretation of anorexia as a cultural phenomenon. He claimed that individuals were not eating disordered in isolation—that we lived in a culture that had an eating disorder, that an eating disorder was the embodiment of minimalism as an artistic form. He argued that the person engaged in disordered eating behavior was in rivalry with others—that this competition was based on renunciation rather than acquisition: "To abstain voluntarily from something, no matter what, is the ultimate demonstration that one is superior to that something and to those who covet it."

Girard spoke of anorexia in the voice of a man who had, perhaps, never gone on a diet himself, had never had more than a cursory conversation with a woman who had. In other words, his voice was distant—and this did not seem to be just an extension of the genre in which he was writing, critical literary discourse. He referred to bulimics as "failed anorexics," invoking the language of competition in his discussion of mental illness. I found myself disliking him, though I was drawn to his reading of a phenomenon that I, too, believed was widespread rather than singular. If only we were more open to talking about it. And though his interpretation of the behaviors was less than flattering, I did not believe he was wrong.

"My main experience is that I read other people's books about it," one woman said as she discussed her struggle with an eating disorder on *This American Life*'s episode "Secrets." "I don't talk to other people about it." Perhaps to quiet the voice that tells us our struggle is superficial and vain, we aim to intellectualize it.

One feature common to those who struggle with eating disorders is that the behaviors are done in secret. It is as if one takes a vow of silence. There is no water-cooler diet talk. There are no public fitness challenges.

For those without eating disorders, diet talk is out in the open. These discussions often feel evangelistic—with conversion attempts and accountability groups. But disordered eating behaviors—which look very similar to the diets that provoked them—happen in isolation. Discussion of binging and purging is reserved for anonymous message boards. To participate openly would be too revealing, an acknowledgment of the extent of the obsession.

Perhaps we do not talk because we know, deep down, we are in competition. The sort of competition where losing is winning and the opposing side is unaware of the game at all. We say we fear being seen as shallow, but perhaps the bigger fear is that we will be seen as we are: ugly. Not physically, but in the extent of our desire to outdo others. The thin pages of books become a substitute for words exchanged between flesh and blood. In the ritual of reading, a life of the mind, we can escape the mess of bodies, the needs of others and ourselves, while still attending to that aching desire to feel a little less alone.

35

Our pastor resigned and moved away. He was replaced by another man. There was less talk of grace, more discussion of America's descent into liberalism, the massacre of unborn babies and the socialist welfare state. *This isn't what I signed up for*, I thought to myself after several of these sermons. I was slowly moving toward more progressive positions, beginning with *my body, my choice*.

If there's anything someone who's struggled with an eating disorder understands, it's the concept of bodily autonomy.

I started to research the Reformers, beginning with the most famous one, Martin Luther. I stumbled upon something he said about women: "If women become tired, even die, it does not matter. Let them die in childbirth. That's what they are there for."

"Martin Luther's an asshole," I told E.

"What was the context of that quote?"

"Does it need a context? He was a misogynist, just like all the others," I said.

"I don't know if that's fair. He lived during the sixteenth century. You can't expect him to hold all your same progressive views about women. He was a product of his time. Just because he had some sexist opinions doesn't mean he doesn't have important, good things to say about the Bible."

I began paying attention to other Reformed pastors who had

significant platforms. It seemed the movement attracted machismo, sometimes even vulgarity. I had women friends from church posting sermons on social media from Mark Driscoll, lead pastor at Mars Hill, an exploding megachurch in Seattle. He decried the feminization of Christianity. He referred to women as "penis homes." A sort of pastoral precursor to Donald Trump, his "locker-room talk" from the pulpit appeared to be reluctantly accepted by many, fully embraced by some.

And then there was the blatant sexism of revered older pastors like John Piper and John MacArthur. Superficially, they seemed innocent enough, with their gray hair and glasses and book titles like *Desiring God* and *The Freedom and Power of Forgiveness*. On the desires and work of women, a contributor in Piper's edited collection on biblical manhood and womanhood said, "The woman is created be the man's helper (Genesis 2:18; I Corinthians 11:8–9). From these perspectives, the husband's work must take precedence (when necessary) over the wife's, and she must be willing to help her husband fulfill his calling in this realm even if it means she must give up her position." And John MacArthur, whose annotated study Bible was in nearly every church I'd ever attended, went viral on the internet telling famous Bible teacher Beth Moore to "go home" rather than continue to teach the Bible, all because she was acting out of place as a woman.

"These people are disgusting," I told E after watching the video of MacArthur eviscerating Moore's desire to teach others about Jesus. "There is nothing for women in this belief system."

E defended them—to an extent—but eventually conceded that they spoke about women in an insensitive way. "But you can't say that the Bible doesn't empower women," he responded. "It does. It was revolutionary in its view of women at the time. Women were the first witnesses to the resurrection of Christ. Women's testimonies were considered nothing in that culture—but still, the Bible offers their testimonies first. Paul told husbands to love their wives in a culture where women were considered little more than property. And he emphasized that there was no 'male' or 'female,' that we are all unified in Christ."

"I know. And that's one of the reasons I would still consider myself a Christian. But why is there still so much sexism in the church?"

Once, E was in a men's Bible study in college. As usual, the topic turned to porn—how to control a man's temptation to look at porn.

"Typical," I said, rolling my eyes as he told me about it. "Men are such *visual* creatures. What else is there to talk about at Bible study? Boys talk incessantly about porn, and girls are told incessantly not to become porn."

"Yeah, I know how you feel about it. I agree—it's obnoxious. But anyway, I think you'll find this interesting: I remember Andrew told our group, 'One way I manage my temptation to look at porn is by not eating.'"

My eyes opened wide. "So, he'd starve himself? That's probably one of the only things that actually works!"

"You mean, besides prayer?"

"Oh, I guess," I said. "Was this a habit for him?"

E said that it sounded habitual, and when I asked whether anyone seemed concerned that he admitted to using disordered eating behaviors to control his sexual desires, E shook his head no.

"It's probably because he's a guy," I speculated. "So, of course he couldn't have an eating disorder. That's only something stupid, vain girls develop."

"See—men suffer in Christianity, too, Anna. Well—I'm not going to call it Christianity. That's not *true* Christianity. In perverted religious systems."

I argued that everyone suffers in patriarchy. And there sure did seem to be a lot of Christianity that was perverted. E countered that this perversion was because humans are sinful, and their sinfulness makes systems broken.

"That's why it's so important to constantly look to Christ," he added.

I paused. "It all feels hopeless."

"Well, what's your alternative?" E asked me. "Do you have a better place you're going to look for hope?"

I shrugged my shoulders. "I don't know where else there is to go. But it also feels like there's nothing here."

"Maybe you should pray about that, then," E said.

"I have."

"Good." He paused. "That's the most you could do." He walked into the kitchen and filled up a pot of water to start dinner.

MOTHERHOOD

36

I went to a Bible study with a group of young stay-at-home moms roughly my own age. I was the only one in the group who did not yet have children. I could tell it was just as much work for them to draw me into their conversations as it was for me to participate.

E and I had been trying for a baby for a little over a year. I'd decided we should look into things. The day of the Bible study, I received a phone call with lab results from the doctor's office. My husband's test results came back fine.

As I considered the reasons for my own infertility, I was surrounded by women whose days were filled with mothering. Bible study was usually the first time in the day when the rest of the women in the group were able to interact with other adults. Small talk lasted for at least an hour. Then, the hostess hesitantly volunteered to pray. "I get so nervous praying out loud," she said.

We talked about a chapter from a devotional book. Several of the women had not had a free moment to make it through the whole chapter. We totally understand, the rest of us said, nodding our heads. One woman quoted a passage she had underlined, something about how we needed to be bolder in our witness for Christ. "This made me feel really convicted," she said. Everyone nodded their heads and bemoaned their own timidity.

The hostess who was hesitant to pray read a passage of Scripture aloud. She was struck by a particular word. *Dynamis.*

She'd looked the word up in the original Greek and wrote it on her bathroom mirror. It meant "power, potential, ability." "So I can meditate on it each morning," she said. "I used a black dry erase marker."

She suggested we could maybe do the same at home on our own mirrors. No pressure—only if we wanted to. "Maybe it's a stupid idea, actually," she said.

"No!" the room erupted. "It's not!" "I loved it!" "I was so inspired."

This discussion of Scripture felt like enough for one session. We all started talking about our upcoming weeks: swimming lessons, play dates, batch cooking. Somehow, the conversation shifted to how unsafe our town had become, specifically about the rising threat of sex trafficking.

Each woman had a story about her safety—a situation where she was on the edge of critical danger but was saved by her own foresight and caution. One woman was shopping at a craft store after her children's bedtimes. As she left the store, she saw a white van parked just beside her own car in the nearly empty parking lot. "I just had this feeling," she said, and we all nodded vigorously. She walked back inside the store and asked for an employee to escort her out. "Thank goodness you did!" several women said.

Another woman described a strange car driving down her dusty county road while her children played in the front yard. This happened around the same time each day. "One day, I'd finally had enough," she told us. "I unlocked the rifle from its safe. I went down to the bottom of the driveway and just stood there and waited."

The car came slowly down the road while she stood positioned with her gun. "It's been several weeks since then, and I haven't seen that car again," the woman said.

The stories continued. I couldn't think of any real threat I had experienced in our community. I scoured my memory and tried to think of any story I could contribute. I found myself feeling bitter toward these women. *Oh, everyone is after you and your beautiful children. Your family is irresistible!* I thought to myself. They had so much. Their stories of threatened loss felt like bragging.

As we left at the end of the night, we all hugged one another. I'd met the majority of the women only twice. The hostess apologized for her food not being elaborate enough, for her house being messy. "Stop," we all said, "your house is perfect." "It makes me want to set my own house on fire." "Your food is delicious." "I ate way too many of those cupcakes." "Diet starts tomorrow!"

I walked to the end of the dark driveway with a bounce in my step. When I made it to my car, I sighed deeply. I pressed the button on my car key to unlock the doors and noticed that the back window was rolled down. I held my breath. I hadn't remembered doing that. I gripped the metal of my keys between my fingers and peeked into the back seat—no one was there. The front seat—also empty. I looked beneath the car, by the wheels. One woman had just told a story of a couple who hid beneath vehicles in parking garages, slit women's ankles as they climbed into their cars. No one was beneath my car. I paused. I climbed in and started the engine to drive home. *If only this had happened before our Bible study*, I found myself thinking. *I could have told everyone about it.*

37

Time passed. There were more lab tests, more results. Nothing abnormal. I made an appointment to discuss more direct interventions, like intrauterine insemination. The morning of the appointment, my period was several days late. I retrieved one of the bulk strips I kept in the linen closet. I'd taken hundreds of these tests—all negative—but that morning, two lines appeared. I called E at work. I canceled the appointment for the intervention. I scheduled a prenatal appointment instead.

At my first appointment, I considered asking the nurse to weigh me blind. Backward. And please, never share the number. I'd read online that this is a practice suggested for people who have struggled with eating disorders.

Of course, I'd never had an eating disorder, I quickly reminded myself after having read articles online for hours about pregnancy after an eating disorder. I'd had hang-ups with food, sure, and maybe I could get a bit obsessive with numbers and exercise—but an eating disorder? I'd used this label once or twice before—but anytime I'd mentioned my problems to someone, they told me that my feelings and behaviors were normal. An eating disorder was serious stuff. And I would have had a diagnosis. No, I was just a woman, and all women had issues with their bodies.

The nurse handed me a glossy folder filled with literature and coupons for diapers and baby wraps. There was a list of pregnancy-approved medication—"keep that one on your fridge," the nurse instructed me. There was a list of all the banned foods. No soft cheese. No deli meat. No sushi. No ramen. No under-cooked meat. No high-mercury seafood. No alcohol. The list continued—it was nearly a full page. Even though I knew these restrictions were for the health of my baby, they reminded me of my previous struggles with food. I'd worked hard to reduce my anxiety at mealtimes, and now—just as my body was about to change even more drastically than it did during puberty—I was being told to fixate on food again.

I was familiar with this list already, and I took seriously the directive to modify my diet. Since I learned I was pregnant, I'd given up my glass of wine with dinner. And then, several weeks later, I felt that familiar shiver of pleasure when I saw that I was down a pound.

I'd felt I had a leg up searching for a medical provider when we decided we wanted to try to have a baby. E had completed internships with the academic OB-GYN service.

When we began trying to start a family, the first thing my husband told me was to switch OBs. "You don't want anyone in that practice delivering your baby," he told me over dinner one evening. "All they do is cut women open over there."

He suggested I try an OB who was more progressive, open to natural births. "He's a great physician," my husband said. "A bit kooky. Like the sort of guy you'd imagine has model trains and clown collections in his basement."

I decided this was not the provider for me. So, I asked around: the moms at church, the women in my running group. Over and over, I heard similar names, all of whom belonged to a particular practice of four. One of the OBs in this practice had been in medical school with my husband.

"What do you think of her?" I asked one night.

"I'm sure she's great," he said simply. This was enough of a recommendation for me to go ahead and make an appointment.

When I met her during our appointment, the air conditioner blowing through my paper gown to my bare breasts, I couldn't help but notice how cold she was. Curt. She had a pinched face, stony eyes. She placed her stethoscope to my midsection to listen to the baby's heartbeat for mere seconds. She seemed relieved when I told her I didn't have any questions.

"She seemed very . . . stoic," I said to my husband that evening.

"That sounds right."

"I thought you said you liked her?"

"I don't think I said that. I think I said that she was probably good."

"So . . . you don't like her?"

"I didn't know her, really," he said. "The longest interaction I ever had with her was when she made fun of me in class for still being a virgin."

"What!?"

"Yeah. Somehow—I don't remember the circumstances—she and her friend learned that I was still a virgin. She thought it was ridiculous and mocked me for several days. But she's smart. She'll do a good job."

"She'll do a good job delivering the virgin's baby?"

"Exactly," he said with a laugh.

38

E and I went out to dinner with another couple, friends who were also expecting their first child. We were both still in our first trimesters, that stage of precarity and invisibility. It felt so good to share future dreams with friends, to imagine a companion from birth for our seed-sized child.

Still, I felt a pang of fear as we talked about our lives to come—fear that we were all becoming too comfortable in this happiness, that our hopes had become oversized when we may soon experience loss.

I ordered my dinner: salmon, a baked potato, a side salad. The waiter brought the salad first, bleu cheese dressing on the side. I began to drizzle the dressing over the salad, until my friend very politely cleared her throat: "That's unpasteurized, right? Soft cheese?"

I realized my mistake. "Oh, yeah," I said. "I can't believe I wasn't thinking about that."

"I mean, it's probably fine," she said.

"Probably," I said, but still I picked the dressing-smeared leaves off the bed of lettuce. I ate the rest of the salad plain. It was tasteless. It reminded me of the years when I'd order no dressing at all, ever.

I don't like any dressings. I like how it tastes on its own. I hadn't told this lie in years. I continued eating my disappointing dinner. *Well, it's not like you need it anyway*, I heard in a voice familiar but not my own.

The rest of our food arrived. I picked at the baked potato. I refrained from adding butter or sour cream on top, even though I knew these items were pregnancy approved.

I remembered a dinner years ago: I was a child, and my uncle's new wife was pregnant and large. My mom and grandmother, still consumed in grief over the loss of my aunt (my uncle's former wife) and the dreams of her own future children, looked my uncle's wife up and down with sneers.

"Did you see her eat two baked potatoes?" my grandmother said on the car ride home. "Did you see all that butter and sour cream and cheese she packed on top? No wonder she looks the way she does."

"I wonder how big that baby will be," my mom quietly replied. "I wonder if she'll have to have a C-section."

That night, I lay awake in bed. I reflexively rubbed my hip bones, a decades-old habit. When I was sleepless or lonely or scared, my hands migrated to those sharp edges, and I felt comfort.

I wondered how long I would still be able to find them.

39

I met with a doula during the first trimester of my pregnancy. This doula was recommended by one of my coworkers at the university where I taught. Our conversation centered on my upcoming birth. She'd had a home birth the year before, and I thought that sounded messy.

"The most important thing is that you go to a provider who cares about your priorities," she said. "Who are you going to?"

I told her the name of one of the providers in the group—not the woman my husband had gone to school with.

"Have you asked about their C-section rate?" she responded.

"I did," I replied. "But he told me he didn't have a number. He said the best thing I could do to avoid a C section was to stay in shape."

"Well, the fact that he doesn't have an answer to your question shows where it fits into his priorities."

I nodded my head. She then began to talk about the importance of supportive providers, the benefits of natural birth. "Of course, an epidural in the late stages of labor can be a beautiful thing," she added.

I was intrigued by the idea of an unmedicated birth, mostly because I was interested in it as a challenge. But I never actually considered going medication-free during labor. Married for half a decade, I could still hardly have sex without pain. If I could barely have intercourse, how could I possibly have an unmedicated birth?

The doula began to talk about painful sex after birth. She initiated this conversation. Episiotomies without consent. Significant tearing. I tried to keep my face blank. I didn't want to explain to her that, really, even though it was better than at the beginning, I was basically already there, had always been there, experiencing painful sex.

It had taken some time to get pregnant, and I assumed that the painful sex was likely the reason. It felt as if there was some obstruction. Each time we came together, I couldn't breathe through the pain long enough for him to stay in there and make a baby.

Eventually, I began to grow. It was what I had been waiting for—I could tolerate it. Temporary, I reminded myself. Rather than obsessing about my expanding body, I began to think constantly about what I would do with my baby when I was back at work teaching English at our local university.

At a birthday party with family, I made small talk with my father-in-law in the kitchen. He was dismayed that I planned to go back to work after the baby (a boy!) was born.

"But y'all can afford for you to stay home," he said. "What will you do with the baby while you're away?"

I paused. This question had been gnawing at me since the beginning of the pregnancy—how to do anything aside from staying home with the baby. I'd really only ever seen moms full-time at home. I'd really only ever heard moms away at work talked about by those moms at home.

"I think we'll use daycare," I said. I was unsure but knew that I wanted an identity outside of dutiful motherhood.

"Daycare," he snorted. Then he paused. "Well, of course, you still have time to make that decision."

My mother-in-law, Kate, began distributing dinner, slices of pizza on paper plates.

"What kind of cravings are you having?" my father-in-law asked me.

"I don't have any cravings," I said.

"None? Nothing at all? Kate," he called, "weren't you always craving sweet tea when you were pregnant with E?"

"Oh, yes," she replied.

"Well, I don't have any," I said again. But of course I did. Fried chicken dipped in ranch dressing. A chicken salad croissant. Peanut butter chocolate ice cream. Pregnancy meant all my senses were heightened. The right meal left me doubly satisfied. I could enjoy my meals most when I was away from others, when I was not in fear of potential judgment. I found myself eating, often, in my car, in parking lots. I looked out the window to my left, then to my right, and when I confirmed that I was not being observed, only then could I fully indulge.

But in that moment, I convinced myself that I did not have cravings. *No way would I tell him, regardless*, whispered that little voice in my head.

I looked down to my slice of pizza. I'd eaten half. Suddenly, I felt sick. The tomato sauce, I decided, was too acidic. I tossed my plate and the remainder of the slice in the trash. Then I walked outside to my nieces and nephews. They were playing tag in the backyard.

"Can I join?" I asked, and suddenly, I was it. I chased them all over the grass. We were giggling and breathing heavily. We were not discussing all the expectations that had grown along with my pregnancy.

40

In my second trimester I lay awake for hours every night imagining daycare: my baby strapped down in a sterile room, crying, while a faceless caregiver soothed other sobbing children. I became obsessed with intrusive images of neglect. I made a list of nearby daycares. I polled friends for personal recommendations. Still, I was paralyzed with fear. I could not bring myself to make a call or to schedule a tour. I could not find energy to fill out applications.

The thoughts followed me through the day, too. They played like a repeated recording as I marched bleary-eyed to the basement, pushing play on my workout video for the day. As I mentored at-risk students and taught them about organizational habits or plans of study, I worked hard to pay attention to their faces and their concerns. I was distracted by images of my baby, alone and uncared for.

When I taught class, I stuck close to my lesson plans. I could not incorporate spontaneous instruction in the way I could before pregnancy. I needed a script. My mind was occupied and loud.

After several months of this rumination, I finally said to E, "I don't feel good about daycare."

"I don't feel good about daycare, either," he replied. He, too, was raised by a stay-at-home mom.

I paused. "I don't want to, but I think I have to quit my job," I said.

He smiled. "I think that's the right thing to do, too. You don't need to work. There's no need for you to take on that additional stress. And then, with your free time, we can focus on building relationships with people at church. We can minister to people, have others over for dinner, or just take more time for hospitality."

"That sounds like replacing one job with another," I replied. "I don't want to quit my job and then be expected to host dinner parties all the time."

"Oh, I wouldn't expect you to do that. But I agree—I think this will be best for Graham." Graham. We'd decided on a name for the baby.

"I do, too," I said after a moment. "I really just don't see another way."

I loved teaching. In graduate school, I'd read an article that described teaching as performative—and I found this description to be true. But the act I was putting on in the classroom was the best version of me. Teaching writing and literature, I was able to talk about my true interests. There was no other sphere of my life where I felt free to discuss things I actually cared about.

My favorite students to teach were the ones who were quiet, insecure because they feared that their voice didn't matter, that no one was interested in what they had to say. As a writing teacher, I could show them that I was interested. That I cared. That I wanted to read their words, to hear them speak. In the classroom, I could be the person to others that I had always longed to have for myself.

The next day, I scheduled a meeting with my department chair. I'd just learned that I'd won a campus teaching award. Along with the honor, I would receive a modest cash prize. I decided to use the money to buy a bright-green crib.

My chair invited me into her office, congratulating me with a smile. She was an older woman near retirement, kind but ferocious. She had one sticker on her office door, and it said, "I stand with Planned Parenthood." I tried to maintain my composure. I'd coached myself all morning to act professional and convinced.

"I think I need to quit," I said abruptly. I'd articulated my resignation more eloquently in my brain, but that is what came out.

She stared at me for a moment. She responded, "Anna, you just won that teaching award."

I began to stammer. "I just, I can't. I can't leave my baby. And so I don't see how I can keep doing my job. I don't want to quit, but I think I have to. I can't leave my baby."

There were several moments of silence. Then, she replied, "You're not going to quit. You will teach online. I will fill out paperwork for a modified work plan. You will receive a salary reduction, but you will not quit. How does that sound?"

"That sounds . . . perfect," I said.

"And after a year, if you still want to quit, you can quit. But I don't think you'll want to. I think you'll be more than ready to come back to work." And she was right—I was.

Years later, I recounted this scene to my therapist. This moment when my life could have taken a bleak turn, but it didn't because of the kindness of one woman, her willingness and ability to bend institutional policies to accommodate me and my fears and my mental health.

"You were very lucky," my therapist said to me. "Most bosses would have fired you." I nodded my head. I agreed. This moment, though, felt special: a moment when my emotions were seen and not punished, a place where my weakness was not grounds for my rejection.

Months later, Graham emerged and was placed on my chest. He was tiny, pixie-like, perfect. His cry sounded like a cat's. Just above his earlobe was a small oval birthmark. I checked it each time the nurses brought him to me in the hospital just to be sure he was mine, my Graham.

41

When Graham was a baby, I attended a dinner party with some of my husband's colleagues. I sat at the table and tried to enjoy a lavish meal I did not cook, a glass of wine, and time away from the relentlessness of nursing and diapering and soothing.

But I couldn't enjoy it. My breasts were hard and tingling, aching to be pumped. The zipper of my pants dug into my belly. Being in the world without the weight of my baby in my arms made me feel dizzy, panicky even. My brain felt foggy and slow.

My husband's colleagues spoke of crises at work, of the TV shows they were binging on the weekends, of trips they were planning, of hobbies. It was as if they lived in another world, the world of adulthood. I, too, had been part of it, but I felt I'd left the day I gave birth.

I didn't feel transported to some elevated plane. I believed I had become the most boring person on the planet.

"How was your day?" a woman beside me asked. I struggled to form a response. I began talking about my son's feeding schedule, his sleep schedule, his bowel movements. His bowel movements! Why was I speaking about my baby's bathroom habits at a dinner party?

I was sure I'd lost my mind. I was convinced that my temporarily contracted world of early motherhood had made me regress, too. When I returned home, I thanked our sitter, who sat on the living-room couch with our sleeping son. Then I settled back in to the monotony of motherhood, that three-hour routine on repeat.

The next day during one of Graham's brief naps, I found myself consumed with anxiety—not about my baby but about my identity. What little there was left of it.

I thought, *I'm going to become interesting again.* But this time, I didn't try to improve myself with a diet or exercise plan. I tried to fix myself with words.

I opened a notebook and began to write. *Something interesting!* I coached myself. But a sentence or two into my exercise, I found myself circling around the same topic I kept discussing at that dinner party: minutiae about my baby.

After about a page, Graham began to coo in his crib. That was that. My fleeting minutes of "me time" were gone. I retrieved him from his crib and held him in my arms.

The house was so quiet—just me and my baby—so I turned on some music. And the two of us had a dance party with Beyoncé to fill the hours until our next feeding, diapering, and sleeping session.

I remember this dance party because the next day I wrote about it. Writing made me happy, so I decided to keep journaling during my brief pockets of free time. I didn't have anything interesting to say about the world, so I gave myself permission to lean into what occupied my headspace: my baby. I wrote about our dance parties. His favorite picture books. His first words.

In writing, I discovered patterns. His favorite word was "bird." He used it to identify anything fascinating or beautiful. A tree was a bird, and a bird was a bird, and so were flowers and the wind. At the grocery store, Graham pointed to a man's baseball cap and exclaimed, "Bird!" And when he nursed, he made me re-see my own anatomy when he paused from his feed to point to my nipple and cry out, "Bird!"

The year when I taught from home passed slowly. Some days felt like weeks. But soon enough, it was time for me to return to my regular work. I enrolled Graham in daycare. We left our nest and both learned how to fly.

Though my life contracted after Graham's birth, E had become more involved in church. I spent most of my day alone with Graham. E left the house early in the morning and would not return until eight or nine. Sometimes, work kept him out late—but often, he wouldn't return in the evening because he was volunteering with various ministries at church. He'd gotten to know several of the regulars at the city mission, including Nolan, a man who used a wheelchair.

In the evenings, E drove over to Nolan's house to administer his insulin shots. Nolan was afraid of needles. And his apartment was so messy that his landlords had complained. So about once a week, E visited with our vacuum to clean the carpets. E brought our dog, Rory, to accompany him for the outing. Nolan loved dogs, and Rory liked to lick Nolan's open wounds.

Many weeks, Nolan texted us his grocery list whenever we were out to dinner on a Friday night: five pounds of ground turkey, four cans of tomatoes, chili powder, an onion, and a bag of beans.

"Don't worry, I'll just be ten minutes," E would say as he swung by Kroger on our way home.

E began donating large sums of money to various religious organizations. Some were places I was familiar with, local ones, but others were nonprofits—Bible translation companies, a group serving hungry widows in Jerusalem—advertised on a Christian TV channel.

"If you want to donate money, can't you just give to the city mission? To hungry people? Can you try to not write checks to fringe groups advertised by that crazy television network?"

When Graham was almost two years old, E attended a conference retreat with several pastors. His sleep was disrupted on the trip—his roommates' snoring and the tiny beds had kept him up most of each night. Though exhausted, he returned from the trip and said it was "completely life changing."

"What changed?" I asked.

"The way I think about God. The way I hope to serve God."

Shortly after the conference, E became convinced he'd committed the unpardonable sin, the sin of blaspheming the Holy Spirit.

"When, exactly, did you do that?" I asked him, casually sipping a beer on the porch one evening after putting Graham to bed.

He did not have a specific answer. He flipped through the Bible feverishly for hours on end, looking for an answer, looking for relief. Sometimes he found verses that filled him with hope. Minutes later, those same verses became prophecy that predicted his damnation.

He began struggling to function with basic, daily tasks. Giving Graham a bath. Reading a bedtime story. Grocery shopping. He requested sick leave from work. *Physician burnout*, we both thought. *Or perhaps paternal postpartum depression?* I wondered. Eventually, he checked himself into an inpatient psychiatric unit. He was there for a week and was diagnosed with a severe mood disorder.

Our family knew, and a handful of friends knew, but otherwise, I worked to keep the experience private and hidden. "This isn't something you need to let other people know about," my mom advised me. "He's a doctor, after all. You have to think about his reputation. You have to think about your futures."

"I think I need to see a therapist myself," I said to a nurse one day when I was visiting E on the unit. "Can you connect me to someone?"

In that moment, I was not thinking that I needed to see someone because of my husband's diagnosis—I thought, *I need to see a therapist to talk about my issues with food.* I'd thought this for years. I'd convinced myself I was making a big deal out of nothing at all. Sometimes my issues with food felt nonexistent, like a distant memory. But then, with little warning, they would return and take over. When a meeting ran over time, for instance,

I might start perseverating on something I'd eaten earlier, food I needed to burn off. My eating issues tended to flare up under stress, whenever my schedule was thrown off.

This period when my husband was receiving inpatient care felt like a time when that might occur.

So standing in the lobby of a psychiatric institution, discussing the reduced cognitive capacity of my physician husband, I finally felt I had an excuse to talk about the thing I'd wanted to talk to somebody about for two decades.

"Absolutely," the nurse said. "That's really wise." She gave me several recommendations. The next day, I made myself an appointment. I was able to get in quickly.

During the first appointment, we mostly discussed my reaction to E's mental health diagnosis. "How's your appetite?" she asked me.

Is this it? No, I decided. "Fine," I said. "Normal."

"How about self-care?" she asked me.

"I care about myself very much," I replied. She laughed. I told her I'd had coffee with a friend several days ago. I didn't mention that I'd brought Graham along because I felt too guilty to use childcare for anything other than work, that I never mentioned my husband's mental-health crisis, that my friend and I discussed only gossip surrounding our Bible study and our children's developmental milestones. I didn't tell her that I ordered only coffee at the get-together, even though I was hungry, even though it was time for me to eat a meal.

Maybe next time, I told myself at the end of the session. There were several next times. But I just kept talking myself out of it. I wondered whether my issues with food were all in my head—I wondered whether I'd made them all up. *You're not even that thin! Your therapist will think you're ridiculous, saying you might have an eating disorder, when you're the size of a normal, average person. Plus, you can't possibly have an eating disorder. You ate a burger and fries last night. People with eating disorders don't eat burgers and fries!*

Because sometimes I was fine—and sometimes I was more than fine—I questioned whether my problems even existed. I questioned whether they had ever existed in the first place.

Besides, what would a therapist possibly tell me that I didn't already know? That I deserved to eat? That my worth was not in my body size? I already knew that stuff. I just didn't always believe it.

Anyway, the topic just never came up.

Once released from the unit, E seemed tired and changed. We went out one afternoon to the mall with Graham. As we walked from store to store, E was quiet, going through the motions of caring for a toddler in public.

On the way home from the mall, we stopped at a red light. The car was quiet, radio off, Graham content in the back seat playing with his stuffed fox. E looked out the window to a bare plot of grass.

"I feel like my brain has broken," he said. "I feel like something split apart, and I will never be the same."

I believed him—and I began to weep.

When we arrived home, E bathed Graham. I nursed him and rocked him to sleep.

When I left Graham's nursery, I found E downstairs reading on the couch, Bible in hand. I walked up to him and rubbed his shoulders, kissed his neck. "Come upstairs," I said, and he followed me.

Two weeks later, I peed on a stick. *Positive.* I'd purchased the pregnancy test that morning at the Walmart by Graham's daycare. I was going to the gym before heading to the office, and I decided to take the test after changing into my exercise clothes. I slipped the positive test in my purse and headed toward the elliptical. I worked out a bit longer, a bit harder.

I called E to tell him the news as I drove to the office. "Wow!" he said. "Well, that was fast." It had taken several years to conceive Graham.

"Yup," I said. "Really fast."

"I'm really happy!" he said after a moment.

"I think I am, too," I said.

But I spent most of my pregnancy crying and compulsively weighing myself and reading articles on the internet about how to hide one's baby bump, with intended audiences of teenage moms or women in hostile work situations—not thirty-something-year-old doctors' wives.

I worried about my body changing when I was pregnant with Graham—but my worry multiplied during my pregnancy with Alex. Fear consumed me. With E's new mental-health diagnosis, my entire world felt unstable. In the past, the way I dealt with a world out of my control was by trying to control my body. But I couldn't do that while I was pregnant.

After my pregnancy with Graham, I'd returned to my pre-pregnancy weight, and then I dropped below it. I was busy and nursing, and I hadn't even really been trying that hard. But the compliments flooded in. At church, at work, at the grocery store, I'd run into friends and acquaintances, who told me how good I looked, even better than before!

Had I really looked that bad before? I found myself thinking after hearing these comments several times. *Have people really been inspecting me that closely?*

I'd never received so much praise in my life. No accomplishment at work, no kind deed, not even creating an entire human being with my body seemed to elicit as much applause as I received for shrinking myself. It was delicious and disgusting. I resented people who said these things, but having had a taste, I craved more.

While pregnant with Alex, I had a perpetual sense of dread. That the thing expanding was going to make me explode. "I'm sorry, buddy. I love you, I promise," I'd whisper between my tears to the baby kicking below my ribs.

I had seen my therapist the week before. I told her my fears, though I said nothing about my body. Could there be anything more cliché than body-image issues during pregnancy?

"I worry that E will get sick again after the baby is born," I had said instead.

"That makes sense to me. Is he still taking his medications? Going to therapy? Prioritizing sleep and self-care?"

"He is. He's doing everything he's supposed to be doing."

"So he's doing everything to keep something like that from happening."

"That's true," I had said.

At the end of the session, she had told me, "It sounds like you are navigating some unique situations with your husband's diagnosis—but otherwise, this is pretty typical pregnancy anxiety."

"Okay," I had said, nodding my head.

I kept my rules for recovery while I was pregnant. I had intrusive eating-disorder thoughts, but I wasn't going to engage in the behaviors, like skipping meals or spitting out food. *I'm not a monster*, I told myself. I didn't really believe that people who continued to struggle with eating disorders during pregnancy were monsters. I believed they were human, that I was human. I believed that pregnancy was hardly enough to fundamentally change someone's psychology and addictions. Still, I was well enough to care about someone other than myself, my baby, even when my brain was screaming at me not to.

I was careful. I ate my meals mindfully. I cut sandwiches into tiny pieces: *a third of the sandwich at eleven o'clock, a third at noon, and then the rest at one*. I didn't skip meals. I didn't cut out food groups. I even kept my rule of exercising only four days a week—though I added in some long walks and yoga on days off. *Those things don't count*, I told myself.

42

Women from church wanted to throw me a baby shower. At first, I refused. "It's our second baby! We don't need anything," I insisted. Really, I didn't want everyone looking at me, commenting on my body. I didn't want their blessings over my baby. I didn't want to answer their questions about how I was going to manage two children *and* a career. I didn't want to eat food in front of an audience.

I really didn't want to be at church at all. Since E's illness, it felt impossible. During each sermon, everything that came out of our pastor's mouth sounded like the language of my sick husband. Even the most innocuous of phrases—*may we remain faithful in all we say and do*—felt loaded with potential destruction.

E was committed to treatment, and he was resolved to do everything possible to keep us from going through the turmoil of untreated mental-health issues again. He imposed his own set of rules. He now rarely drank alcohol, and he'd reduced his intake of caffeine. He kept a consistent sleep schedule and aimed for a full eight hours. He was back at work, and he was doing well—a dutiful and attentive father to Graham.

To be honest, he seemed more stable and mentally well than I was.

While I wasn't the most enthusiastic congregant, I did have several close friends, and E was beloved—always the first to volunteer to bring a meal or bake a pie, to help someone move, to lead a Bible study, to watch children in the nursery, to donate money to a cause.

I ended up agreeing to the baby shower. I felt ridiculous and ungrateful resisting the insistent generosity. As I pulled tissue paper from the bags of presents, I looked in the corner of the room to see my friend, Fran, smiling and remarking upon each onesie, each teddy bear. She had no children. She and her husband had been trying for years. She'd miscarried for the second time several months before, and when she sent me a text, told me she was doing okay, I had a vase of flowers delivered to her doorstep. Still, I found myself avoiding her most of my pregnancy. I couldn't bear the idea of standing before her, knowing how fully I resented my body in its present state, knowing how much she longed for precisely what was happening to me.

For the shower favor, the hostesses distributed mini bottles of hand sanitizer. My friend, Sarah, winked at me: "I thought to myself, what do I think of when I think of Anna as a mom? And the first image that popped into my head was you wiping down restaurant tables with Lysol wipes, coating Graham's hands with sanitizer."

"You know me," I laughed. When everyone left the shower, few remembered to grab their party favors, so I was sent home with a gallon-sized ziplock bag of mini hand sanitizers. The party favors would last us through the whole COVID-19 pandemic two years later.

43

One day at work, I was putting off emails by scrolling through social media instead. I saw a photo of a childhood friend from church, Kirsten, pop to the top of my feed.

I had many memories of Kirsten and her mom, Jill. Jill had been a single mom who served as music minister in our church. "Served" was the operative word—she did not receive compensation for her work, despite her repeated requests to the elders. She was at church all the time, between directing choir and volunteering for her daughters' activities. She also worked full-time in an office doing who knows what. As a child, I couldn't imagine what moms did in offices all day. I just envisioned them constantly adjusting their navy dress suits, tugging on their stockings as they swiveled in their cushioned desk chairs.

Sometimes Jill served as a substitute for our youth Sunday school class on mornings when the regular teacher was out of town. She wore a work suit, as she always did on Sunday mornings, and walked us through the usual curriculum. I don't remember much about anything we were taught in Sunday school. I just remember that I knew most of it already due to my private Christian school education, that I could turn to the assigned passages of Scripture more quickly than anyone else in the room. Even when I didn't raise my hand, Jill still felt comfortable calling on me. I had learned that it was impolite to seem too eager, but I was always happy to offer up the correct answer.

During Sunday school one morning, an ambulance's siren sounded in the distance. Jill stopped the lesson immediately and began to pray aloud for whoever needed the ambulance's services. When she concluded her prayer, Kirsten chimed in with an explanation: "Anytime we hear an ambulance, we always stop and pray."

In the first grade, Kirsten and I recited Luke 2 from memory in the annual Christmas cantata. We wore our holiday dresses, stood by a cluster of red poinsettias, and shared a microphone as we spoke our assigned verses aloud. Kirsten was a year older than me, and she'd been given slightly more verses to read than I had, which I took as a small insult. Still, I memorized both her verses and my own, not because I cared so much what they said but mostly to prove to myself that I could. After our performance, Kirsten gave me a small present—an ornament—and a card that said how much she enjoyed reading with me. I didn't have a gift ready to exchange with her.

Though Kirsten was older than me, she was always shorter than me, a feature that would come to define her: her petiteness. "There's little Kirsten," I heard a mom say as Kirsten bounced through the aisles of the church—those big barrel blonde curls and bright red cheeks were hard to miss.

When Kirsten reached middle school, she was still short—she would never reach five feet, even in adulthood—but people no longer called her little or small. She had hit puberty, and she'd grown hips and average-sized thighs that seemed large on her small legs. "I bet you're going to shoot up any day now," I heard one youth worker say to Kirsten, a weird aside, a remark about a problem that wasn't actually a problem.

Kirsten never shot up, but in high school, she did slim down, significantly. People in youth group made concerned comments that actually showed no concern at all, but at the beginning of youth meetings, Kirsten piled her plate high with pizza, eating every single slice. *Maybe she is just lucky*, I heard someone speculate about Kirsten growing into herself without ever growing at all.

The summer I was fifteen, we went on a mission trip together. Kirsten was still friendly, but we weren't really friends anymore. She was one of the popular public-school girls, outgoing, a cheerleader. Before the trip, Jill made an offhand comment in front of the whole congregation during the evening service about how Kirsten would likely need two suitcases to get her through one week of missions.

"I keep saying, Kirsten, you don't need your hair curlers to volunteer with hungry children. You don't need that big bag of makeup. But you all know Kirsten. . . ." Jill laughed, and the congregation laughed. That vain little cheerleader—it was so pleasurable to poke fun at a girl who obviously cared that much about appearances.

I remembered dreading the mission trip for all my usual reasons, and I made my typical plans to survive it: hidden workouts during free time, small portions, lots of vegetables. During the week, I'd receive offhand comments (*that's* all *you're having?*), but mostly I'd learned how to make myself quiet and small so that I escaped much notice. On our van ride to the mission site, we stopped for lunch at a Subway. I ordered a veggie sub and tore up the bread into tiny crumbs with some degree of vengeance—it was helpful to have something to do with my hands. Kirsten sat at another table with Mark, laughing loudly, eating a pizza and meatball sub and some of her friend's chips, too.

She excused herself to go to the restroom, and around the same time, I did, too. There were two stalls in the women's room, and when I entered, I heard retching that seemed to quiet upon my arrival. I used the bathroom, and I saw Kirsten exit the second stall. Her eyes were bloodshot. The room smelled like vomit. I paused.

"Are you okay?" I said after a moment. She looked away from me and at her own reflection in the mirror. She tucked a stray strand of hair behind her ear and evaluated the burst blood vessel in her eye. She retrieved some nude lip gloss from her purse.

"I'm fine," she said as she twisted the applicator from the bottle. She turned to me. "Are *you* okay?"

I looked down to my chest with embarrassment. "Yeah, I'm fine," I replied. Then we exited the bathroom together quietly to board the van. We were driving to hand out snacks to children at a park in a low-income neighborhood.

Apart from following each other on social media, Kirsten and I didn't keep up after high school. But occasionally, I scrolled through her page out of curiosity. There was something about her that I had always been drawn to watch; she had always been such an interesting character in our church microcosm. I saw pictures of her at college parties, plastic red cup in hand. Then, several years later, I saw a photo of her with a newborn—her baby, it seemed—but no photos of the pregnancy. I read the comments on the photo, hundreds of congratulations, dozens telling her, "You look great—like you never had a baby at all!" This pattern repeated itself two more times: two more babies, no documentation of any pregnancy, Kirsten looking like nothing had ever happened to her at all.

Then that morning at work, that photo of Kirsten with her children popped to the top of my feed. I read the comments. Hundreds of "thoughts and prayers" and "RIPs." I felt dizzy. I clicked on her profile to find out what had happened.

I learned through an update from Jill that Kirsten's body had been found on the floor of her bathroom, that she'd been there for several hours. Her children were in bed; her husband was working the night shift. After an autopsy, they found that she'd died of an aneurysm, a blood vessel bulging in her brain, a berry born to burst, so small with such power.

I sat in my swivel chair and stared at my screen. She was so young, neither of us even thirty yet. I looked to a photo of Graham taped up behind my office computer. In it, he wore a green cardigan, and he held his precious stuffed fox that had lost a limb due to his excessive love. I rubbed the bulge of my growing baby in my abdomen—Alex, we'd decided. I looked back up at the screen, at Kirsten's tiny smiling face and rosy cheeks and carefully curled blonde hair. I imagined her in her bathroom, her boys asleep with no warning, no alarm to alert them. I imagined her quiet, a sudden headache, perhaps. Maybe she looked to her phone, thought about making a call—but that would be silly, I imagine she thought, to make such a big deal of something that was probably nothing at all.

44

Just before Alex was born, E began having another severe mood episode. It presented similarly: no sleep, feverish praying and reading, relentless volunteerism, impulsive donations to religious organizations.

"Do something to get this under control," I hissed at him one night. "I'm about to have a baby!"

He requested time off work. Went for long runs. Booked a massage. He was about to walk into the massage just as the OB sent me to the hospital for an induction: I had high blood pressure.

It was early March in West Virginia, lonely and cold with perpetual gray skies. We checked in to labor and delivery. I changed into a gown and extended my arm for an IV.

"Can I just go ahead and order my epidural now?" I asked my nurse. I'd attempted a natural birth with Graham, but this time, I wanted to feel nothing at all.

"Good for you!" my nurse said. "No need to be a hero."

I smiled and reclined in the hospital bed to watch the curves of my contractions rise and fall on a dark screen. I received my epidural. Hours passed. E paced the room, adjusted the many cords hooked up to my body. He held my hand as he glanced out the window, attempting to be present despite his mind being somewhere else entirely.

When it was time to push, I gripped E's hand with vengeance, gazed into his bloodshot eyes.

"It's all going to be okay," he murmured.

"I don't know why you couldn't have gotten this under control," I growled. "I'm about to have a baby!"

Though I knew he was sick and felt sorry for him, I was angry that all of the preparation and lifestyle changes we'd made seemed to have little effect. I couldn't believe that my worst fear—that E would get sick when I had the baby—was coming true, despite all our efforts.

"You know this doesn't always work that way," he said as he looked away from me to the screen monitoring my contractions.

My labor was four hours long. It was easy. I remembered feeling fear during Graham's birth, but during Alex's, I felt nothing but rage. Rage, I came to believe, was what pushed him out so quickly.

The nurse laid Alex on my chest. I stroked his head, kissed his cheeks. *I love you, my boy. What a mess you've been born into.*

At discharge, my blood pressure was still high: 160/110. Concerning, but not quite preeclampsia. "We're going to keep a close eye on it. You're going to need to take medication. And you—" my OB looked at E—"take her blood pressure every morning and every evening." E nodded.

When medical professionals entered the room, E was calm and composed. A bit tired looking with glazed eyes, but otherwise, his normal self. When they exited, his facade collapsed. His breathing turned heavy. He paced frantically. Then he would fall down on the couch.

"We probably wouldn't discharge you this early if you didn't live with a doctor," my OB laughed. "But there's no need to keep you here just to monitor what your husband can keep a watch on at home."

I laughed and nodded and wondered whether leaving the hospital was wise—but, I told myself, maybe if we got home, got into a routine, got a handle on our sleep, then maybe we could cut this episode off before it exploded. I had a whole plan with dozens of rules I was using for newborn sleep. I believed if I could control our sleep, then I could control E's mental health.

We returned home. The grandparents held Alex, and then they waved goodbye to Graham. Just us. A family of four.

The next day, E woke and drove Graham to daycare. Upon returning home, he descended into the basement with his Bible.

"Let me know if you need help," he said, still my loving and thoughtful husband. "I can hold Alex if you need to nap."

"We're fine," I said as I held Alex to my breast. He was nursing fully with a strong latch. A dream. Breastfeeding had never been this easy with Graham.

I heard Mozart blaring from the basement speakers. I'd come to recognize the music as accompaniment to my husband's moods. It comforted him, or it heightened the sensations. I began to dread it, tensing my whole body as the notes played, wondering what was to come next.

Alex was ready for a nap. I swaddled him and placed him in the bassinet. I kissed his soft, still-not-washed cheek. I walked to the bathroom. I changed the bloody pad out of my mesh underwear. I sprayed my stitches with Dermoplast. I washed my hands. I turned to the side, evaluating my profile in the mirror. My belly had shrunk, but it was still protruding. There was still a small bump.

I lifted my T-shirt, pushing my soft flesh forcefully in. *Go in. There's still time*, I thought to myself. *He's only two days old.*

The nurses warned me that afterbirth pain was worse with each subsequent baby. I noticed the intensity of the contractions. They woke me from sleep and forced me to pause, but I loved the discomfort of them—it gave me a rush. I knew what it meant, that I was shrinking, and I felt this way in labor, too—each contraction meant that I was one step closer to no longer being full.

I went to my bedroom. I thought about taking a nap. But I felt pretty good. I didn't feel tired. *Maybe, if I just do one*, and I loaded a postnatal workout video. Half an hour. *I'll stop if I start feeling too bad.* So I squatted and lunged and kicked. I completed the video and grabbed my phone. *One more*, I thought as I pressed play, and this time, I targeted my arms. The video ended and Alex was still asleep. *What an amazing baby*, I thought to myself as I glanced at the monitor and loaded another video, this one for abs, for my "mummy tummy."

By the end of it all, I'd broken a cold sweat. I was a little bit dizzy—but they told me that was a side effect of the blood-pressure medication. I heard Alex begin to stir. Mozart was still blaring from the basement. I lifted Alex and pulled my sweaty sports bra up and pushed his small head against my engorged breast. He began to suck, to empty me.

I loved how it felt to be empty.

In the middle of the night, I woke—not to the cries of Alex but to a pain in my calf, sharp and debilitating. I held my leg and massaged the muscle. I heard E outside the nursery door, pacing, muttering, praying. I checked the time. Three a.m. I tried to go back to sleep.

The next morning, E took my blood pressure: 170/110. "That's high," he said. His eyes were bloodshot with dark circles beneath them. "Try to lean back and breathe for a few minutes. We'll try again." High again: 165/110.

"How about you take two, rather than just one?" he said as he handed me the bottle of blood-pressure pills.

I felt dizzy the whole day. I had a pounding headache. When Alex napped, I lay in bed and closed my eyes and massaged my calf—it still hurt. I had an itch to do another workout video—just one, it could be a short one that day—but I was winded carrying Alex down the stairs to the living room.

It's fine, I told myself. *You need a day off. He's only three days old.*

E scribbled feverishly in a notebook, Bible open beside him. He appeared to be in another world entirely.

"Can you hold Alex while I go to the bathroom?" I asked.

"Of course," he said, laying aside his notebook, extending his arms toward our baby. I didn't really need to use the bathroom. I just wanted him to stop writing. I just wanted to bring him back.

The next day, I woke with another dull headache, dizzy, short of breath: 170/110. I took two pills. I looked down to my still-tender calf and noticed it was swollen.

"These are all signs of a blood clot," E said.

"I did a few workout videos," I admitted, and E shook his head.

"Do you think that could be why my calf is swollen?"

"Maybe," he said, "but it doesn't explain everything else."

"Well, you're making me stressed!" I said. I'd been trying to tiptoe, to be kind. "Your crazy religious fervor is making me really stressed!"

"I can't help it," he said quietly. "I think you need to call your OB."

I dialed the number. "I hate to say this," the OB said over the speaker, "but you need to go to the ER. As a precaution."

I hung up the phone, gathered my breast pump, my purse.

"Can you handle taking care of Alex?"

"Of course. I can take care of a baby—I'm a doctor."

"I mean, in your current state."

He hesitated. "I'll call my sister to see if she can come over as backup."

"You don't really think I have a blood clot, do you?"

"I don't know. You have all the symptoms of a blood clot. Postpartum women get blood clots. It's one of the most common causes of maternal death."

"Holy shit. Do you seriously think I could die?" I looked at Alex; he'd fallen asleep without any rocking or bouncing or milk. He'd just dozed off, and he was so perfect and peaceful and new. He had no idea.

"God's ways are not our ways. His thoughts are not our thoughts. Who can comprehend the ways of the Lord?"

"What the hell? I just had a baby. You just told me I might die. Comfort me, dammit!"

"I don't know what to tell you, Anna," he said with no emotion, eyes still glazed. "You need to go to the ER."

I drove to the ER. I wore a backpack with my breast pump. I brought a book for the wait. *This is almost like a break. Or self-care*, I thought as I read pages of a novel I couldn't really comprehend. I applied hand sanitizer compulsively, anytime I touched the arm of a chair, a pen. It was still flu season. I was terrified of bringing something home to Alex.

A nurse called my name. "Describe your complaint." She took my blood pressure—still high.

"How much do you weigh?" she asked as she scribbled in a chart.

I didn't know. My scale had broken during the last few weeks of pregnancy—a gift. I'd been weighing myself dozens of times each day; the number was almost to a digit I'd feared—but what could be done? The scale broke unexpectedly. I took it to the trash. *You can have some time off until after the baby's born.* I breathed a sigh of relief. I drove to work, taught my classes. Midday, I ordered a cherry pastry from the campus coffee shop.

"I don't know. I just had a baby."

"Want to find out?" the nurse said, pointing to the scale.

Hell no.

"Okay," I said as I stepped on. The number blinked. The nurse made a note in her chart. I made a mental note about how much I still needed to lose.

The nurse wheeled me back to radiology. "We're going to do an ultrasound on your leg." I nodded. "Would you like a blanket?" she asked.

"That sounds nice."

She walked to a closet—"it's still warm from the dryer"—and she laid a blanket across my lap, swaddled it around my hips, and I felt as if I was going to cry.

In the exam room, I changed into a paper gown and a pair of socks. "How many children do you have?" the tech asked as she probed my leg.

"Two," I said, and then she told me about her two children.

"I'm not seeing anything concerning," she said. "Of course, the doctor will review it."

"That's great," I said. *I can't believe I did those stupid exercise videos.*

But it shouldn't have been hard to believe. It's what I did to deal with life. It had always been the way I coped.

I was wheeled to another room. After several minutes, the doctor entered. "Nothing concerning on the ultrasound. There are still other tests we could run, but they are invasive—expensive." I looked at the clock. I'd already missed a feeding of Alex's—maybe two.

"I was probably too active too soon," I said vaguely.

"I suspect this is a muscle sprain," the doctor said. "But I want you to know there's still a possibility you have a blood clot that's traveled to your lungs. We can still run more tests."

I paused. "What would you do if it was you?"

"My wife and I have a three-month-old. I think I would advise her to go home to the baby."

I drove home. E's sister was in the nursery rocking Alex. He was awake but content.

"Think he's hungry?" I asked.

"I was just about to give him a bottle," she said, and she handed him to me. I placed him to my breast. He latched right away. "He's the best baby," I said.

"He's perfect," she said. "Are you okay?"

"Fine—they said it was probably a muscle sprain."

"That's scary. I'm glad you got it checked out."

45

Alex was ten days old the morning E walked into the nursery, his eyes beyond bloodshot, and asked, "Are we prepared to count the cost?" I was in bed with the boys, Alex nursing, Graham lying across my feet.

"What do you mean?" I was tired. I hadn't been sleeping much either. I was breastfeeding a newborn every two hours around the clock.

"I think God is calling us to give all of this up." He gestured broadly to the room around us.

"This—what do you mean, *this*? Our children?"

"No—not them. Of course, not them. I mean, *this*. Our house. Our cars. Our lifestyle. I think I may need to quit my job. I think God is calling us to give all of this up. To sacrifice for the sake of the cross. Are you prepared to do that?"

I looked around Alex's nursery, a new wooden crib with a Crate and Barrel comforter, Dollar Store frames showcasing homemade art. We lived in a modest but beautiful brick Tudor home, three bedrooms, one bath, in a hilly tree-lined neighborhood. We had our two kids, two dogs, and extended families an easy drive down the interstate. *All of this* was pretty nice. If I'd been another sort of evangelical, I may have described myself as *blessed*, but I'd given up that language years ago. Besides, my fundamentalist upbringing had instilled a persistent fear in me that the easiest way to invoke the wrath of God was to become too happy.

I paused. "I . . . hope that if you lose your job, or if we had to give things up that I would be able to adapt. I hope I'm not that materialistic. But I don't think we need to punish ourselves preemptively. Life is hard enough. We're going to lose things naturally. I don't think we need to inflict pain on ourselves—we're already going to encounter pain."

He shook his head. "I'm hurting our family. Your soul. The boys' souls. I'm afraid you will all be damned because . . . I don't love the Lord like I should." He began to cry. "I know you all would be better off without me."

I rubbed my tired eyes and gritted my teeth. I'd been up breastfeeding Alex most of the night. I'd been trying to tread lightly, to support my husband. But I was angry—I had too many people to care for and not enough resources for the job.

"No, we wouldn't be." I took a deep breath. "I need you. Our boys need you. We love you. I love you."

"I know you do. I don't deserve it."

"Yes. You do."

"I . . . don't want to do this. But I'm afraid. I'm afraid of what I could do. I think I need to go to the hospital."

I began to sob. "Okay," I said, shaking. "I'll drive you."

"No. No way are you driving me with the two kids. I would feel terrible about that. I can drive myself."

"Are you sure?"

He nodded. "Call someone to help you. Your parents. My parents."

"Okay," I said, though I'd already decided—I didn't want anyone else in the house.

E left. I fed Graham lunch in his high chair—mac and cheese—as I nursed Alex.

We're doing it! I thought. *I'm doing it!* It had been only ten minutes, but I was managing the boys by myself. I called my parents briefly. They would stop by for a few hours to watch the boys so that I could get some groceries and walk the dogs. But otherwise, I wasn't going to ask for help—I didn't want to take the time to tell others what was going on. I didn't want to think about what was going on. I was going to mother. And I was going to diet.

46

I set my alarm to dress and fix my hair and put on makeup before nursing Alex and driving Graham to daycare. I was not quite two weeks postpartum—lots of women in the US were already back to work at this point! *Quit feeling sorry for yourself, Anna.* I loaded the boys in the car.

I dropped Graham off and began to drive home. *I don't want to go home. I don't want to be in that house with my baby all alone.* I pulled off the road and began to cry. *Stop it! Get a hold of yourself. Pretend he's at work. If you start crying, you may never stop. You have to take care of your baby.* I thought about going to a coffee shop. But what was I going to do with a baby in a coffee shop? He'd probably cry, and I'd need to nurse. And the germs. All those germs! The flu. I couldn't go to a coffee shop. I thought about going to work—to my office. I could send some emails. Talk to coworkers. *And say what? I have a perfect baby. My husband's in an institution. There are germs there, too, you know.*

You need to exercise, anyway. Alex's about due for a nap. Go home, put him down in the crib, and then do a few workout videos until he wakes up. Then nurse him. Then take him on a walk. Fresh air for you both—and more exercise. You can call the hospital—talk to E's therapist, see how he's doing. Then Alex will nap again. And then he'll nurse. Then you pick up Graham—a full day, right there.

Women from church were bringing meals to our home at night, and I was grateful to not think about what to feed Graham.

"I'm not going to stay long—I know how busy you are. You look great!" they'd say.

"Thanks," I'd say as I carried their Tupperware to the kitchen.

"Where's E? Working?"

"He's in the hospital," I'd say.

They'd leave, and I'd place food on Graham's high chair and make myself a carefully portioned plate. I'd load the leftovers into gallon-sized ziplock bags and haul them to the deep freezer. *We'll have all sorts of meals ready for whenever E gets home.*

The week went smoothly. I called the hospital each day, apologizing for having not attended visitation hour.

"E is doing well," his therapist said over the phone one afternoon as I strolled with Alex through the park. "We changed some of his medication. He's really working in therapy. He wants to get back to help you and be with the baby."

"You're sure he's doing better?" I asked. Alex was napping, a warm breeze was blowing, all the trees were blooming with bursts of pink. I wasn't eager for discharge. The week had been so peaceful.

"He really is! I'm proud of him. Before we discharge, I want to have a family group therapy session."

I'd expected a group therapy session from the beginning of his hospital stay. It was required prior to his first discharge nine months earlier.

It became imperative to me that for this session I fit back into my pre-pregnancy jeans. Nothing was more critical—not childcare for Graham, not the happy disposition of Alex, not the health and recovery of my husband. Just that those jeans would slide past my postpartum hips, that they would zip over my belly without a bulge. So I was careful. So I exercised compulsively. If I could fit back into my old jeans, perhaps that meant my old life, my formerly healthy husband, would also return.

But really, whom was I trying to impress? Not my husband. He couldn't see past his visions of the fiery wrath of God. I wanted to impress his therapist. I wanted to look as though I was handling an impossible situation, as though I was completely put together.

After a week, his therapist called me to schedule our discharge session. "You pick the time," she told me. "Whatever's best for you and the baby's schedule."

I chose a time in the morning that would allow me to drop Graham off at daycare and squeeze in a few workouts.

"You look fantastic!" the therapist said as I strolled into the meeting room with Alex asleep. "How old is he, again?"

"Seventeen days."

"Wow!" she said—and I felt smug. As though I'd accomplished something important. I also felt sick. *What am I trying to prove? Why do people keep praising me for this? Why doesn't anyone see me and call me on this shit?*

The session went well. The therapist was impressed with the good heads we had on our shoulders, with how well we communicated. I talked a lot about sleep schedules, and the therapist liked this. We discussed medication, meditation, more therapy, continued self-care.

Then we were free to go. A nurse escorted us to our car. I fed Alex in the back seat, and then we picked Graham up from daycare. E took Graham to the playground. Afterward, they went out for milkshakes. Then, they stopped by the pharmacy to pick up E's new prescription.

I stayed home with Alex where I climbed into bed and didn't move for the rest of the day. I just held my baby and nursed him and sipped from a glass of water on the nightstand.

47

During church shortly after Alex was born, I wandered the stairs behind the pulpit, baby in my arms, searching for a place to nurse. I walked past old church directories and musty books, stacks of aged Sunday school material, and finally, I'd settle into a small storage closet where Christmas trees, garland, ornaments, and tinsel were stored. I sat on the unvacuumed red carpet, leaning against the bare portion of one wall. I placed Alex on the floor briefly. I removed my dress, and in my bra and underwear and heels, I sat and nursed my baby for the whole of the pastor's sermon. I could hear the pastor's voice booming in the background, though I could not hear the content of his message. Shortly after the pianist began to play, signaling the end of the service, I re-dressed and returned with Alex to the sanctuary.

"Where do you go to nurse?" the pastor's wife asked me. She was just a few years older than me with toddlers of her own.

"I've been going to the Christmas closet," I told her.

"Oh, honey," she said. "There has to be a better place than that."

"I kind of like it. I think it's peaceful."

She shook her head. "I think we need to make a mother's room. A place where nursing moms can go, and there'd be a rocking chair and a couch, and we'd put some speakers in there so that moms could still hear the sermon. What do you think of that?"

"I like the closet," I said.

She rolled her eyes. "Well, we need something."

I continued to retreat to the Christmas closet for months, usually exiting the sanctuary just as the sermon was about to begin. I left even as Alex grew, as he began nursing less frequently, as he began eating table food. As the pastor ascended the stairs to the pulpit, I descended into the basement of the church and sat undressed in that quiet, dark space with my baby.

"Isn't it about time you started sending him to nursery? Have you even been able to attend an entire service since he's been born?" the pastor's wife asked me after church one day. Alex was nearing a year old.

"I don't think Alex's ready," I said. He'd been in daycare for months. The pastor's wife knew this—she was a stay-at-home mom with convictions about working outside the home.

"I think you need to start sending him," she said.

I looked past her face at the table of refreshments, strawberries and crackers and chicken salad and cookies. Graham was grabbing a handful of each, touching everything on the table in the process. I ran to him. "Here, Graham"—I carefully picked up several crackers—"let's just start with these."

My friend Sarah approached us. "Hey!" she said, "we're thinking of going out for ice cream later. Would y'all be up for it?"

The pastor's wife shook her head. "We're doing Whole 30," she said.

Sarah nodded. I liked Sarah—but I needed to exercise. It was my day off—but I felt fidgety, very much as if I needed to run far, far away.

"I wish we could!" I said, "But this week's been crazy, and we're playing catch-up today. Also, I've had to cut dairy since I've been nursing Alex."

Alex hadn't actually shown any signs that he needed me to abstain from dairy. Graham was sensitive when he was a baby, and I'd cut dairy, and I'd resented cutting dairy—I liked pizza and ice cream. I didn't want to restrict those things from my diet. But several weeks after Alex was born, I decided to cut dairy preemptively. Just in case. I didn't even miss it. I was probably depressed. I didn't like much of anything at all, anymore.

"Maybe we could meet up at a playground later this week," I said to Sarah.

I'd begun breaking some of my rules for recovery when Alex was born.

It started with exercise. It moved from *only four days a week* to *only five days* and then *never more than one workout a day* to *you can work out as many times in a day as you want, but you can't consciously be compensating for something you've eaten.*

One evening I ate a Snickers bar. Then I went for a brisk walk. The two were not related. Another evening, I ate a Snickers bar. I was tired. But I realized I needed to go for a brisk walk. Soon after that, I ate a Snickers bar, and then I thought, *that will cost you 1.8 miles*, and it was raining outside, but I grabbed an umbrella and laced up my shoes to go for my walk.

Though exercise had always been tangled up with food, in adulthood, I'd mostly rid myself of explicit food rules. I'd developed a degree of quiet superiority to those I heard cutting food groups for nonspecific gastrointestinal complaints. *Sure, food is medicine, but everyone's really just trying to disguise their eating disorder, right?* I could hardly see past my own experience.

I looked for my own pathology in the lifestyles and behaviors of almost all others.

I cut dairy because Alex was nursing. This was something most nursing moms did—I'd rarely met a lactating mom who hadn't nixed dairy from her diet. I bought a cookbook that was marketed toward moms short on time but interested in healthy, efficient meal prep. All the recipes were gluten-free. They substituted zucchini for noodles, cauliflower for rice. I piled my grocery cart with produce, returning home to place pounds of vegetables in my food processor. *This is pretty good*, I thought one night after eating marinara over zoodles. *Maybe I should use this substitute for noodles more often. Maybe I'll never eat pasta again. Maybe I'll never allow myself to eat pasta again.*

I was able to convince myself that it was normal. *Every woman is like this sometimes, right?*

E was back working long hours in the hospital. He was often not home for dinner. On the many nights he wasn't home for dinner, I wasn't motivated to cook. I cracked some eggs. I ate a vegetable. I did a quick calorie count in my head. I smiled—the numbers were low. *You don't keep track of those things anymore*, I chided myself. But I didn't think about the numbers long—it was time to give Graham and Alex a bath.

When I woke in the morning, my whole body was in pain. Not just my muscles, but my bones—my fingers, my toes. I lifted Alex from his crib, placed his mouth to my engorged breast. He nursed, and it was relief—but also, it felt like the life was being sucked out of me.

"Everything hurts," I moaned as I slowly strapped Graham and Alex into their car seats for the ride to daycare.

In the morning, Graham would sometimes wake early and climb into our bed. He snuggled his head against my chest, and I softly rubbed his arms. "I love you, Graham," I whispered into his ear.

"Are you hurting again today, Mommy?"

"Yes, buddy—Mommy just hurts a lot."

"Maybe Daddy can fix it," Graham said after a moment. "He's a doctor. He could give you some medicine."

48

When E was home, he was cooking or cleaning or caring for our children. He was incredible. He wasn't manic, but he cared for us as though he had something to prove.

When E was in the hospital, I'd been frustrated—but I felt sorry for him. He was so sick. He'd missed out on Alex's earliest days. Once he was released, once he began to improve, I was furious—seething, constantly. The smallest disruptions set me off. I was obsessed with controlling every part of my schedule and my life—not just my food. Any interruption to our routines—a knock on the door, a longer-than-normal grandparent visit, an abbreviated nap—upset me. I began exercising constantly, even more than ever before. I could never get my workout over with because it was never enough.

"I need to run," I'd say the moment E returned home from work. He'd nod his head as I passed off Alex. I was still wearing my athletic clothes from my workout earlier in the day.

At night, I bathed and read and rocked and nursed Alex. Bedtime. Sound machine on. I snuck out of the nursery and down to the basement. I started another workout video. E was in the corner of the room, typing patient notes on the computer.

Suddenly, a cry from the nursery. My fists clenched. *He's supposed to be sleeping!* Another cry. I screamed. Another cry. I grabbed a nearby toy, threw it against the wall. Another cry. This time, a chair: small, wooden, and light. I tossed it gently toward the wall, still in control, but wanting to make a point.

"I'll go rock him," E said, rising to stand.

"He might need to nurse," I muttered.

"You're not going anywhere near him right now."

After some time, E returned.

"I don't want to be here anymore," I said.

"Here—where? Like, in our home?"

"On this planet." I began pinching and pulling at the flesh on my arms. "In this body. I don't want to be here. I hate it here."

"Okay—then you need to get some help."

"No one can help me. I don't even have a real problem. You're my problem! You're the one who did this to me."

"I was sick, Anna. I got some help. You probably need to get some help, too."

"No one can help me."

"That's pretty arrogant. Maybe you just don't want to change. You've been so irritable. Your mood has been volatile. I think you may be depressed. I think you might need medication."

"I can't take medication. It'll make me gain weight."

"It might not. I mean, my medication did—but I just try to manage it. I just have to watch what I eat more. You know you'll do something about it if you do gain weight."

"I can't do that. I'm already doing that enough. I couldn't possibly do that more."

"Well, that's another reason you probably need medication. Your body's an idol. Your body's going to change, eventually. You'll get older. You'll gain weight. Who cares! Our bodies are temporary."

"I care!"

"Well, maybe you should try to care about something more than yourself. God. Me—"

"I don't give a shit about you. You left me. You left me when I needed you."

"I didn't leave you. I was sick. I know you know that. And I know you care about Graham and Alex."

"Yes. I do."

"Maybe for them, then."

"Yes. I'm sorry."

"It's okay."

"I love you."

"I know you do."

And E left the room to check in again on Alex.

49

Finally, it was fall in West Virginia, the air crisp and cool with hillsides ablaze in yellow and red. Alex turned six months old. His first half-year had been healthy. Not even a sniffle. He slept through the night early on and rarely cried. *A dream, this baby.*

I'd been training for a Halloween weekend half-marathon, compulsive exercise funneled toward a socially acceptable goal. The day before the race, E was working in the hospital. Alex had been sick—a small cough, a low fever. His face was a bit pale when I lifted him from the crib that morning.

I took Alex to a walk-in clinic for an evaluation. The pediatrician listened to Alex's lungs, evaluated his throat, and peered inside his ears. He gave me a look of concern.

"Keep a close eye," he said after wrapping the pulse oximeter around Alex's big toe, evaluating the reading—an almost, but not quite, unacceptable oxygen saturation.

"Right now he's stable—but it could turn quickly."

I nodded as I held Alex on my lap, patting Graham's blonde head as he wriggled in the chair beside me. The pediatrician gave me a box with a blue nebulizer shaped like a seal. He sent in a script to Walgreens for cartridges of an inhalation steroid.

We left the clinic and walked out to our SUV. I fastened Alex and Graham into their car seats, smothering their hands with sanitizer to hopefully neutralize any germs they picked up in the waiting room.

It was about lunchtime. On the way home, I drove past Fazoli's. Even though I knew their pasta was substandard, I loved the chicken alfredo. I allowed myself to eat it only whenever I ran a race with double-digit mileage. I'd been looking forward to this meal for months. I turned in to the drive-through and ordered. I had a moment's hesitation. *What if he's too sick for you to run tomorrow?* But I reassured myself. *E has the day off. Even if he's still sick, you can run your race quickly. E can handle it. He's a doctor.*

We returned home, and Graham and I ate our pasta. As the day wore on, Alex's breathing turned to panting. It was time to trick or treat. But instead of dressing him up in his pumpkin costume and going door-to-door, I bribed Graham with Skittles to sit in our basement and watch *The Incredibles*. Alex struggled to suck in air, belly breathing, unable to drink milk without vomiting.

I turned off all the lights in the house and placed a large Tupperware container of chocolates in our front garden, notebook paper taped to the side. "Have At It!!!" the sign read, the number of exclamation points mirroring my desperation.

That night, E returned from work and counted Alex's respirations. He watched Alex vomit each time he nursed for comfort. He strapped him in the car and drove straight to the ER.

Alex was admitted to the ICU and diagnosed with respiratory syncytial virus (RSV) and pneumonia. That next morning, I didn't run my race. Respiratory therapists dropped orange tubes down Alex's throat to his distended belly to release accumulated air.

And as they did this to my baby, all I could think about was that pasta in my own belly.

Phlebotomists pierced his doughy skin with needles. *That pasta.* Nurses casually mentioned that he would probably need to be tubed. *I should've known. I can't believe I ate that fucking pasta.*

Grandparents offered to watch Graham. "I'll drop him by their house," I told E as we sat in the ICU.

"That sounds good," E said. "I'd feel more comfortable staying here and watching Alex closely, anyway."

"I might stop by our house for a little bit, too," I said. "Get my breast pump. And I might take a nap. I'm really exhausted."

"Absolutely," E said. "I'm sure you are. I'll call you and keep you updated."

I dropped Graham off at the grandparents' house. I drove home. *Just one*, I told myself as I walked through our front door. I streamed an exercise video on my phone. *I have to get rid of some of that pasta.* I jumped and kicked and lunged and squatted. I finished the video. *Another.* More kicking and jumping. *Another.*

Eventually, I decided I'd done enough. *Surely that took care of it.* I took a quick shower. I packed myself an overnight bag. I drove back to the hospital.

"They're going to see how he does with a BiPap," E said as I walked back into Alex's hospital room. "He might be able to dodge intubation."

"Oh, that's such great news!" I said.

"You look so much better!" one of the nurses said to me. "I'm glad you were able to go home and rest a bit. This looks like it might be a long haul."

50

The trees were autumnal and bright when Alex was admitted to the hospital. When he was discharged, the horizon was bare and gray. I was by his side most of the day and night for the two weeks he was in the hospital.

Machines monitored Alex's health—improvement and decline—at all hours of the day and night. Lights flashed and alarms sounded when those numbers veered from an acceptable range. At night, I slept on a foldout couch. I did sit-ups in bed in the dark as I gazed at the numbers on his monitor.

Throughout the day, I hooked myself up to a hospital-grade pump. My breasts were engorged and inflamed. I massaged them as the machine triggered a letdown. I watched the milk accumulate quickly in bottles, and I thought, *I wonder how many calories this is burning.*

When Alex fell asleep, I darted to the bathroom and streamed workout videos, shutting the door quickly to hide what I was doing when any medical personnel entered the room. Friends from work and church sent cards and food and money and flowers. They wanted to help with Graham. They offered to cover my classes. They were incredible and kind, and I was so grateful, but I couldn't stop thinking about E's hospitalization from months before. How hardly anyone knew. How I felt I couldn't talk about it. How much lonelier and scarier it was than Alex's hospitalization.

What did I do wrong? I asked myself repeatedly. *It's because I send him to daycare*, I thought. *It's because I'm a working mom. A selfish one, too, because it's not something I really have to be doing. We could get by on E's salary.*

It's because he was induced. His lungs hadn't formed fully, but we induced his birth anyway—and now he has pneumonia and RSV.

It's because I couldn't control my stress when he was born. The high blood pressure. It's because my mental health was in shambles while I was pregnant. It affected him in utero. It's because my mental health is in shambles now. It's all my fault, and everyone knows it. If he dies, I'm the one to blame.

I shared my anxiety with E. "I don't know why you think you had any control over this. God's in control—not you," he said. But controlling the uncontrollable was always my problem. It had been what had plagued me my whole life: my incessant attempts to stay in line, to do everything right.

"God's the one who gave us Alex," E said. "He's the one who sustains his life. Eventually, you're just going to have to trust him. You're going to destroy yourself until you do."

After Alex was discharged from the hospital, I finally had the conversation with my therapist. I'd injured myself from overexercise. I could barely move Alex from one breast to the other when I fed him. I was seeing a chiropractor and trying home remedies, but I knew what had caused my pain. I knew I needed to talk.

Right at the beginning of the conversation, I tried to show her that I had thoroughly intellectualized my disorder. That I was not stupid or vain—the stereotypes—but thoughtful, despite my persistent struggling. I wanted her to believe I had figured my problems out—despite the continued existence of those problems.

I told her that I believed a big reason I developed an eating disorder was that I grew up in an environment where bodies were bad. Women's bodies, especially. Desire was demonized. Appetites were, too. And I subconsciously applied everything that preachers said about sex to food. I was scared of growing into a woman, a sexual being, and so I tried to starve away my libido. I tried to halt puberty by not eating enough to continue getting a period. I tried to make it easier to adhere to the strict dress codes and standards about modesty by making my body smaller, by reducing the size of my curves.

"I think my eating disorder was tied to my religious environment," I said.

My therapist gazed at me for a moment. Then, she said, "I know you'd like to find a reason. But it was very likely not just one particular thing."

I was hoping for a compliment on my insight. "That makes sense," I said.

"The cause is not black-and-white," she continued.

But I wanted it to be. I wanted to deconstruct my pain, to find the root of the weed and pluck it—though this was probably not possible. I wanted to say, *I struggle with food because of religion.* Or *men.* Or even, *I struggle with food because of black-and-white thinking.* But this also was too black-and-white. It would never be just any one thing.

I could not go on an elimination diet to cure my eating disorder.

51

I spent the winter with one major goal: to protect our bodies. A slightly updated version of the goal I'd had my entire life—to protect my body. I lived in fear of germs. Danger lurked at Christmas gatherings and birthday parties, in trips to the grocery store and to playgrounds. I feared the sneezes of strangers, the coughs of neighbors. I baptized my hands in sanitizer after exiting small seminar classrooms. I sat at my work computer grading papers, coaching myself to keep my hands from touching my face in moments of distraction or contemplation.

Despite my efforts, Alex got sick again several months later, this time on his first birthday in March. We raced down the road to the hospital before we could slice into his cake. More needles, more oxygen, more tubes.

The timing felt significant and cruel. I spent the night in his hospital room watching numbers turn red on the monitors. I relived his birth—and those weeks after—that whole sleepless night.

Alarms would sound. Nurses would rush in. Early in the morning, a resident physician visited the room to ask me questions about Alex's symptoms. I could not form answers. I could not construct a complete sentence. I groaned like an animal, threw my phone across the room while the doctor was still present. She raised her eyebrows and exited quietly. I'd never acted this way in front of a stranger before. I couldn't continue keeping up appearances. Everything inside me felt as if it was breaking.

Alex was discharged after about a week, on March 10, 2020. And then, on March 15, the world shut down due to COVID-19. I sensed that everyone else on the planet felt my fear—of mortality, of ever-present, invisible danger. As we sheltered in our homes, I breathed a sigh of relief. I was isolated but no longer alone. It was a strange comfort to experience shared, not just individual, trauma.

At the beginning of the pandemic, my new neighbor asked me to join her on a socially distant jog. We walked up the hills. "I hate having to walk," she said, "but I hurt my back about a year ago. Hills aggravate it. I have to be careful."

She began talking to me about her anxiety, about how much she'd struggled during her injury. I tried to reciprocate in conversation. Then, as we rounded a corner, she said, nonchalantly, "I struggled with bulimia in grad school. It got pretty bad. I had to be hospitalized, eventually."

I felt my breath catch, felt that I'd been exposed. And then, that voice in my head: *But you weren't bulimic. You didn't throw up. Quit being dramatic, pretending that you had a problem. That you have a problem.*

She continued to tell her story. She turned her head. We made eye contact. *Does she know something? There's nothing to know!*

"Jerry and I were engaged, but he broke up with me for a while. He said he couldn't deal with the fact that I was destroying myself. He couldn't build his life with someone like that. But I loved him—that made me motivated to get better."

She said it all with no emotion, no tears, no catch in her own throat, as though she'd told the story dozens of times to others in the past.

Why is she telling me this? Why does she think that she's allowed to tell me this? You're not allowed to talk about this stuff!

After she started working toward recovery, her fiancé took her back. They got married. They had children. Now here we were—

running through a cemetery beside an upper-class neighborhood at sunrise in the middle of the pandemic.

I didn't say much during the run, but I thought about her story for days. I wondered what kind of person could tell an acquaintance such intimate details about their life. I became jealous of her hospitalization. It felt like bragging. That she was sick enough for care. That she had a narrative with an ostensible ending. It seemed that to have a conclusion, you had to reach a particularly low point, a crisis that involved another's noticing. I never could seem to reach that point. I never was quite sick enough. I just hovered constantly, endlessly, in an uncomfortable status quo, just barely cause for concern.

"I wish I'd thrown up," I told E one night after putting Alex to bed. "Maybe then I would have been sick enough to get some help."

"You probably didn't throw up because you knew throwing up was *bad*," E replied. "And you were *good*. And exercise was *very good*. So that's how you purged instead."

I nodded. There was a name for this: exercise bulimia. If I'd gotten a diagnosis, that's what it would have been. When I'd restricted, being disciplined with food was a point of pride: a sign of my self-control. The binges were what gave me the most shame. Ultimate defeat. But now I was trying to recontextualize them. They were a sign of my body's resilience, my body's insistence on living a full life, despite how much the rest of me wanted to shrink.

52

That first COVID spring I began trying to process E's and Alex's hospitalizations through writing. During naptime, I'd sit down with a cup of coffee and a notebook and try to make sense of these experiences. Each time I wrote, no matter the scene, no matter the situation, the story morphed into a narrative about my body. I tried to stay on track. *Focus*, I told myself. *You're not writing about that.* But I kept veering away from the hospitalizations.

This veering had happened in the past. I'd sit down to write—about motherhood, about vaginismus, about God—and the content would shift into some reflection about food or exercise. At one point, I'd decided to quit writing. *No one wants to read about your eating disorder. Quit focusing so much on your body.*

This time I decided to embrace the detour. It was April 2020. *The world's suffocating. We're all locked in our homes. What else do you have to be afraid of?* I decided to write about my body, food, and exercise—I was going to write about it to death. I was going to write about it until it was no longer inside me. I was going to write about it so that I could, eventually, write about something else.

Maybe you'll even write a book, I thought as I lifted Alex from his crib. *That would actually be pretty easy. That book's been in your head your entire life. A book about eating disorders. There's nothing in the world you know about more than that.*

I wrote every day. Twice a day. I wrote when I wanted to overexercise. I replaced one compulsion with another. *A health-*

ier one, I thought to myself. I wrote thousands of pages, scenes from my adolescence, moments of starving and then binging in fugue states. I scribbled furiously as I took sips of coffee, bites of a donut.

I asked several people I'd decided were safe to read my work, people I believed might be able to guide me out. I was ashamed. *What if when they read this, they'll see I'm just using writing as therapy?* Eventually, I decided, *Who cares if I'm using this as therapy? So what? I need therapy. I need things!*

53

While I was nursing Alex before bed, a post popped up on my Instagram Discover page: "Weight loss observed outside the context of diet culture is indicative of risk." The meme was created by Dietitian Anna, an anti-diet practitioner whose close family member died due to complications related to disordered eating.

I was reminded of a recent Sunday at church. Our pastor's wife complimented my friend Sarah's weight loss. Sarah seemed uncomfortable with the comment, with the confirmation that others had been not just noticing but assessing her body.

I wondered what had been happening with Sarah. Was she trying to lose weight? Was she hungry doing so? Was she sick or depressed or stressed or unable to afford enough groceries?

When others had walked away, I pulled Sarah aside and said, "Hey! You looked great before. I hope you're feeling okay now."

I was introduced to the anti-diet world on Instagram. I clicked through posts that said things like "your body is the least interesting thing about you" and "you don't have to have a diagnosable eating disorder to deserve help and support." I learned that girls start wanting to be thinner by six years old and that most start dieting by eight years old. Slowly, the algorithm stopped showing me weight-loss befores and afters, replacing them with content from dietitians, therapists, and everyday people who want to dismantle the chokehold of diet culture.

Around this same time, I began searching online to have conversations with women who'd grown up in similar environments or had similar experiences. I joined some online groups focused on recovering from the impacts of purity culture and diet culture.

One community I joined was focused on parenting children from a Health at Every Size (HAES) paradigm.

To align oneself with HAES, a person does not necessarily believe that a person *is* healthy at every size but rather that a person's size does not tell us much about that person's health status. Individuals aligned with HAES believe in the beauty of body diversity. Just as canines include chihuahuas and Saint Bernards, people, too, take on a variety of shapes and sizes. A husky could not and should never strive to be the size of a beagle—and this same principle can be applied to humans, too.

Yes, even baby humans. This parenting community was filled with moms experiencing medical bias against their children. Moms who had given birth to big babies watched those same children follow their expected growth trajectory—and still, pediatricians would suggest restrictive diets. In this group, moms discussed ways to advocate for their children against medicalized anti-fat bias while still caring for the health and well-being of their kids.

The common feature uniting most of us was that we all, at some point, had struggled with disordered eating. And we desperately did not want to pass the same fate along to our children.

In the group one day, I asked a question: "How many of you grew up in purity culture? If so, what overlap do you see between purity culture and diet culture?"

The responses flooded in. I began having private conversations with individuals in the group. "Yes," one woman replied. "I began deconstructing my faith at the same time I began unraveling my own fatphobia and healing my relationship with food."

This connection between faith and fatphobia, she believed, was not a coincidence.

I continued to correspond with about a dozen women, and I spoke to many of them over the phone. This is how Cali and I began discussing how our experiences in purity culture affected our relationships with our own bodies.

Cali narrated the landscape of her childhood to me. Midwestern, small-town, Baptist upbringing. And then she launched into a description of her dress code. Knee-length shorts. No two-piece swimsuits. No tank tops.

The list was familiar, an exact description of the stipulations I adhered to at my fundamentalist school. As she talked about covering her shoulders, belly, and knees, a contrarian voice in me silently countered, *Were these rules* really *so bad?*

And I couldn't help but consider that it was the effect of the rules that left such an indelible mark. The experience of looking *other*, those glances from the grocery store cashier communicating they believed your dress quietly said that you thought you were *better than them*. The visual representation of being in the world but not of the world. The confirmation of that peculiar teenage angst that you would never actually fit in.

And, of course, there was the surveillance. We both learned early and often that someone was always watching your body, assessing it. If it fell out of line, it would be punished. The safest thing to do was to learn to administer the surveillance—and punishment—ourselves.

"I hid my body—and I hid my eating," Cali said.

In secret, Cali binged in closets. Not at family meals, not at the church potlucks. There, she could perform—arranging her plate perfectly, purity ring gleaming from her right hand. An impressive number of vegetables. Not too much starch. She could feel the eyes of the congregants examining her lunch, determining whether she was following the rules there, too.

"All that peer pressure of having your plate look a certain way. There's no more judgy place than a potluck," Cali groaned.

This struggle was a theme in many of the conversations I had with women about their experiences with food in church. So much of the church's social life revolves around food. And these situations are often fraught with pressure.

54

When Megan told me about her family's schedule at their evangelical, nondenominational church in upstate New York, it sounded consuming. She was a worship leader, and her husband was a youth leader. They were at church four nights a week.

At church, she felt pressured to perform: to be soft-spoken and thin, to dress conservatively and make sure that her children were tamed and well-behaved because "children are like spiritual currency," she explained.

Each year, she and her husband participated in a Daniel fast, loosely based on the type of fast practiced by the prophet Daniel in the Old Testament. This partial fast (lasting for several weeks) was not tied to the liturgical calendar, and it involved avoiding things like meat and other animal products, along with processed foods. This practice was recommended for all adult parishioners. But in between those fasts? She and other women in church kept dietary accountability by participating in the Weigh Down Workshop, a pray-yourself-thin, non-diet diet that focuses on feeding a person physically and emotionally.

"It was something you did with your accountability partner or closest gal pals," Megan recounted. "Nearly all the women in the church participated. There was definitely FOMO. If you weren't doing it, it was like, you weren't spiritual enough. Or you weren't going to hear from God."

Though Megan was raising three children, she also endured seventeen pregnancy losses over a ten-year span. She watched other women at church experience similar issues with fertility. Megan said that most of the women in her community viewed their losses as results of the choices they made, and their first line of recourse was to make dietary changes.

As Megan processed her grief, she still felt the pressure to keep a perfect home, perfect children, and an unrelenting church schedule. She had to keep her husband's eyes from wandering while also keeping herself from being lusted after by other men. She confessed that, by the end of the day, she was often screaming at her children and crying in the shower; her reactions seemed logical to me.

She didn't need more accountability for her behavior. She didn't need more rules. I wanted to give her a snack, a nap, and a hug.

Most of the women I spoke to described implicit messages regarding the importance of thinness and dieting in church settings. Still others (like Megan) spoke of more overt lessons in the form of church-sanctioned diet programs. It's no surprise that many of these health programs target women in the church. Busy moms desperate for some "me time." Postpartum women looking to shed the baby weight. Frustrated wives hoping to reinvigorate their marriages.

Brooke went on her first diets at church, a Daniel fast and then one called the Holy Diet. She explained the premise: "Basically, they said, 'Let's learn to eat the way they ate in the garden [of Eden] and see your body transform.' It tied together holiness and thinness. There was the impression that, 'Well, fat people are fat because they're undisciplined and irresponsible.'"

Brooke noted that after these church diets, she started to struggle with disordered eating—a struggle that would last fifteen years. She began restricting food—either the amount or type. For years, she never considered this restriction a real problem. She believed that thinking about food excessively and becoming obsessed with controlling it was just how good people were supposed to live.

Institutionalized religious diets are nothing new in American Christianity. There have been multiple waves in church diet culture. While fasting in early modern Anglo-American Protestantism was often guided by asceticism and repentance, diets in the church after the Civil War era were "typified by obsession with perfect health and slenderness as physical signs of regeneration," writes R. Marie Griffith. A thin body has been treated as an outward manifestation of an inward reality: The willpower and discipline shown in dieting are correlated with one's obedience to God.

America's thin ideal really emerged in the 1890s to 1910s and has had a hold on the country ever since. There is significant speculation as to why that ideal has persisted. During the Reconstruction period, fatphobia was racialized. Sabrina Strings writes that by the 1890s in America there was "a growing praise of slenderness in parts of the South [and] a growing relationship between Nordic/Aryan heritage, slimness, and beauty." In other words, thinness became associated with whiteness and American exceptionalism.

Some contend that as consumerism increased, one way to demonstrate physical restraint amid material abundance was an intensified focus on disciplining the physical body. Likewise, as society became more individualistic rather than communal, we directed our efforts toward perfecting the self. In this same environment, Christian literature became more concerned with transformation via self-realization rather than salvation.

"I once was lost but now am found" had shifted into "I once was fat but now am thin."

55

I spoke to one woman who characterized her years of starving in response to an abusive romantic relationship as an attempt to "make [herself] less juicy" to men. She feared men as predators, herself as prey, and she longed for safety. She wanted out of the hunt entirely. Perhaps skipping meals would give her another place to go.

And yet, while some women turn to disordered eating to divest themselves of sexualized power and remain innocent as girls, there is still a grasping for another sort of power. They—we—are tapping in to other means of dominance.

We are not actually subordinating.

Perhaps we are reaching for the privilege of learned men. By denying the body's hungers, we demonstrate a command of mind over matter, achieving "the ascetic aesthetic," or the thin ideal for men of the Enlightenment era.

People of all races use thinness to access racialized power. Thin bodies have long been associated with Whiteness. There is a relationship between Protestant moralism and race science. Fat bodies were associated with Blackness, and White Anglo-Saxon women were encouraged to use thinness to distinguish themselves from Black women. Sabrina Strings argues that "two critical historical developments contributed to a fetish for svelteness and a phobia about fatness: the rise of the transatlantic slave trade and the spread of Protestantism. Racial scientific rhetoric about slavery linked fatness to 'greedy' Africans. And religious discourse suggested that overeating was ungodly." As I continued to read about how racialized beauty ideals are often associated with White Protestant women, I couldn't help but consider the directives eerily familiar, so similar were they to what I learned in Grace and Dignity, my fundamentalist school's class for middle-school girls, with advice ranging from ordering abstemiously on a date at a restaurant to maintaining an attractive but demure appearance.

In other words, when a woman makes herself small, she is simultaneously trying to become big.

While folding laundry in Alex's nursery, I turn on *Maintenance Phase*, a podcast that debunks wellness scams and junk nutritional science. I start following the work of one of the show's hosts, Aubrey Gordon. Prior to the podcast, she wrote a column for *Self* magazine and used the pen name Your Fat Friend. She delayed using her given name for years, in part because what she wrote about was so vulnerable but also because the subject matter—the harm others had done to her body—opened her up to abuse. She received harsh comments, doxing, and even death threats after writing essays about weight stigma in the doctor's office and fat shaming as being bad for public health.

In one essay of Gordon's on weight stigma in the doctor's office, she writes about how, when making a visit for an ear infection, she was told to lose weight. At one annual checkup, she witnessed a doctor recoiling from her, refusing to touch or examine her body, and she received no instruction other than being told to lose weight. At another appointment, when her blood pressure read as low, the nurse checked the reading again. And again. And again. Because "obese patients don't usually have low blood pressure." Not only was Gordon's body maligned but her health was also disbelieved.

I continue binging episode after episode of *Maintenance Phase*, and I listen to one entitled "Eating Disorders." "Fat people have them too!" the show description reads. Many people who have eating disorders don't look skeletal or even thin, the episode contends. Many people with eating disorders are fat.

Not all bodies react to starvation the same way. The *New York Times Magazine* has also reported on the prevalence of atypical anorexia: patients who have all the behavioral and physical symptoms of anorexia nervosa but who are still overweight.

Still, disordered eating is associated with people who have bodies like mine—thin, white, upper-middle class, and female. This stereotype is not accurate because "eating disorders don't discriminate." The association between the pursuit of thinness and white bodies, though, is likely due to the fact that our fear of the fat body is rooted in racism.

We haven't always idealized thin bodies. One of the earliest surviving pieces of artwork, the Venus of Willendorf (created about twenty-five thousand years ago), is a fat female figurine. She has full, pendulous breasts, a round belly, and thick thighs. This figure is not an outlier—hundreds of similar pieces of art have been found from this era across Europe and Asia.

Even though gluttony was considered a sin in the Hebrew Bible, fat bodies were not connected with the vice in ancient times. Historian Susan E. Hill writes, "Anyone can behave gluttonously, and fat people are not inevitably gluttonous." Part of the gift of the promised land, a land of milk and honey, was that the Hebrews would reach a place where they would "eat their fill" and become fat (Deut. 31:20 NIV).

Sixteenth- and seventeenth-century European artists like Dürer, Raphael, and Rubens all idealized fat female bodies in their work. European beauty standards at that time upheld figures that were abundant, fleshy, and round. The shift in ideals happened in the eighteenth century, at the same time the transatlantic slave trade was growing rapidly. The thin ideal became associated with upper-class white women because it was a way to distinguish themselves from Black people. As Sabrina Strings writes,

"With women commonly being used to represent the nation, the emerging face and figure of American exceptionalism as seen in mainstream art and media was the trim Nordic woman."

A thin body, in other words, signals both power and privilege.

Fat people are discriminated against harshly. They are less likely to be hired and to be paid a fair wage, and they can be fired at will in the workplace. Infrastructure is rarely built to accommodate their bodies. In health care, they often receive shame and blame for their medical problems and concerns. Fatphobia is the one prejudice that has grown in the twenty-first century rather than shrunk.

56

A former student, also raised in purity culture, sent me a text: She and her husband wanted to have a baby sometime soon. She was excited—but she was also scared. Would I ever be up for talking about motherhood with her?

"I'd love to," I responded. "What are you scared about?"

She replied with the usual list: work-life balance, money, attaching to the baby, and at the very end, she said, "And I know this is vain, but I'm really scared to gain weight."

I decided I would not do what everyone had done to me—*oh, you'll be fine. It's only temporary. You'll bounce back right away! It'll be worth it when you see your precious baby.* I said, "I completely understand your fear about weight gain. It was a significant struggle for me. I've had an eating disorder most of my life, and it didn't go away during pregnancy. If that's something you relate to, I'd love to talk about it."

This was, in fact, something she related to—something so many women relate to but never really talk about aside from brief conversations about body image. We texted for several hours. We talked about OCD and calorie counting. I talked about what had helped me in therapy: establishing boundaries, diversifying the type of media I consumed, not attaching too much meaning to intrusive thoughts, and speaking to myself kindly, even when it felt false. She said she felt less scared of pregnancy and told me that my admission gave her permission to share.

Our conversation reminded me of a discussion I'd had with Linda Kay Klein, author of *Pure: Inside the Evangelical Movement That Shamed a Generation of Young Women and How I Broke Free*. Klein now works as a coach with individuals struggling to disentangle their belief systems from what they'd learned about gender and sexuality in purity culture, and I asked her whether she'd noticed women in purity culture having unique reactions to pregnancy.

"Absolutely," she said. "Some feel their protruding bellies announce their sexual activity to the world, which they feel is shameful. And many have a strong aversion to the patriarchal expectation that they have to give themselves up completely in order to be a 'good mother.' For some, this aversion extends to pregnancy, which they may see as the first phase of giving themselves up in the form of literally sharing their body."

Of course, it's not as if pregnancy anxiety is limited to women who grew up in purity culture. In all of culture, motherhood is both praised and punished, often in the same breath. The larger culture treats the pregnant body as a public entity that needs both regulation and protection. Pregnancy, for all women, often means no longer being seen or treated as an individual person with rights, needs, and desires.

I spoke to several women from purity-culture recovery groups who described pregnancy as a healing experience. They learned how to marvel at, be with, and trust their own bodies. Several of them became doulas. Kinsey, now a doula, described her mindset shift to me this way: "My trauma from purity culture impacted my decision to be a doula too. Growing up I had so much shame and fear around my body. Being able to witness birth and the incredible things our bodies can do was so healing for me. I'm angry that I spent so many years of my life in fear because I was lied to."

Pregnancy, in many ways, made me realize how much healing I needed to experience in relation to my own body. It made me understand the extent to which I feared myself and any situation where I did not have perfect control. And ultimately, it made me want to heal.

I spoke to another student via email: She was writing a book. Could she share portions of it with me? she asked.

"Of course," I replied, and she responded with pages devoted to processing her sexual trauma and her eating disorder. I felt privileged that she was inviting me into her writing as therapy. I knew how people often critiqued this sort of writing: as navel-gazing. This judgment was why it took me decades to write about my own experiences. I knew that issues related to women's experiences were often received with scorn. In a chapter of *Body Work* titled "In Praise of Navel-Gazing," Melissa Febos reflects upon the tendency for others to disparage women writing about their own personal experiences: "I don't think it's a stretch to wonder if the navel, as the locus of all this disdain, has something to do with its connection to birth, and body, and the female." Still, Febos continues, shame is a way of silencing, and a patriarchal society benefits from the silence of victims. I was excited to think about coming alongside this student as she processed her experience, as she revised her essay into something new and polished that she could share.

In the fall, I attended a virtual faculty orientation. All the panels centered on the pandemic, supporting students as they learned at home, as they juggled an impossible load. A representative from the counseling center spoke. She talked about referring our students to their services: "for their struggles with depression and anxiety, time management, and, you know, if they need support losing the weight they've gained in isolation: the COVID-19." She chuckled.

My facial expression shifted—I was angry. I turned off my webcam to keep up appearances. I still cared so much about appearances. *Maybe college students don't need to be shamed for gaining a few pounds during a global health crisis. Maybe the counseling center should focus on students who are coping with this impossible world by developing an eating disorder.*

I knew if I were more recovered, I would have spoken up—maybe not in a public meeting, but perhaps in a politely worded email. I promised myself that, in the future, I would not be silent.

57

"If you could have three wishes, what would those wishes be?" My therapist asked me this question during intake. I paused, head static and palms sweating. I tried to brainstorm wishes. I listened to the tick of a wall clock. I asked whether I could skip the question. I wasn't able to say what I wanted most, even as a hypothetical exercise.

When I was a child in Sunday school, whenever the teacher was too tired to prepare a lesson, we watched VeggieTales on a rollout box television set. As we drank from Dixie cups full of apple juice, cartoon vegetables acted out juvenile versions of biblical stories. One episode of the show is about the book of Esther. In it, Queen Vashti is banished from the kingdom because she will not make the king a midnight sandwich.

In the actual biblical text, Queen Vashti is not even asked to perform a task. She is asked to appear. To be gazed upon. To be seen. She refuses this request, vanishing into smoke for the rest of history.

After the video, my Sunday school teacher taught us that Queen Vashti was a bad woman, a warning to wives everywhere. She was disobedient. She acted out of place. If she had obeyed her husband, she could have kept her beautiful life.

The historian Josephus is kinder to Vashti. Persian women, he explains, were raised to value modesty, to not be seen. Vashti chose to follow the teachings of her youth, rejecting the demands of her husband.

The narrative of the book of Esther hinges upon the fulfillment of a wish a woman dared speak aloud. "What is your request? Even up to half the kingdom, it will be given you," the king says to his new wife, Esther, Vashti's replacement, as she appears before his throne (Esther 5:3 NIV). He offers her 50 percent, an equal partnership, just because she shows up.

Esther refuses the kingdom. She requests a feast instead and invites to her banquet Haman, a man who has committed violence toward her and her people. Proud and full, he loosens his belt and leans back to relax. Bloated from meat, wine, and ego, he is hung on the gallows—a pig plumped for slaughter. Esther's request leads to Haman's death. And by taking this risk and indulging in these feasts, she is rewarded further still: by opening her mouth, she saves her people.

Months later, my therapist asked me again, *three wishes.* This time, I gave her fake wishes, safe wishes, wish equivalents of "thoughts and prayers." The wishes we all have. For health and love and safety. Wishes that obscured me and made my true desires totally unidentifiable. To be honest, I wasn't even sure what my true desires were, but I knew I wanted more than just the basics.

Why could I not identify or say my wishes out loud, even in a clinical setting, even to a person who had no ability to grant or deny my desires? Why was I so fearful of the power in want?

Maybe this inability to name my desires is why I was very, very, very angry, as my therapist observed.

That evening, after feeding Alex in the dark of his nursery, I undressed and climbed into the shower. Naked and alone, I thought, *Three things. What three things do I really want?* I pushed down my fears of disappointment. I relaxed in the heat of the water. I knew my desires would follow me, even if I shrank them, even if I buried them. My silence wasn't going to protect me.

I want to write a book someday, I thought to myself in the shower, even as I wondered whether I really had anything to say.

"Women should remain silent in the churches" (1 Cor. 14:34 NIV). This verse was the passage up for discussion in my parents' Sunday school class. It's not that anyone liked this particular command. Except for those who did: the male Sunday school teacher, the women in the room who felt they they'd worked pretty hard to become good at it.

Only one woman in class had the audacity to call the author out. "He's a misogynist," Kirsten's mom, Jill, said.

"It was hard to listen to Jill this morning, calling Paul names in church," my mom said on the ride home. "Doesn't she realize she's talking about Scripture? This is God's word, after all." My mom paused, sighing. "And Jill's a leader in the church, too! Just one more example of why we need to be providing better education at church about theology."

As a teenager, I began to question my own training in theology. Mine was a quiet deconstruction. Someday I would learn hermeneutics that emphasized the importance of context, but that had not happened yet. I was still grappling with how I, as a Christian woman, could give voice to something without going against the commands of God. Though I fantasized about speaking—about telling speakers, *no, you're wrong about me, and I think you hate many of the people you pretend to love*—I rarely challenged authority. I communicated my displeasure with my body during sermons—about modesty, the importance of evangelizing the lost, the total depravity of man. I sat straight in my hard metal chair, crossing and then recrossing my legs. I drew circles repetitively in the journal where I was supposed to be taking notes. This drawing was a place to go, somewhere rhythmic, mindless, away from this stern God and his hells both here and to come.

Some days, dissociation was enough. I could manage my anger and perform, good and quiet and kind. I could keep my feelings under control. On other days, it was a little less dinner that kept me in check.

This refusal was my protest. Without the power to speak up and challenge religious authority, I communicated my rejection of this world by trying to disappear my body. I dissented with a quiet, "I'm not hungry."

58

What does health look like? If I follow the signs I see on social media and maybe even my doctor's office, health looks a lot like my eating disorder. I can hardly spot the difference, though I know there must be one, a thin line one crosses when moving from "choosing healthy habits" to having no choice at all. This line seems so slight, barely the width of a foot. How does one not cross over? The path to health seems totally consuming and suspiciously abstinent.

Of course, maybe the depictions of health aren't the problem. Maybe I am the problem. Maybe the diet is neutral, with potential for problems or joy, in the same way a glass of wine is neutral with potential. Both are loaded, and it can be difficult to know which way it will all go. Maybe you have an inkling: *This seems like something that could tip me over*. But you don't really know until it does.

But here's one difference: The wine has a warning on the label. The diet does not. My friend selling superfood shakes and rainbow portion containers does not have to reference the surgeon general in her sales pitch. It is not general wisdom that restriction can impair judgment and make you dizzy behind a wheel, too. The diet industry receives pushback for false promises, for its proclivity for disappointment, but there is such little concern for the people who succeed. And by succeed, I mean lose. And they are praised for their success—I mean loss. And they become addicted to less feeling, less food, less skin, and they find beauty in nothing, and they become hard and sharp as bone. I become hard and sharp as bone.

When I pour myself a glass of wine, I do not feel preoccupied by it. I do not feel that I am on some edge. With wine, I can take it or leave it. I do not have that luxury with food. When I restrict food, I will think of nothing else. I will try to consume just a little bit less, exercise just a bit more, target a number lower and lower, but no number will ever be low enough. This endless pursuit is what I find intoxicating. And my first step toward recovery was to be honest about this fact. I had to acknowledge that for me a diet is dangerous, that I find disappearance a most interesting project, that I have the tendency to communicate my emotions not by opening my mouth but by shutting it up, not allowing anything or anyone in.

Out to dinner with a group of E's colleagues, I ate with no fear and no plans to compensate later. I was in a good place. I began talking to a loud woman beside me. At the time, I thought of her as confident, assuming the volume of one's voice correlated positively with confidence. This woman began speaking to me of a liquid cleanse she was about to start; toxins, digestion, headaches—all of it would be improved. Cleanses were unusual then, not yet ubiquitous. The woman did not mention weight-loss goals, though I could not imagine that this was not the main point, all else a smokescreen—or was I seeing only myself in this judgment?

As this woman spoke to me of the number of days she would sip liquid kale and bone broth, I felt overcome with emotion and unable to form a response. I found myself repeating, "Oh, wow. I wouldn't be able to do that." It was all I could bring myself to say, and I kept saying it: "I wouldn't be able to do that."

Finally, the woman looked at me—she was angry now—and said, "Well, guess what! You don't have to." I stammered and apologized and blushed furiously. I wanted to leave that dinner and go for a long run to a place far away.

I was trying to say something about myself, and in my poor communication, she understood these expressions as critiques of her. Which they were. But they were rooted in my awareness of my own weaknesses. How do I say to someone else that their pursuit of health would be unhealthy for me? That I suspect it may be unhealthy for them, too? Why do I feel compelled to attempt this communication at all?

At that same dinner, there was a man at our table who had not ordered a drink, though the rest of us at the table had several glasses of wine and cocktails. I placed my order for a mojito with little thought. Some of us made remarks about the bartender's mix of our cocktails. This man, I learned later from my husband, had struggled with alcoholism in the past. I began to think about him as I replayed the events of the evening in my mind. Did he feel like me at this dinner? Did he feel as if we were taunting him with our freedom? Did he worry about us the way I worried about that loud woman?

"I'm so happy kids today have body positivity," a friend says at brunch one morning.

I almost choke on my mimosa. "You . . . think it's better now?" I ask.

"Well, sure," my friend replies. "We had Kate Moss, 'nothing tastes as good as skinny feels,' and low-rise jeans. Now we get to see and celebrate way more body types."

I know I have benefited from seeing a variety of bodies celebrated. As I've diversified my Instagram feed, I've learned that the narrow ideals for beauty I've held are very much conditioned. Just as reading literature from a variety of subject positions has broadened my perspective of the world, of who is good and who is bad and whether such binaries exist in the first place, so, too, has consuming content that celebrates a variety of bodies expanded possibilities for beauty.

Body positivity used to be radical with roots in Black feminism. But now that it's mainstream, it's been co-opted by white women. If I click on #bodypositivity on social media, I see photos of young, thin women posting shots of their midsections before and after lunch. Or of themselves in a seated position with a single belly roll spilling over the top of their jeans. To be frank, the movement feels silly, filled with body checking and comparison, just with slightly less exacting standards.

If I look away from my feed and out at the world, body positivity hasn't appeared to do much for people's lived experiences in their bodies. Despite the rise of the body-positivity movement, the number of people hospitalized with complications from eating disorders doubled after the COVID-19 pandemic. A 2023 study published in *JAMA Pediatrics* found that one in five kids shows signs of disordered eating. Anorexia is the deadliest mental illness, but health professionals still receive little training about eating.

There is still a multibillion-dollar weight-loss industry; there is still size-based discrimination. The punishing standards for women's appearances haven't gone away. The thin ideal still exists. We're just told that it no longer does. Or, rather, we're no longer allowed to *say* that it does.

Body positivity, to me, feels like slapping a bandage on a hemorrhaging ulcer. It's being told to smile while you're grieving because your sadness makes others uncomfortable. It's adding another layer of deception to an already exhausting game.

Some propose body neutrality as an alternative. This mindset is supposed to function as a middle ground between loving and hating your body. Rather than focusing so much on appearances, body neutrality encourages a person to consider what their body can do or how their body feels.

Or, as Lexie Kite and Lindsay Kite say in their book *More Than a Body*, "your body is an instrument, not an ornament." Rather than getting caught in self-objectification, body neutrality encourages valuing how you feel over appearances. And it doesn't ask for you to maintain a perpetually sunny perspective.

But this mindset isn't entirely realistic. It's challenging, if not impossible, to feel neutral about something—especially about something as central as our own bodies. Neutrality is, in a way, asking someone to not feel at all. But feelings aren't things we want to do away with—feelings give us information. Feelings are worth considering so that we can take better action. They're not things we need to squash down and ignore. I don't feel neutral about my children, my job, my marriage, the church, or even the weather. Why in the world would I feel neutral about my own body?

Both mindsets involve some degree of ranking. But the philosopher Kate Manne's proposition—body reflexivity—dispels the idea of hierarchy. It proposes the idea that my body is for me. It does not exist for the purpose or pleasure of anyone outside myself. My body is not for my husband. Or the church. Or my children.

My body is mine.

And immediately, I think—no, it's not. I recall a verse: "You are not your own; you were bought at a price. Therefore honor God with your bodies" (1 Cor. 6:19–20 NIV). When I hear this verse, it comes to me in the voice of an angry preacher. He says it to me as if he's saying, "Gotcha!"

It's enough to make me want to curl up into the fetal position and cry. I wish this reaction were not my inheritance: my tendency to hear Scripture weaponized, something that tears me apart, cuts me down, makes me small.

The concept that my body is mine sounds selfish, at first. But it's not as though living to please others has made me selfless. Ignoring my own needs and desires has not made them go away—and it's kept me from showing up in the world as the unique person God's created me to be.

I consider what it might mean to believe that my body is for me. It might mean that I don't have to keep up, shape up, fix up. It might mean that I no longer need to try so hard to be a better Christian, to have a better body, to live a better life than everyone else. It might mean no more worries about being good or bad at parenting, or sex, or eating food. It might mean less judgment, less competition. It might mean more rest.

It might mean love.

If I believed my body was for me, I could just *be*. And I could believe that I'm already enough to be held. Just as I am.

Body reflexivity resists the idea that bodies should be ranked and compared, that there are good bodies and bad bodies. It encourages appreciation over critique.

Kate Manne invites us to consider our experience of sunsets. We don't rank or judge them against each other. We don't offer up before-and-after photos of the sky. As night falls and the sun dips below the clouds, as color illuminates the horizon, we simply look up. We behold the pink and the purple, the orange and the red. We gaze in awe and complete satisfaction as we marvel at each one's exquisite, unique design.

59

I spoke to Malerie, a pastor's daughter, on the phone in early spring of 2023.

"How did your experience in purity culture impact your relationship with your own body?" I asked.

She recounted the story of a boy when she was eight years old. An assault. She told her parents—and while they were concerned, they didn't want to make it too big of a deal. The boy's family was part of the church, and her mom and the boy's mom went to fitness classes together. They were always talking about their diets together.

This same boy assaulted Malerie a second time when she was a young teenager. She described herself as a little bit chubby then. She had just started developing breasts.

"I had a strong feeling that no one else would want me," she said. "This is something I don't like. This is something I'm being coerced into. But maybe this is the only way I'll ever experience something sexually—because I'm not worthy. Because of my body."

Malerie became obsessed with her body after that second assault. She lived in a perpetual state of contradiction. She'd learned that focusing on her body was a sin, but she had to think about her body all the time to guard it, to keep it.

When she began struggling with disordered eating, no one seemed to notice. She never really got *that* thin. She just became thinner than before. She knew she was suffering, that she had a problem, but she also wondered whether, perhaps, this was just what women were supposed to do. To always be on a diet.

"I didn't have a diagnosis," she said. "But if I'd gotten one, it probably would have been anorexia."

Later that evening after my phone conversation with Malerie, I looked out my window to watch my sons playing in the yard with their best friend, the girl next door. They swung and kicked soccer balls, drew chalk portraits, and played tag. One of my sons began shoving the other, roughhousing, and I called from the window, "Keep your hands to yourself!" He listened—but minutes later, they began pushing each other again.

Eventually, I called them in for a break.

At bedtime, we talked about consent. "Do we ever touch somebody without their permission?" I asked my sons, and they shook their heads: *no, of course not.* They touched each other, without permission, even as they assented to my direction.

I told them "no means no" and "stop means stop"—we'd discussed this before—and I gave them an object lesson about boundaries.

I kept thinking about Malerie, about her needs that were ignored and minimized. About how people who had power did nothing to help her maintain hers.

I desperately wanted to raise kind sons, sons who respected others and themselves. I wanted to teach them to control their passions and desires.

I felt a chill when I considered that this control of desire was the urge that had dogged me, frustrated me, my whole life.

60

Fitness influencers on social media talk about how to fit exercise in with children. They post videos of themselves in toy-strewn living rooms, wearing sports bras and leggings, children playing independently with blocks while they do burpees. Then, in the next frame, children sit spread-legged across their backs as they assume a plank position. Then children pull their sweaty hair from their top knots as they bend into downward dog. Their children are giggling—no, they are crying, they are screaming, they are smiling; it does not matter. These moms still get it done. There is so much praise for their resolve.

These women have toned abs and herniated belly buttons. They break their fasts not with breakfast but with lunch, usually a smoothie, and the ingredients cost nearly ten dollars, so they call it a meal. Sometimes they take a photo of themselves eating pizza just to show their followers that they are real, loose, and flexible.

When I first began struggling with disordered eating around the age of twelve, my days looked like a teenager's version of these influencers' lives. I didn't work out with children bouncing on top of my head—I was still a child myself. But I was always playing a game of how I could bend my day's responsibilities to meet my body's strict demands. I was fearful of anything unexpected that might force me to consume more or move less. I lived in a world I wanted to escape, and so I tried to create my own world, a small and uncomplicated existence, all anxiety confined to numbers: inches, pounds, calories, and hours.

Despite my efforts, gravity pulled me back into the real world, and I was forced to grapple with life's dirt and messiness. I feared fevers because even a high temperature did not alleviate the compulsion of counting. I found myself doing leg lifts and sit-ups in secret, covered in a cold, clammy sweat—illness was no excuse. If I was too sick to white-knuckle my way through it, my hours would have to be added to later in the week when, I hoped, I would feel better, would be able to tackle four hours that day rather than the normal two.

Intermittent fasting wasn't a phrase thrown around yet, but if I could have explained away all my skipped meals as being for my health, to rid my body of toxins and to slow the growth of tumors, I would have been relieved for the excuse.

I ate pizza for show, as do the fitness influencers I see on Instagram now. It felt like an exhibition, so awkward and uncomfortable consuming such decadence for other eyes to see. But more often, I ate pizza in private late at night sitting in my underwear on the tile kitchen floor. The room glowed with the light of the cracked refrigerator. I grabbed a Tupperware box of leftovers, and I ate half of each slice because I did not want to admit to a full piece, and I ate it cold, not because I liked it that way but because I was ravenous, and my body was making the decisions now, and it was all happening so fast, it was happening to me, and I had no control. And when it was over and I was back, I was full, and full of shame. The noise returned: *You'll have to pay, you know.* And of course I knew. My whole life was a ledger of deposits and withdrawals.

I read the comments on these fitness influencers' posts, and so many people view them as inspirational, as healthy.

I feel terror. What they are doing seems very much like walking on the edge of the world, the insatiable maw of body obsessions and disordered eating one wobble away. Maybe some people are so sure-footed they can live here without fear, without stumbling. But I couldn't, still can't. I know how it feels to fall. It's similar to flying, at first. But then you are gone. And it's so hard to climb your way back to life.

At mealtimes with my children, I berate myself for speaking about food *incorrectly*.

I accidentally tell Alex, "No, honey, you can't have soda pop before bedtime because it's *bad for* you." And then I fear that calling food *bad* will create a bigger problem.

At dinner, I try to practice *division of responsibility*, a strategy that is meant to show respect toward a child's autonomy and appetite. I offer a variety of foods on a plate. Vegetable, fruit, meat, starch, dessert. I let them decide what to eat. I refrain from calling anything on the plate *bad*.

But then Graham insists on eating just the noodles. Night after night after night. And I can't help myself—I beg him to eat a vegetable. Then I make him eat a vegetable—just one. And at night I worry—*is this it? Is my force feeding my kid a single broccoli floret going to give him an eating disorder?*

I don't want my children to have a messed-up relationship with food. I know how critical it is that I model good behavior and say the right things to my children. I know this truth, even as I also continue to feel strongly that my mom pretty much said and did all the right things, too—but then look how all that worked out for me.

And then, something clicks: *Isn't this the exact same thing my mom dealt with? The pressure to parent perfectly so that she would raise perfect children?*

Everyone blames moms for their children's problems. Moms are blamed for obesity. Moms are blamed for eating disorders. Moms used to be blamed for autism and schizophrenia. For homicide and suicide. For all the ills—physical, criminal, psychological—in society. If the mom could be perfect, perhaps, finally, we would achieve peak civilization. Moms are blamed everywhere—and I never saw relief from this blame in the church.

And maybe this pressure, too, is what I was feeling during pregnancy. The need to be perfect, not just on behalf of myself but for the sake of my children.

During the COVID-19 pandemic, I tried to make it back to a good place. Still, the noise was not gone. I suspect I will always be reckoning with a compulsion for counting, radio static in my brain—some days the volume is turned up, other days it is turned down, and I cannot predict which days will be loud.

Sometimes moving relieves the static. But equally often, it only turns the volume up more. I am not relieved. I am still distracted by noise. And then, maybe, I try to do a bit more in another attempt to quiet the static. And the volume turns up louder still.

My children are hungry. It is time for lunch. I set them down at the table with a sandwich and some chips, and I sneak off to an adjacent room to fit in a bit more exercise, just to take the edge off. It does not work. They want to read now, and we are on the floor with books. I start doing leg lifts as I read aloud. Alex is climbing on top of me. An annoyance. No, a challenge. Additional resistance. I read *Peter Rabbit* with inflection and manipulated voices—"but naughty Peter squeeeeeezed under the gate"—as my leg moves up and down, my toddler riding my limb like an attraction at an amusement park.

"Let's go for a walk!" I suggest soon after, and Graham groans. I feel desperate. "I'll give you chocolate chips!" I say, and he is persuaded with this bribe. We walk hilly roads near our neighborhood, Alex sitting in a stroller, Graham lagging behind with chocolate smeared all over his face.

"Can you walk any faster, Graham?" I ask, while still trying to sound light, carefree. It is a beautiful day. It is not always this way on our walks.

"I'm out of energy," he says. "Let's go home."

The static is still loud. It is practically crushing me. "Can you find more energy?" I ask, pushing the stroller up a hill I purposefully choose to break more of a sweat.

"I don't think I can," he says, sounding exhausted, and I don't want to be cruel, so I make a new plan. Television for them at home. Just a bit of it. And another workout video in the corner for me. Surely this will take care of it.

But it does not. I feel guilty now. A full day at home with my children, and all my energy has been spent manipulating our activities for more exercise.

Do they know? Can they tell that my allegiances are elsewhere? Do they feel neglected, despite my presence?

Will all their childhood memories feature Mommy maniacally jumping up and down?

One day in spring 2020, the temperature was just warm enough to go without jackets. After breakfast, Graham told me that he was ready to go for a walk. He said it this way: "I want to get some exercise." I looked at him, startled to hear my words come out of his mouth, a walk referenced in the language of duty rather than pleasure. Though most adults I knew would feel excitement or pride that their child, so young, was already interested in healthy habits, I felt a shiver of fear: *Is this where it begins? Will he be overcome by the noise, too?*

Still, the sun was out, and I heard birds chirping in our front yard. Graham had already grabbed his own shoes and his brother's shoes, too. We headed outside. There were few cars on the road, but I directed us to a cemetery near our neighborhood so that we could roam freely without worry of traffic.

We arrived at the cemetery, and after some time, Alex began wandering off the paved path into the grass, stepping on gravestones, resolved to steal a bouquet of artificial flowers from a copper container.

"No, Alex!" Graham yelled. "We don't step on gravestones."

Alex, just a toddler, bumbled straight to the graves despite the warning. I lifted him swiftly from his intended path of destruction and jogged back with him to the paved path. Still, his gaze was fixed, and immediately, his steps turned to his previous destination, to the place where the dead lay.

Graham called to Alex again: "No, Alex! It's disrespectful," and I grabbed Alex around his waist and carried him back once more to the path we were meant to travel.

He began to veer again—what should I have expected? There was noise in his head, too. It was in his toddler nature to explore.

A bell in the cemetery began to ring loudly in the distance. We each stopped and turned our gaze up toward the direction of its sound. The bell played a song I often hummed to both boys just before bedtime as their eyes grew heavy and their bodies lay relaxed, the soundtrack of their dreams.

Years ago, when I fought my way back to earth, to the place where people eat and drink and make love and war and feel regret and sorrow and pain but also bliss and intimacy, I learned that I had to say no to the noise of legalism and perfectionism. I had to resist its call to move further into myself and away from others. To gain the courage to feel the hard things rather than running away from all feeling. I learned that, as much as I needed to say no, I also needed to say yes. Yes to risk. Yes to hope. Yes to uncertainty. Yes to possibility.

Each time I said no to the noise, the volume turned down, and I could hear the sound of other, beautiful things. I began to move in the world freely knowing that I would always be a body, but never just a body.

As we listened to the cemetery bell's song, its distant power and intimate familiarity, my boys and I stood still, gazes fixed to the horizon, so taken were we with this noise outside ourselves. When the song concluded, I looked at my boys, flesh of my flesh, and both of their bodies turned to the place ahead. I grabbed their hands, and together, we could move forward. I knew being focused on something outside myself would help when I heard the call to drift away.

61

I keep publishing essays online to try to get an agent to notice my writing. Many of the pieces are about disordered eating. I publish a dozen articles. Two dozen. Fifty within two years. I am showing my ambition. I am insatiable, and I am indulging it.

At first, I think—*this*. *This* is what will heal my disordered eating. Taking up space. Being seen. Allowing myself to be big.

But I do not feel healed. I do not feel satisfied. My desires just keep growing, bigger than me, bigger than my own body. They feel like something I'm unable to quench or reduce.

I read my work, and sometimes the clickbait is cliché. Occasionally, I roll my eyes at my own words. My dogged attempts to find moral high ground. My claims that I am good, we're all good, everything's good.

I turn on the news and hear about the latest political scandal, the rising temperatures, a school shooting.

We are definitely not all good, I think to myself.

For Alex's birthday, I order a cake from a local microbakery: cookies-and-cream marshmallow, chocolate ganache, fresh cherries, and buttercream. It's a breezy, warm spring day, and we eat slices of it on the porch.

It is so good—and yes, we are good, too.

But here's something else I know: I'm not *all* good.

I'm no angel in the house, no innocent little foal in need of shelter. I have been both hunter and prey. I have just as much desire for power as any man.

I've been begging for someone to tell me this my whole life. That my problems are *not* just women's problems. That they are *not* nothing. That my compulsions are not actually virtue. That when I look in the mirror, there actually is a problem: me.

I'm not pure. I'm a sinner.

In *Attached to God*, Krispin Mayfield argues that, just as we form attachments to our caregivers in childhood, our religious environments foster different styles of attachment to God. Why does God feel so far away? The answer depends on one's style of attachment: anxious, shame-filled, shut down, or secure.

In his work with those who experience religious trauma after being raised in purity culture, Krispin sees cognitive patterns: rigidity around ethical and moral rules; a presumption that there's one right way to live; the inability to trust oneself—neither one's own experiences nor feelings; a belief that pleasure is bad and pain is good.

Religion certainly doesn't have to result in disordered behaviors. In fact, there is research to show that secure spiritual practices lead to healthier relationships with food. However, those who have anxious attachments to God experience higher levels of disordered eating. And for many of the women who came of age in religious purity culture of the '90s, their relationship to God is marked by embodied shame and anxiety. The cognitive patterns a person develops in the midst of fundamentalism can make something like intuitive eating—or eating based upon natural hunger cues—incredibly difficult.

I asked Mayfield what actionable steps he recommended for individuals who grew up in high-control religious environments who wanted to heal.

"Pay attention to what spaces feel safe. That might mean changing your faith community, but not necessarily your faith tradition entirely," he told me. He said you could continue to engage in normal faith practices but also reflect by asking the question, "What was that like for me?" Rather than ignoring or shaming our feelings, we can think of them as information about what we need.

This evaluation is different from what high-control religion encourages. High-control religion involves evaluation—but this evaluation is often in terms of, "Am I following the community rules?"

When we are in a mindset of grading ourselves and judging ourselves, we can't get in touch with self-compassion. And self-compassion is just being able to turn toward yourself and say, *This is really hard.*

If you're able to do that, it helps reduce anxiety and depression. But you can't get into a space of self-compassion if you're constantly worried about whether you measure up. High-control religion strongly encourages you to be in that headspace of judgment all the time.

Even though I've written about and talked through my problems to death, I haven't been able to think my way out of disordered eating or my issues at church. The difficulties I have with my body are deep within my body—and so I decided to book an appointment for eye movement desensitization and reprocessing (EMDR) therapy. This therapy is often used to treat trauma and phobias. EMDR is different from cognitive behavioral therapy (CBT). Both have the aim of changing negative mindsets into positive ones, but CBT focuses on fixing thought processes, whereas EMDR focuses on retraining the body's subconscious reaction to trauma. CBT focuses on talking through an issue. EMDR involves embodied therapies like eye movement and tapping.

During the intake, I told my therapist I wanted to work on the trauma responses I have at church. I described how I felt in church settings: heart racing whenever the pianist played hymns from my childhood. Palms sweating when the pastor invoked anything that seemed like an altar call. Sometimes on Sunday mornings in anticipation of going to services, I'd stomp my feet and yell about how much I hated church.

One morning while I was throwing a fit, Graham moved his little body in front of mine and acted like the adult in the room: "I know you hate church. But I love it!" he cried.

I decided I couldn't live in the in-between anymore. For my own sake—and for the sake of my children. I needed to either stay in or get out. My unwillingness to choose a path wasn't just causing me psychological stress; it was confusing and damaging my children. I had to take some responsibility.

I thought about what it would look like if I left: Would I teach my children about God? If so, what would I say?

I believed in God. I also believed I was a sinner—that my body was simultaneously good and affected by sin. And the only thing that gave me the courage to admit my sin was that, deep down, I also believed in forgiveness.

Forgiveness was something that Christianity offered me.

Just because church has hurt me, just because it can be bad, doesn't mean I have to give my religious tradition up. I don't have to abstain. I can reject the black-and-white binary of all good or all bad.

And so I chose to stay. I wanted to try to heal my embodied responses to church.

My therapist instructed me to envision a scene where I felt triggered. "Now," he said, "I want you to follow my fingers with your eyes. Don't move your head." He raised his pointer and middle fingers and began quickly moving them from one edge of my peripheral vision to the other. After about a minute, he stopped and instructed me to take a deep breath. "How did you feel?" he asked.

"I felt disgusted. And guilty."

"Okay," he responded. "Sit with that. Let's do it again."

Then we kept doing this cycle of exercises. For an hour, we did it. After I trembled and cried, I felt tense in my head, then my chest. When we concluded the session, I still felt disturbed at the triggering scene—but less so. I felt safer and safer each time.

62

In the same way that I will never escape my problems with food by giving up a relationship with food, I cannot heal my hurt with religion by giving up my relationship with God.

I feel stalked by the divine. I see the face of God in my sons.

"Describe when you feel happiest," my therapist asks me in a follow-up appointment: *in the morning, when I am in bed with all my boys.*

"That's what you said last time, too," she says, smiling, reviewing her notes.

In the mornings when I wake, my husband and sons pile in our king-sized bed. E pours coffee from the French press into mugs. I lean back against a pile of pillows to drink it while I nurse Alex. Graham eats a granola bar beside us, leaving a pile of crumbs on the sheets. Our children climb over our limbs as we read the Bible—not for long, just a chapter. Sometimes I read that chapter aloud. I do not read devotionals. I have little tolerance for the book genre of Christian living. The neat bows these books tie around any given situation make me angry, in the mood for argument, but I can start my day with a psalm. "Give thanks" or "In my distress" or "I lift my eyes," they begin. And then a range of emotion, a lack of perfection, few clear-cut answers.

There is so much about Christianity that I am tempted to pick apart. I have moments when I want to reject it entirely. I can become consumed by all the ways men have used this religion to hurt me and those I love.

But I know it's not perfect out in the world, either. If I left the church, it's not as if I would escape sexism. It's not as if I struggle with disordered eating *just because* I was raised in conservative Christianity. There is no perfect place, and there are no perfect people.

I'm not perfect either—and that's okay. That's why I need God. Just because the church isn't perfect isn't a reason I need to reject it completely.

I don't have to be perfect to be loved by God.

I have a wish: to be enamored with something outside myself. To step away from the mirror and see the face of God in all the bodies in this world, the way I see the divine in my children. To see others the way I so desperately want to be seen myself.

When Esther appeared before the king, when she allowed herself to be seen, she did it for herself and for her own revenge—but she did it for those she loved, too. I want to be seen for my sons. I want to be seen for all the women who have been told that God wants them to be quiet, to be small. I want to be seen so that we all might have life—right here and eternally—and have it more abundantly.

63

As a child, I knew I didn't want to go to hell—but heaven didn't sound all that great either. At first, I thought my aversion to the idea of heaven was because I was so earthly and depraved. So tied to my flesh, I couldn't fathom the riches that awaited me. Streets of gold. Pillared mansions with ornate roofs. The celestial city. Even a perfect body. Whatever that meant.

I couldn't imagine what I would *do* in heaven. It seemed to be a perpetual church service or a crowded potluck: the two places on earth that gave me the most anxiety. No one seemed to imagine that feasting might be a pain point, but there was some honesty about the prospect of heaven as a church service. "I know it sounds boring," a teacher would say in a moment of candor, "but we will all be changed. We will be without sin. This will allow us to feel full joy praising the Lord."

The only authentic longing for heaven that I saw came from those in grief. Our eternal dreams were for our parents. Our babies. Our blood. My mom's own grief hung heavy upon my childhood. Her sister was her best friend, her only friend, really. And she died at thirty-four.

"A parent should never outlive her child," my mom would say as she stroked my hair at night. She was speaking of her own mom. She was speaking of herself. A single tear rolled down her cheek. I was her best friend now—but I was also her daughter.

Those who could remember only a sense of their own possibility spoke wistfully of afterlife. The elderly in wheelchairs. Those with degenerative sight. People who had, for a time, moved through this world with ease.

But there were plenty more, I'd learn as I grew, who were in significant pain and found no comfort in the idea of heaven. People whose bodies had long been the site of oppression. Friends who had no memory of their own former power. For so many, even if the church had not been complicit in their suffering, the church still had not seen it. Their testimonies of struggle had been received with suspicion—if they had been listened to at all.

When I consider heaven now, I do not think of a place far away. Heaven is my baby in the middle of the night waking me with cries. All he needs is my chest, the rhythmic motion of rocking and the vibrations of breath and heart. Heaven is my toddler plucking tomatoes from the garden and taking a big, juicy bite. Heaven is watching a storm from the porch and considering how the whole world can appear both green and pink. It's a run that feels like flying. It's the grace to stop when you are tired. Heaven is enjoying all that is good, and knowing that it is good, and that you are good, and believing that you won't be made more holy by restricting yourself from all that goodness.

Heaven is a revelation: God cares about life on earth right now. The life that we live in our blessed bodies.

Heaven is the hope that even the imperfect and broken religious systems we have could someday be made new. Heaven is not just the taking down but the building up. Heaven is not empty. It is full. It is here.

64

I wake to the sensation of touch. Aunt Catherine, my mom's sister taken too young from a battle with stomach cancer, is beside my bed. She is the same size that I am now, not the shrunken skeleton she became.

She smiles at me, bone-white teeth shining in the dark. She smells of roses and ivy. "I didn't mean to startle you," she says with a laugh, "but since I've got you here—come on!"

She pulls me to standing on the creaky wooden floor of my childhood bedroom. I reflexively glance in the mirror, and before I can get a proper look, she takes my hand to hers. With a tight squeeze she says, "Your nightgown is perfect. No need to change."

She pulls me out of my room with a leap, through the hallway by the whir of the grated vent, past my parents' desktop computer in the den, and to the kitchen. I can smell marinara bubbling on the stove, manicotti with ricotta cheese baking in the oven—the last meal we shared together, our final Christmas—and she feeds me.

I skate along the freshly dusted hardwood floors in my white cotton socks by the geraniums insulated on the porch. We stop at the top of the basement stairs. Slowly, with a certain reverence, we descend together. My old jump rope rests on the cold concrete, its ends frayed from so much use. She turns on my father's stereo, adjusts the volume so it is loud, loud enough to wake the house, loud enough to wake the whole neighborhood. "Go ahead," she yells over the noise. "Show me what you got!"

I hesitate. "You don't really want to see this," I say.

"But I do," she replies. "It's the whole reason I'm here." She pauses. "Go ahead. You know you want to," she says with a wink.

I pick up the rope and begin to jump. After a single jump, the basement vanishes—the chipped green concrete, the stereo speakers, the porcelain scale in the cupboard—and I am flying. She is with me, but quiet, though I can still smell her perfume as we move through the dewy morning air. Past the creek filled with crawdads, past winding mountain roads, past steeples, past highways, and up up up, and the higher we fly, the brighter everything appears. We are in heaven—but heaven is here.

"There's a place I've wanted to explore with you," she says to me. We are lounging on a cloud. She grabs a handful of its fluff and places it to her lips. I do the same. "Mmm . . .," she says with satisfaction, and I, too, am satisfied. Moments pass. I look at her, taking in the marvel and wonder of every inch that is her. "I've missed you so much," I say. "I can't believe you're here. Will you stay forever?"

"I'll see what I can do," she says with another smile, as if it is all a joke, as if so much gravity has no place this high in the sky.

Below my feet is blue ocean. And then there are hills of green. We are moving back to earth, and the air feels heavy with salt. We land on pavement. Surrounding us are shops of many colors, red, light green, yellow, blue. I hear waves crash in the distance. Along the horizon are cliffs covered in grass.

"I know where we are," I say looking around at the town. She nods her head without remark, and together, we walk toward the sound of the sea. The ground feels gritty beneath my feet, my white socks dirtied from the asphalt. As we approach the shore, I discard my socks in a bin, eager to feel the smooth sand against my skin.

A ruined castle stands on top of a dune. I look to my aunt for direction, but she has none. Still quiet, she turns neither left nor right but hikes up, away from the sand, away from the sea, to the castle in the sky.

The castle is all brick, its sharp, gray edges curved and green with age. There are no rooms, only windows. The cracks glow with the light of the rising sun. I can feel the breeze blowing against my thighs, expanding the range of my flimsy nightgown. I shiver with cold. My aunt takes me in her arms, and she holds me. "We'll stay warm together," she says.

After some time, my aunt moves her hand to scratch her head. "Oh, forget this," she says, taking her synthetic bob from her head. I have forgotten her hair is not her own. She evaluates the wig, and after a moment, she pitches it with all the might she can muster over the dune into the sea. Her bare, bald scalp shines with sun, and I kiss it.

"Is this what you imagined it would be?" she asks, looking straight into my brown eyes.

"No," I say simply.

"Good. Me neither," she replies.

Crowds form behind us. Tourists, all here to see the beauty of this wreck, this structure crumbling in the elements.

Hours pass. My stomach grumbles. My aunt retrieves a loaf of bread from her pocket, somehow still hot with butter. I eat it, and I see that it is good.

We continue to curl into the heat of each other. Clouds accumulate on the horizon, and I smell drops of rain.

"When will we go home?" I finally ask her.

"Wouldn't you say this is home?" she says after a pause. And I realize that it has to be, home, right here, on this rock, in this flesh, there is no other place, and I am so glad to be back, again, with her.

65

I still consider Christianity to be home. I am tempted to present an apologetic: the logic in my staying. But really, studying theology and church history is not what makes me stay. Despite the pain, Christ still gives me hope. He calls me to look up.

My husband and I don't see the world the exact same way, and we've learned that's not required to be in a loving partnership. To believe that there is no room for conflict and disagreement in a relationship is to follow the same thought patterns I was raised with: that we all have to be the same, that we all have to get in line to be safe.

And as much as E and I are different, we are also the same. We come from the same place, and we identify the same hurts, and we share similar fears, and no one understands me the way he does. In this way, we are one.

At church, we say the Apostles' Creed aloud. I want to believe it—the forgiveness of sins, the resurrection of the body, life everlasting.

The sermon is on *the gospel*. Our pastor reminds us the word means "good news." He speaks of evangelism, how natural it is to tell others about what is *good* and *true* and *right* in our lives. *I am desperate for good news*, I think. *I hope Jesus will someday save me from myself.*

The pastor announces that after the service, the youth will be having a special gathering: lunch followed by a Bible study.

I wonder how many of the teenagers are most nervous about the portion of the event that involves eating. *I bet there's at least one*, I think.

It is hard for me to volunteer in church, and is hard to make myself attend. But, here's a wish: Perhaps I begin to really believe and become convinced of God's love. Maybe I will volunteer with the youth. And maybe when I eat with them, I will see that girl in the corner with a paper plate, pizza torn to bits and a nervous look behind her eyes. Rather than ignoring her, I will talk to her.

And I will not say, "Aren't you hungry?" because I know of course she is. And I will not say, "Just eat!" because I know she's carrying enough shame already. I will not tell her, "You're beautiful," and I will not assure her, "This is a phase you'll grow out of." I will just let her know that I want to hear her voice, that I will listen to her speak.

And perhaps, eventually, when she gives me the hint, when she throws out that small cry for help, I'll say, "Hey, me too." Maybe then she'll feel free to open her mouth.

66

In regions where water levels test high with lithium, there are lower rates of depression, of suicide. In these towns, a middle-aged woman fills up a tall glass at the kitchen sink. A man sips from the rusty YMCA water fountain. A toddler guzzles from the backyard hose on a scorching hot summer day. I imagine them all smiling, white teeth gleaming in the sun, and when a passerby asks how they are doing, they respond with the word "blessed."

Lithium, a metal found in nearly every rock, is the most natural of medications. It halted E's madness. The valleys of depression and mountains of mania leveled to something traversable and tame. The drug evened him without flattening him. It made him calm—not numb. It gave him his mind back—our marriage back.

But like any good thing, lithium, in excess, can turn toxic. Lithium's power to soothe the storm of mania feels miraculous. This power is bound up with danger. As a precaution, those on the drug must have their blood drawn and tested regularly to avoid a lithium overdose. An overdose can lead to myriad complications: nausea, vomiting, seizures, paralysis.

E noticed his first side effect several months into taking the drug. He stood in an exam room suturing a patient's wound. He looked to his hands; he'd hardly even noticed them before, so youthful and steady; they'd served him his whole life. But that day, they were trembling.

"I eventually had to ask a nurse to take over," he said, shaking his head as we lay in bed that night. "I think I'm developing a tremor."

"What can you do?"

"It's one of the side effects. Not much that can be done unless I just stop taking the medicine."

He continued to shakily grab that green pill bottle and place that small white capsule on the tip of his tongue, night after night after night. He did it for his mind. But mostly, he did it for us—his family. To spare us potential future pain, he took on the present consequences.

One June, we were packing for a vacation to the beach, SUV bursting with luggage, play yards, and toddler-friendly snacks. We were about to head out on the road when E received a call: After a routine blood test, his results showed concerning levels of lithium. He needed to report as soon as possible for another blood test.

"So, what does that mean?" I asked. "If your levels are high, what happens?"

"If they're high for too long undetected, you could have kidney damage. Renal failure. You may need dialysis."

I gulped and nodded my head as E hopped in the car to drive to the lab.

He wasn't gone long. When he returned home, I was in the backyard with Graham and Alex, pushing them on parallel swings.

"Faster!" Graham yelled.

"Faster!" Alex repeated.

"When will you get the results back?" I asked E as he joined us by the swing set.

"Soon. There's a chance the test was wrong. That happens sometimes. Maybe I was dehydrated. I'd worked out just before, so it very well could be wrong. The tech said they will call with the results soon."

"But this is always something you're going to have to worry about, isn't it?"

"I mean, yeah. I'd like to go off the medication eventually. The longer I'm on it, the more likely I am to have long-term side effects."

"I hate this. I don't blame you for wanting to go off it," I said.

"Push me harder!" Graham called.

"Daddy, push me!" Alex chanted.

I glanced at our dogs on the porch. "While you're waiting for the call, would you be up for playing with the boys while I take the dogs for a walk?"

E nodded his head.

I hooked the dogs up to leashes and started down the road. I imagined our future unfolding. E off lithium. Mania. Another breakdown. Shielding Graham and Alex from the madness, parenting all alone. And then I imagined another future: E continuing to take those pills, hands trembling, kidneys failing. No matter our next step, so much could go wrong.

I felt the pull of my zipper against the flesh of my belly. For a moment, it was relief to turn my attention there, to the familiar desire to shrink away from potential pain.

But nothing bad has actually happened yet, I reminded myself as I turned up an oak-lined hill. *You don't really know what will happen, but if you spend this walk, this vacation, worrying about it, you* do *know you'll lose the present time you have with your boys.*

I looked out over the ridge, sun setting, light dappled through the leaves of trees. *I want to be here fully now*, I decided.

Perhaps this is what it means to have faith.

I pulled my phone from my pocket to turn on a podcast. I found an interview with George Saunders. He spoke on the topic of the profound upside of self-diminishment.

"Can you say more about this process of turning down the volume of you and what it is that rushes in when that volume goes down?" the interviewer asked.

"Yeah, you know, in the Catholic faith, they used to have a hymn that went, 'We must diminish and Christ increase.' I just thought that was really beautiful," Saunders replied.

The dogs pulled hard on the leash toward a squirrel darting through our neighbors' yard. Holding them back, I bristled at the suggestion that these words were beautiful. The lyrics transported me back to the shame of my childhood, to chapel services with loud, burly pastors yelling at me to "give it all up for God." I envisioned myself sitting in those gymnasium bleachers, legs crossed, arms pulled in, blue glasses dangling at the tip of my nose. I saw myself age in that same seat, growing bigger and taller, from a girl to a woman, trying so desperately to diminish. *What part of this is beautiful?* I thought to myself.

Just as I turned the corner to our home, the interviewer clarified: "Self-diminishment is not running yourself down. It is not self-flagellation or self-deprecation. It is turning down the volume on self-centered thinking. That might be synonymous with love."

"Hey!" E called as I approached our front porch. "They expedited my test. My levels are normal this time."

"Oh, what a relief," I said.

"I'm going to make an appointment with my psychiatrist. Just to discuss options for the future."

I nodded my head, kissed his cheek. "That sounds good," I said. Then we headed off to the beach.

Our vacation is perfect. Each morning, we wake to Graham's and Alex's squeals and cries—alternatively ecstatic and bereft. The four of us lounge in our king-sized vacation bed as I hold a mug of coffee and a plate of pastries, glazed and jelly-filled. We bought enough for the whole week.

Alex wants bites of mine, and I'm happy to share—not because it is less for me but because it is more for him. I no longer see virtue in taking as little as possible.

We lotion up and walk to the shore. Our condo is several blocks away from the beach. I am tempted to check the number of steps we've traveled on my phone. I zip the device in my bag instead. I want to enjoy the walk. Or, I want to negotiate with my toddler melting down on the walk. Mostly, I want to be here now, not making meaningless calculations.

We play at the beach—building sandcastles with moats, jumping waves, digging for shells. A walk to the pier. Eventually, I pull snacks from my purse. They have crumbled and are melting in the heat. We eat them anyway because we are hot and hungry. We feel good once we do.

A body, no matter its size, is so vulnerable and visible. So needy. So uncertain. But having one is the only way to be here. And standing in the surf in my black swimsuit, the sun shining on the faint stretch marks left from my pregnancies, I am so glad to be here.

This sentiment is easy to say when *here* is good, and right now it is—my doughy toddler in a pair of tiny trunks, a perfect breeze on a shaded patch of sand, the hand of my partner interlaced in my own. *Here* can change so quickly though. I know. My mind is still eager to warn me about all the ways the sun, or those snacks, or this water—all natural and necessary—will be the things that get me in the end. If not them, shadowy men lurking in the middle distance are always on standby.

But I'm not here to engage those fears, to argue about all the ways I can stay safe or good or pure. I'm here beside my boys. Graham wants me to bury him in the sand. "You sure?" I ask as I start to dig. He nods his head, giggling in anticipation.

"Hop in," I say after minutes of excavating earth. He lies down shirtless in the ground, and I pile the sand on top of his small body. He continues to laugh. "I love the way it feels on my chest," he says. And I smile at him—my firstborn son, fearless as he takes on the weight of the world.

ACKNOWLEDGMENTS

For my mom, who was radically present, who loved me with every part of herself, who gave me safe spaces to question and exist, who made me feel secure, regardless of my behavior, appearance, or performance: I am the most fortunate daughter. When I think of what I want to give to my own children, I look to you.

For my dad, whose calm presence and sense of humor gave me steadiness. Who, when I said, "You're actually not in my book much at all," responded with a smile and a sigh, saying "Oh, that's probably a good thing." Thank you for all the ways you show me love, including how you walk into my house and automatically fix whatever has been broken.

To my brother: thanks for giving me so many good stories (that I have not included in this book). Your sense of humor is unmatched. I love you.

To Morgan Strehlow and the entire team at the Bindery Agency: thank you for taking a chance on me and my proposal, for treating this work as a passion project, for advocating for me tirelessly, and for mentoring me with wisdom.

To the team at Eerdmans—Laurel Draper, Amy Kent, Jeff Dundas, Jason Pearson, Clare Galloway, Claire McColley, and most especially Lisa Ann Cockrel. This manuscript is so much better because of you (and so am I). I am forever grateful to have been matched with an editor who shared such a similar vision for this project.

To friends and early readers: Kristen Lillvis, Kara Angus, Joy Callaway, Joy Haser, Mary Beth Ferda, Daniel O'Malley, and Rebecca Minardi.

To Rachael Peckham and Kelli Prejean, whose impact on my writing and my life cannot be overstated.

To my former students, tutors, colleagues, and department chairs, especially Allison Carey, Jane Hill, and Jana Tigchelaar.

Thank you to the Faculty Senate at my former institution for awarding this project with multiple summer research grants. And thank you to Phi Kappa Phi for the Love of Learning Award that also helped fund this project.

To my brilliant critique partners, Sarah Canney and Amre Klimchek.

To Courtney Maum, Cassie Mannes Murray, Sue Shapiro, David Hochman, Estelle Erasmus, and especially Jill Rothenberg. To the Binders, #WomenWriters, and UPOD Academy.

To the women in purity-culture and diet-culture recovery groups who made me feel less alone by speaking and sharing their stories.

To dear friends who were not early readers but who heard me talk about this project way too often: Chessa Emerson and Michael and Meagan Valentine.

To all of my children's teachers at school and church who show extensive love and care toward our whole family.

To my husband, whose generosity, love for others, and creativity inspires me. Thank you for wanting more for me than I've had the courage to want for myself. Thank you for loving me, for not always agreeing with me (because I do like a good debate), and for knowing what I'm writing about, often even before I do.

And finally, to my children, whom I love with every part of myself. Being with you is heaven.

NOTES

xvi **Mark Driscoll's *Real Marriage*** Mark Driscoll, *Real Marriage: The Truth about Sex, Friendship, and Life Together* (Nashville: Thomas Nelson, 2012).

Stephen Arterburn's *Every Man's Battle* Stephen Arterburn, Fred Stoker, and Mike Yorkey, *Every Man's Battle: Winning the War on Sexual Temptation One Victory at a Time* (Colorado Springs, CO: WaterBrook, 2000).

xviii ***Everything Happens*** https://tinyurl.com/4ayvt2cz.

Blessed Kate Bowler, *Blessed: A History of the American Prosperity Gospel* (New York: Oxford University Press, 2013).

The Wisdom of Your Body Hillary McBride, *The Wisdom of Your Body: Finding Healing, Wholeness, and Connection through Embodied Living* (Grand Rapids: Brazos, 2021).

4 **"She's taken to wearing socks"** "The Science of Fat," *The Spark*, archived June 2, 2001, https://tinyurl.com/4z99zvab.

6 **She "has ridges"** "Day 3: Fat Science," *The Spark*, archived August 15, 2001, https://tinyurl.com/yyrnwv4m.

7 **"visibly much fatter"** "Day 10: Fat Science," *The Spark*, archived August 5, 2001, https://tinyurl.com/mrxpn895.

"She used to be a homecoming queen" "Day 22: Fat Science," *The Spark*, archived June 11, 2001, https://tinyurl.com/3877tsus.

"Bloated is not really a strong enough word" "Day 17: Fat Science," *The Spark*, archived August 7, 2001, https://tinyurl.com/35eumxy3.

10 **"'the ultimate expression of the self.'"** Joan Jacobs Brumberg, *The Body Project: An Intimate History of American Girls* (New York: Vintage Books, 1997).

55 **Elisabeth Elliot's *Passion and Purity*** Elisabeth Elliot, *Passion and Purity: Learning to Bring Your Love Life under Christ's Control* (Grand Rapids: Revell, 1984).

56 **Joshua Harris's *I Kissed Dating Goodbye*** Joshua Harris, *I Kissed Dating Goodbye* (Colorado Springs, CO: Multnomah, 1997).

64 **"nothing tastes as good as skinny feels"** Brid Costello, "Kate Moss: The Waif That Roared," *Women's Wear Daily*, November 13, 2009, archived March 9, 2022, https://tinyurl.com/2bpdkp7c.

"the obesity epidemic" W. Wayt Gibbs, "Obesity: An Overblown Epidemic," *Scientific American*, December 1, 2006, https://tinyurl.com/47rdk3e6.

"[The Millennial] generation was caught in the crossfire Michelle Konstantinovsky, "If You Survived the Early 2000s without Body Issues, Congratulations," *Glamour*, July 15, 2020, https://tinyurl.com/7cbadaup.

66 ***The Best Little Girl in the World*** Steven Levenkron, *The Best Little Girl in the World* (New York: Warner Books, 1978).

Second Star to the Right Deborah Hautzig, *Second Star to the Right* (New York: Puffin Books, 1999).

Stick Figure Lori Gottlieb, *Stick Figure: A Diary of My Former Self* (New York: Simon & Schuster).

Wasted Marya Hornbacher, *Wasted: A Memoir of Anorexia and Bulimia* (New York: HarperCollins, 1998).

87 ***Angela's Ashes*** Frank McCourt, *Angela's Ashes* (New York: Simon & Schuster, 1996).

Breathing Lessons Anne Tyler, *Breathing Lessons* (New York: Knopf, 1988).

96 **Gnosticism—not Christianity—is America's real religion** Harold Bloom, "The American Religion," *New York Times*, October 25, 1998, https://tinyurl.com/3vv8wsem.

97 **"For figures like Plato"** Emmeline Clein, *Dead Weight: Essays on Hunger and Harm* (New York: Penguin Books, 2023), 60.

98 **"Why wallpaper the house"** N. T. Wright, *Surprised by Scripture: How and Why the Bible Is Essential to Our Faith* (New York: HarperOne, 2014), 85.

As a reaction to both the sexual revolution and the AIDS crisis Linda Kay Klein, *Pure: Inside the Evangelical Movement That Shamed a Gener-*

ation of Young Women and How I Broke Free (New York: Atria Books, 2018), 25.

100 **"Secrets"** Susan Burton, "Secrets," February 19, 2021, in *This American Life*, produced by Bim Adewunmi, podcast, MP3 audio, 58:20, https://tinyurl.com/44ahdxje.

"That eating disorder memoir I was writing?" Burton, "Secrets."

121 ***Preparing for Adolescence*** James Dobson, *Preparing for Adolescence* (Wheaton, IL: Tyndale House Publishers, 1989).

"lose the innocence of youth" Dobson, *Preparing for Adolescence*, 68.

123 **We respond as though we've been abused.** Tina Schermer Sellers, *Sex, God, and the Conservative Church: Erasing Shame from Sexual Intimacy* (New York: Routledge, 2017), 21.

128 **an estimated 1 to 6 percent of the general population** Ali Doğukan Anğın et al., "Effects of Predisposing Factors on the Success and Treatment Period in Vaginismus," *JBRA Assisted Reproduction* 24, no. 2 (May 2020): 180–88, https://tinyurl.com/5n7yhe49.

"conservative religious women . . . suffer from vaginismus" Sheila Wray Gregoire, "The Emotional Journey with Vaginismus," *Bare Marriage*, December 6, 2021, https://tinyurl.com/5y6cz2pb.

129 **22.6 percent of Christian women reported experiencing painful penetrative sex** Sheila Wray Gregoire, "The Evangelical Sex Report Card," *Bare Marriage*, October 2, 2024, https://tinyurl.com/bde6xxkd.

131 **lower rates of female orgasm and more sexual pain in marriage** Sheila Wray Gregoire, *The Great Sex Rescue: The Lies You've Been Taught and How to Recover What God Intended* (Grand Rapids: Baker Books, 2021), 42.

I Kissed Dating Goodbye Joshua Harris, *I Kissed Dating Goodbye* (Colorado Springs, CO: Multnomah, 1997).

Passion and Purity Elisabeth Elliot, *Passion and Purity: Learning to Bring Your Love Life under Christ's Control* (Grand Rapids: Revell, 1984).

Lady in Waiting Jackie Kendall and Debby Jones, *Lady in Waiting: Becoming God's Best While Waiting for Mr. Right* (Shippensburg, PA: Destiny Image, 2005).

Boy Meets Girl Joshua Harris, *Boy Meets Girl: Say Hello to Courtship* (Colorado Springs, CO: Multnomah, 2000).

132 ***Come as You Are*** Emily Nagoski, *Come as You Are: The Surprising*

New Science That Will Transform Your Sex Life (New York: Simon & Schuster, 2015).

137 ***Anorexia and Mimetic Desire*** René Girard, *Anorexia and Mimetic Desire*, trans. Mark R. Anspach (New York: University of Chicago Press, 1993).

138 **"To abstain voluntarily from something"** Girard, *Anorexia and Mimetic Desire*, 22.

"My main experience" Susan Burton, "Secrets," February 19, 2021, in *This American Life*, produced by Bim Adewunmi, podcast, MP3 audio, 58:20, https://tinyurl.com/44ahdxje.

140 **"If women become tired, even die, it does not matter"** Martin Luther, quoted in Agnes Arnold-Foster, "The Pain We Don't Talk About: Women's Pain in Childbirth," *The Guardian*, March 17, 2023, https://tinyurl.com/4rdpw6mv.

141 **"penis homes"** Libby Anne, "Pastor Mark Driscoll Called Women 'Penis Homes,'" Love, Joy, Feminism, September 23, 2014, https://tinyurl.com/2k3ps5b4.

Desiring God John Piper, *Desiring God: Meditations of a Christian Hedonist*, 10th anniversary ed. (Colorado Springs, CO: Multnomah Books, 1996).

The Freedom and Power of Forgiveness John MacArthur, *The Freedom and Power of Forgiveness* (Wheaton, IL: Crossway Books, 1998).

"The woman is created be the man's helper" George W. Knight III, "The Family and the Church," in *Recovering Biblical Manhood and Womanhood: A Response to Evangelical Feminism*, ed. John Piper and Wayne Grudem (Wheaton, IL: Crossway Books, 1991), 552.

"go home" Morgan Lee, "John MacArthur and the Beth Moore Controversy," October 17, 2019, in *Quick to Listen*, produced by Matt Linder, podcast, MP3 audio, 53:44, *Christianity Today*, https://tinyurl.com/237u3ebx.

207 **"Weight loss observed outside the context of diet culture"** Anna Sweeney (dietitiananna), "Weight loss observed outside the context of diet culture is indicative of risk," Instagram, March 9, 2020, https://tinyurl.com/ypucyk26.

girls start wanting to be thinner by six years old Jacinta Lowes and Marika Tiggemann, "Body Dissatisfaction, Dieting Awareness and the Impact of Parental Influence in Young Children," *British Journal of Health Psychology* 8, no. 2 (2003): 135–47, https://tinyurl.com/mrx4pwdu.

most start dieting by eight years old Kelsey Miller, "Study: Most Girls Start Dieting by Age 8," *Refinery29*, January 26, 2015, https://tinyurl.com/yefh3x5b.

208 **Health at Every Size** "Health at Every Size® Principles," Association for Size Diversity and Health, https://tinyurl.com/3km2nny7.

212 **Institutionalized religious diets are nothing new in American Christianity** R. Marie Griffith, *Born Again Bodies: Flesh and Spirit in American Christianity* (Berkeley: University of California Press, 2004), Kindle.

"typified by obsession with perfect health and slenderness" Griffith, *Born Again Bodies*, introduction, "Perilous Body Gospels."

"a growing praise of slenderness" Sabrina Strings, *Fearing the Black Body: The Racial Origins of Fat Phobia* (New York: New York University Press, 2019), 162.

213 **People of all races use thinness to access racialized power** Strings, *Fearing the Black Body*.

"two critical historical developments contributed" Strings, *Fearing the Black Body*, 6.

214 **one essay of Gordon's on weight stigma in the doctor's office** Aubrey Gordon, "Weight Stigma Kept Me out of Doctors' Offices for Years," *Self*, June 26, 2018, https://tinyurl.com/57zwhusk.

"obese patients don't usually have low blood pressure" Gordon, "Weight Stigma."

"Fat people have them too!" Michael Hobbes and Aubrey Gordon, hosts, *Maintenance Phase*, podcast, episode 79, "Eating Disorders," May 13, 2021, https://tinyurl.com/mr3xnt8z.

215 **atypical anorexia** Kate Siber, "You Don't Look Anorexic," *New York Times Magazine*, October 18, 2022, https://tinyurl.com/52k45nk8.

"eating disorders don't discriminate" Shereen Marisol Meraji, "When It Comes to Race, Eating Disorders Don't Discriminate," *NPR*, March 3, 2019, https://tinyurl.com/2h8v9szp.

hundreds of similar pieces of art have been found from this era Kate Manne, *Unshrinking: How to Face Fatphobia* (New York: Crown, 2024), 59.

"Anyone can behave gluttonously" Quoted in Manne, *Unshrinking*, 60.

216 **"With women commonly being used to represent the nation"** Sabrina

Strings, *Fearing the Black Body: The Racial Origins of Fat Phobia* (New York: New York University Press, 2019), 159.

less likely to be hired and to be paid a fair wage Areva Martin, "Weight Discrimination Is Real. So Why Aren't There More Workplace Protections?," *Time*, December 6, 2017, https://tinyurl.com/28k5pfzj.

Fatphobia is the one prejudice that has grown in the twenty-first century rather than shrunk Tessa E. Charlesworth and Mahzarin R. Banaji, "Patterns of Implicit and Explicit Attitudes: I. Long-Term Change and Stability from 2007 to 2016," *Psychological Science* 30, no. 2 (2019): 174–92, https://tinyurl.com/2szzdjrk.

218 ***Pure: Inside the Evangelical Movement That Shamed a Generation of Young Women and How I Broke Free*** Linda Kay Klein, *Pure: Inside the Evangelical Movement That Shamed a Generation of Young Women and How I Broke Free* (New York: Atria Books, 2018).

219 **"I don't think it's a stretch"** Melissa Febos, *Body Work: The Radical Power of Personal Narrative* (New York: Catapult, 2022), 18.

227 **roots in Black feminism** Meridith Griffin, K. Alysse Bailey, and Kimberly J. Lopez, "#BodyPositive? A Critical Exploration of the Body Positive Movement within Physical Cultures Taking an Intersectionality Approach," *Frontiers in Sports and Active Living* 4 (2022): https://tinyurl.com/yjuvu4rr.

co-opted by white women Stephanie Yeboah, "Women of Colour Have Been Left Out of the Body Positivity Movement," *Elle UK*, September 15, 2017, https://tinyurl.com/rrm6hvpj.

228 **doubled after the COVID-19 pandemic** Katie Kindelan and Lauren Joseph, "Eating Disorder Hospitalizations Doubled during COVID-19 Pandemic, Data Shows," ABC News, July 12, 2021, https://tinyurl.com/4rcsv64c.

one in five kids shows signs of disordered eating José Francisco López-Gil et al., "Increase in Hospitalizations for Eating Disorders among Adolescents during the COVID-19 Pandemic," *JAMA Pediatrics* 176, no. 1 (2022): 18–24, https://tinyurl.com/54a47pex.

Anorexia is the deadliest mental illness Tom Quinn, "The Harrowing Truth about Anorexia and the NHS," *The Guardian*, January 3, 2020, https://tinyurl.com/y8yy8t6n.

More Than a Body Lexie Kite and Lindsay Kite, *More Than a Body: Your Body Is an Instrument, Not an Ornament* (New York: Harvest Publishing, 2020).

229 **body reflexivity** Kate Manne, "The 5 Words That Help Me Accept My Body," *Time*, January 9, 2024, https://tinyurl.com/2s3f6fr7.

230 **Kate Manne invites us to consider our experience of sunsets** Virginia Sole-Smith, "You Cannot Fight Misogyny Without Fighting Fatphobia," January 11, 2024, in *Burnt Toast*, podcast, MP3 audio, 56:21, https://tinyurl.com/3y4haa6t.

235 ***division of responsibility*** Virginia Sole-Smith, "Is Mealtime Miserable? Try This," *New York Times*, April 17, 2020, https://tinyurl.com/4mxyvnx5.

240 **our religious environments foster different styles of attachment to God** Krispin Mayfield, *Attached to God: A Practical Guide to the Theology of Attachment* (Grand Rapids: Zondervan, 2021).

those who have anxious attachments to God experience higher levels of disordered eating Daniel Akrawi et al., " Religiosity, Spirituality in Relation to Disordered Eating and Body Image Concerns: A Systematic Review," *Journal of the National Institute of Mental Health*, July 25, 2015, https://tinyurl.com/mtaaavej.

253 **lower rates of depression, of suicide** Lauren Slater, *Blue Dreams: The Science and the Story of the Drugs That Changed Our Minds* (New York: Little, Brown and Company, 2018), 62.

255 **the profound upside of self-diminishment** George Saunders, "The Profound Upside of Self-Diminishment (Ep. 332)," *Ten Percent Happier with Dan Harris*, podcast audio, 1:08:00, March 22, 2021, https://tinyurl.com/mry255xc.